YOU REALLY
HAVEN'T
BEEN THERE
UNTIL
YOU'VE
EATEN
THE FOOD

KEITH FAMIE

YOU REALLY HAVEN'T BEEN THERE UNTIL YOU'VE EATEN THE FOOD

BY KEITH FAMIE
WITH CHRIS KASSEL
PHOTOGRAPHS BY JOE VAUGHN

AN INTERNATIONAL ODYSSEY WITH MORE THAN 130 RECIPES

CLARKSON POTTER/PUBLISHERS
NEW YORK

Copyright © 2003 by Keith Famie
Photographs copyright © 2003 by Joe Vaughn

All rights reserved. No part of this book may be reproduced
or transmitted in any form or by any means, electronic or
mechanical, including photocopying, recording, or by any
information storage and retrieval system, without permission
in writing from the publisher.

Published by Clarkson Potter/Publishers, New York, New York.
Member of the Crown Publishing Group, a division of Random House, Inc.
www.randomhouse.com

CLARKSON N. POTTER is a trademark and POTTER and colophon are
registered trademarks of Random House, Inc.

Printed in the United States of America

Design by Caitlin Daniels Israel

Library of Congress Cataloging-in-Publication Data
Famie, Keith.
    You really haven't been there until you've eaten the food / Keith Famie.
Includes index.
    1. Cookery, International.   2. Travel.   I. Title.
TX725.A1 F28 2003
641.59—dc21   2002034561

ISBN 0-609-61092-9

10 9 8 7 6 5 4 3 2 1

First Edition

CONTENTS

PREFACE

Ever since I can remember, I've lived for the adventure of traveling. There's a nearly indefinable sensation that comes with it—exotic smells, unfamiliar air, new looks and attitudes. And, most important to me, there's the world of indigenous ingredients and new styles of cooking to discover. I'm equally delighted to learn from a four-star chef as from a local homemaker as long as the food used is fresh, grown in the area, and available at nearby markets. No matter how far away from home I am during these moments, I always know I'm back inside my element.

When I began my latest round of travels, producing thirty-two shows for my Food Network series, *Keith Famie's Adventures,* I knew that I wanted to chronicle the journey with pictures, recipes, and stories. I call this collection *You*

Really Haven't Been There Until You've Eaten the Food because I believe that food is not only the quickest way to learn about a place but also the *only* way to get a true feel for a community's sensory history. I love restaurants, of course, but it's within simple homes and everyday kitchens, in backyards and on barbecue grills, preparing and sharing meals with various generations, that I've come to appreciate the incredible power of food.

Touring markets is another way that I've been able to experience a city's most vital energies, especially when the city is near a body of water. There's no group more passionate about their profession than fishermen, and they're always eager to share a fresh catch with traveling chefs like myself, along with their stories and philosophies. You'll find many such adventures in the pages that follow.

This book could not have been possible if it weren't for the team that has traveled with me, helping to capture the visions, the sounds, the tastes.

Chris Kassel is a great friend and fellow adventurist, a true lover of life. Joe Vaughn has the critical eye and boundless imagination of a world-class photographer. When I decided to create a book on the road, I knew that Joe, who shot all the photographs for my first cookbook, *Keith Famie's Adventures in Cooking,* and Chris, a journalist with whom I've worked for years, would have to be part of the team.

Creating a cookbook while producing a travel cooking show meant that I needed someone I could trust to watch my back when it came to collecting recipes. Matt Prested has been cooking with me since he was twenty-one years old. Now, at twenty-seven, he's become a seasoned world traveler thanks to our many journeys. Matt's attention to detail has been invaluable in the archiving of these recipes.

To all three of these guys I say thank you . . . for your hard, impassioned, and dedicated work, and, most important, because we did the journey together. Guys, you've been there and eaten the food, and my memory will forever be etched with the great adventures we shared together.

AFRICA

Nobody presumes to know Africa after a single trip. Nobody presumes to describe Africa in a single chapter. Nobody presumes to understand Africa in a single lifetime. Fair enough?

KENYA

To get from Nairobi to the boundless plains of the Masa Mara, you take a prop plane. The trip lasts less than an hour, but in that time you pass over two of the most significant human landmarks on the planet: Kibera and Olduvai.

Kibera is Kenya's largest ghetto, an unfathomably grotesque huddle of squatter shacks with a population density of a half million per square mile. Gargantuan trash heaps are everywhere, and the preponderance of cheap colorful plastic packaging makes it look gaudy, even from ten thousand feet overhead. Inside Kibera, unemployment is 50 percent, and those who do work rarely earn more than a dollar per day. Disease is so rampant that dying of AIDS has virtually become a normal and universally accepted life transition. That's one landmark.

A short while later, you pass over the Great Rift Valley, formed 25 million years ago. Just to the south is Olduvai Gorge, where Louis Leakey discovered the remains of what may be the first protohumans. Olduvai is the place where all the citizens of all the Kiberas that ever were or ever will be first began their journey. That's the other landmark.

We land in a small, dusty airstrip sliced from the northern portion of the Serengeti Plain. It's obvious from the outset that we've stepped through some time warp. It doesn't matter how many zoos you've been to, how many nature shows you've seen—nothing prepares you for the sight of a trotting giraffe or a lumbering elephant in the wild. The savannah, stretching incomprehensible distances on all points of the compass, shimmers with movement, black stains migrating, scurrying, hunting, passing through constantly shifting relationships. My first view of the Masa Mara National Reserve is of a timeless landscape that's in a constant state of flux.

Near me, a lean red-blanketed youth called Sopia unloads the plane, methodically piling baggage into Stefano Cheli's battle-scarred vehicle, formerly an army ambulance and now a safari truck. Stefano, who has been tracking game through the Mara for twenty years, is not a casting director's image of a safari leader—a dry, formidable Brit with a bushy mustache and a loaded blunderbuss—but is, rather, a small, rotund, clean-shaven, and excruciatingly witty Tuscan. No matter his look, he knows the Mara as well as anyone alive and keeps us entertained throughout the following days with his wealth of tips—"If you notice that I suddenly start running, just get ahead of me and you'll be fine"—his acute understanding of the local wildlife, and, wonder of wonders, his cooking. It seems that Stefano is as accomplished with field kitchens as he is with field glasses and takes special care to re-create some of his family's favorites, including light, flavor-filled ravioli, an unexpected beam of Mediterranean sunshine beneath a sub-Saharan sky.

Game drives under Stefano's leadership are phenomenally productive; in a single afternoon we track down eland, ostrich, topi, water buffalo, baboon, big cats, small dogs, all sorts of gazelle, and wildebeest by the hundreds of thousands. It's migration time for these massive bearded antelope, and they move across the acacia plains in herds that must resemble those of the American bison in the 1800s. Often, they're trailed by endless strings of zebra. Again, no *National Geographic* footage can prepare you for such panoramas. Forget the animals for a second; the space alone is sobering. Its simple encompassing magnificence startles senses numbed by suburbia; it's a landscape unravaged by

MASAI WARRIORS SHOWING US HOW TO THROW A SPEAR.

African Blue Cheese Soup

Joash Omore, chef at Cottar's Camp, made his favorite soup recipe for me.

SERVES 4

6 RED-SKINNED POTATOES, PEELED AND
    DICED LARGE
1 TABLESPOON OLIVE OIL
1 WHITE ONION, DICED
1 GARLIC CLOVE, MINCED
1 QUART CHICKEN STOCK
1/2 POUND BLUE CHEESE, CRUMBLED
SALT AND BLACK PEPPER TO TASTE
4 TABLESPOONS CHOPPED FRESH
    FLAT-LEAF PARSLEY

In a stockpot with water, boil the potatoes until fork-tender. Drain and set aside.

Heat the olive oil in a large sauté pan over medium heat. Sweat the onion and garlic until golden brown. Add the potatoes and sauté an additional 2 minutes.

Add to the stockpot the sautéed onion, garlic, potatoes, stock, and blue cheese. Cover the pot with a lid and simmer for 10 minutes.

Remove the pot from the heat and puree the soup in batches in a blender until smooth. Return the soup to the stockpot and bring to a simmer. Season with salt and pepper.

Ladle the soup into 4 soup bowls and garnish each serving with parsley.

landscaping. There's no reason to assume that these rolling fields looked any different to our ancestors when they first crept here from the jungles. It is, therefore, a glimpse of Eden.

The pace of savannah life seeps quickly inside us, redirecting priorities; Stefano makes sure that we tune to the bush, not it to us. Accordingly, it's fine to spend hours watching a cheetah and her pair of furry-mantled cubs as they preen, yawn, snooze, and ponder otherworldly inspirations. We spend half a day waiting for a cheetah hunt that does not materialize, but none of it is time wasted. We learn rhythms, hierarchies, cycles of survival, and we become some minor part of the African energy flow.

Returning to camp, we encounter a pride of lions sprawled beneath a croton thicket, and drive within ten yards before they begin to shift and grumble. An amazing phenomenon exists between trucks and game here in the Mara; the animals do not associate the sound, smell, or silhouettes of vehicles with human beings and therefore perceive them as neither a threat nor a meal. As long as you remain inside, still and seated, they will permit amazingly close approaches. Keep your head, in other words, and you'll keep your limbs.

We pause beside these tawny monsters, near enough to watch bugs crisscross thick bands of muscle, near enough to count tufts on the male's majestic mane, near enough to catch the glint of failing sunlight in a sulfur eye, nearly close enough to feel gusts of breath. The moment is indescribably potent, soaked in adrenaline. The lion's renown as "king of the beasts" may be incorrect technically, but viscerally it's right on the money. Their carriage is regal; self-confidence percolates through each twitch of the hide. We remain silent and awestruck, and night falls with serene totality.

Something wobbly and warm is waiting inside my sleeping bag: a hot water bottle, placed there by Stefano, who knows how temperatures drop after dark and who also knows that I'm gonna think it's a snake. He snickers like an adolescent, but it's a nightcap of humility after an alpha-male day among the most dangerous mammals on earth.

All night Sopia stands outside the tent, alert and upright, clutching his iron-tipped spear. Masai are thus employed in most safari camps and also by security firms throughout Kenya. These tall, taciturn warriors are reputed to be fearless. Killing a lion single-handedly is a traditional (and still common, though now illegal) rite of passage for Masai boys.

The following day we're allowed a further glimpse into the lives of these proud tribesmen as we visit a Masai village near the post at Keekorok. It's dozens of miles over territory unsuited for mechanical transportation; we're never more than a single lapse of concentration away from a broken differential and a long hike back. The village sits at the crest of a low rise, a crude circle of mud-and-dung huts surrounding a cattle pen. It is populated by a hundred or so individuals under the guardianship of a single chief. It's one of thousands of such compounds throughout the Serengeti. The Masai, having braved disease, famine, warfare, and rapid political upheavals, thrive in the heart of an Africa that has plucked many other tribes from their ancestral lands.

It is supposed that the Masai possess a unique social flexibility that has allowed them to successfully straddle two cultures, two societies, two eras. Except for a dusty souvenir football inside the hut of one senior warrior, there's no sign of Western influence anywhere in the compound. Nor does my face, Western-cut clothing, or Leica backpack elicit any obvious regard from the Masai as I wander through their flyblown, dung-strewn courtyards. There's giggly and wide-eyed attention from the children, of course, but everyone else behaves with pronounced indifference. Women may be restricted from ogling strangers in this highly stratified society, but with the warriors it's testosterone and hubris.

Two basic life lessons are established early in Masai upbringing: Rely on yourself, and take pride in your heritage. It has seen them through plenty, and nothing in my backpack means the slightest thing to them. Later, when I cook by a riverbank with two strapping Masai youth, I watch them manipulate a pair of sticks and a wad of elephant dung, starting a campfire within thirty seconds.

KACHUMBARI

Chef Joash Omore explained to me that this was a simple but delicious slaw. Its flavors develop because the natural juices of the vegetables are extracted by the salt. I have found out that it is ideal to serve with Durban Spiced Shrimp (page 26).

SERVES 4

1/4 HEAD GREEN CABBAGE, SHREDDED

2 CARROTS, GRATED

2 TABLESPOONS CHOPPED FRESH CILANTRO

1 RED CHILE, SEEDED AND CHOPPED

1 WHITE ONION, THINLY SLICED

3 PLUM TOMATOES, SLICED INTO HALF-MOONS

SALT TO TASTE

In a large mixing bowl, combine all the ingredients and season well with salt. Cover the bowl with plastic wrap.

Refrigerate for 20 minutes before serving to let the salt draw the moisture from the vegetables to create its own sauce. Serve as you would a salad or slaw.

MAHARAGWE YA NASI

MAHARAGWE YA NASI IS SWAHILI FOR "BEANS IN COCONUT SAUCE." THIS IS A POPULAR KENYAN DISH.

SERVES 4

1 POUND RED KIDNEY BEANS, SOAKED OVERNIGHT IN WATER

8 CUPS WATER

1 TABLESPOON OLIVE OIL

2 WHITE ONIONS, DICED

3 PLUM TOMATOES, DICED

2 GARLIC CLOVES, MINCED

1 CUP COCONUT MILK

SALT AND BLACK PEPPER TO TASTE

Drain the beans. In a medium stockpot, place the beans and water. Simmer over medium heat for 1 to 1½ hours, or until tender. Drain and return the beans to the stockpot.

Heat the olive oil in a sauté pan over medium heat. Sweat the onions, tomatoes, and garlic until tender. Add the onion mixture to the beans. Add the coconut milk and bring to a simmer over low heat. Cook for 5 minutes. Season with salt and pepper. Serve warm.

Later still, at Stefano's camp, it takes this same duo nearly five minutes to start one with a book of matches.

It's not until suppertime that I notice my reactions are being monitored. Within the cattle pen I'm allowed a rare glimpse of the ritualistic bloodletting ceremony for which the Masai are so famous. During the ceremony a select cow is wrestled to the dust and restrained as a warrior fires a short dart into its jugular vein. The quick spurt of blood is caught in a cup and mixed with an equal portion of milk. In a part of the ritual I have yet to understand, the cup is next handed to me. And now, suddenly, it appears that the Masai women have shaken their lethargy and are irrationally and completely amused. They show miles of teeth, let go loud peals of laughter, and, for some reason, do not appear the least bit impressed with me, with the incredible level of self-control it requires for me to gag down a sip of this vampire's cocktail, or with my magnanimous show of generosity as I leave ample—trust me, ample—for the bloodthirsty children who have gathered for their own dose.

This coagulated, protein-rich transfusion constitutes a portion of the daily food intake for most Masai, but the bulk of their diet, like that of all rural Kenyans, is *ugali*. Similar dishes, starchy mushes made of corn, millet, yams, plantains, or cassava, are known elsewhere in Africa as *masima*, *adze*, or *mealie-meal*—though *ugali* by any other name would be as bland. Frequently it serves as a foundation for stew, sauce, or gravy.

COTTAR AND ME IN KENYA WITH MY GMC ADVENTURE COOKING TRUCK.

At Cottar's Camp, a 1920s-style luxury safari outfit bordering the Loliondo Reserve, I learn this and a pantry of other facts about African cooking from one of the most remarkable chefs I've yet encountered, Joash Omore. He is one of a new generation of Kenyans who have abandoned the traditional constraints and, occasionally, the poisoned politics and bloodshed of tribal life for an expanded worldview. His ultimate goal is to come to the United States, find a kitchen job, and hook into the dream. Tonight, however, his focus is here and now as he attempts to fill in my educational gaps and finishes by preparing an array of traditional Kenyan dishes.

His personal slate of recipes, including these African classics, was what first caught the attention of Calvin Cottar (whose background in the safari business is now three generations deep). Omore's personality also served him well; he's a soft-spoken man who converses in the lilting accent of subcontinental English, though when he directs his kitchen staff, it's in Swahili or Luo. Earlier in the day he'd assembled produce from a well-tended garden in a valley cusp behind the camp, and it now sits on a wooden table: knots of chard, pint-sized potatoes, and the omnipresent pinkish African staple: yams. At Omore's request, knives begin moving rapidly and deftly; it's a vortex of energy as leafy cabbage, crisp carrots, and miniature fiery chiles are transformed into traditional Kenyan coleslaw and as fudge-colored pestles crush cardamom and clove heads into rich and pungent dust. Meanwhile, tended by intense turbaned workers, bubbling pots of red beans simmering in an ever-thickening coconut sauce and steaming cinnamon rice send the perfumes of ancient Africa throughout Omore's semi-mobile kitchen, a twenty-by-twenty structure set up before a wood-fire range.

At dinner, while we enjoy a tumbler of Tusker beer, a pair of red-fezzed attendants haul out heaping bowls of food: steaming rolls smeared with local honey, the variegated raw-vegetable *kachumbari*, spongy stacks of unleavened chapatis, *sucuma wiki* (a creamy cassava leaf concoction, similar to collard greens, that can be made with any leafy

ORZO PASTA WITH PEAS AND ANNATTO-SAGE SAUCE

WALKING THROUGH THE NAIROBI MARKET, I SPOTTED A WOMAN SHELLING PEAS. IT WAS THE INSPIRATION FOR THIS RECIPE.

SERVES 4

1/2 CUP DRIED PORCINI MUSHROOMS

2 CUPS HEAVY CREAM

1 TEASPOON ANNATTO POWDER

1 TABLESPOON CHOPPED FRESH SAGE

SALT AND BLACK PEPPER TO TASTE

1 TABLESPOON UNSALTED BUTTER

1 CUP BLANCHED FRESH PEAS

1/2 CUP JULIENNED SUNDRIED TOMATOES

2 CUPS COOKED ORZO PASTA

1/2 CUP GRATED MANCHEGO CHEESE

2 TABLESPOONS CHOPPED FRESH PARSLEY

Soak the mushrooms in warm water for 30 minutes. Drain and discard the liquid.

In a sauté pan over medium heat, simmer the cream for 3 to 4 minutes. Stir in the annatto powder and sage. Continue to simmer the cream sauce another 2 minutes. Season the annatto-sage cream with salt and pepper. Keep warm.

In a separate sauté pan over medium heat, sauté the drained mushrooms in the butter until golden brown and tender, 4 to 5 minutes. Add the blanched peas, sundried tomatoes, and orzo to the pan. Toss all the ingredients until hot. Stir in the annatto-sage cream and cheese. Stir in the chopped parsley.

Sucuma Wiki

Chef Joash Omore made this traditional Kenyan dish for me. It combines spinach with onions, tomatoes, and a touch of cream. This is a great side dish for your African-themed dinner.

SERVES 4

1 POUND SPINACH OR SWISS CHARD, ROUGHLY CHOPPED

2 TABLESPOONS OLIVE OIL

1 WHITE ONION, DICED

2 PLUM TOMATOES, DICED

¼ CUP HEAVY CREAM

SALT AND BLACK PEPPER TO TASTE

Bring a stockpot of salted water to a boil. Add the spinach and cook for 20 seconds. If you use Swiss chard, boil it for 1½ minutes. Drain and cool the spinach to the point where you are able to squeeze out the water from the leaves. When you have removed as much water as possible, set the spinach aside.

Heat the olive oil in a large sauté pan over medium heat. Sweat the onion until translucent, 5 to 6 minutes. Add the tomatoes and spinach and cook for 2 to 3 minutes. Stir in the cream and cook 1 minute more. Season with salt and pepper.

green), aromatic rice *pilau,* the beans and coconut stew called *maharagwe ya nasi,* and *nyama kuku,* which is richly sauced, fire-roasted chicken.

Dinner at Cottar's is served within an open-air tent, but in cordon bleu style, with gloved waiters and white tablecloths and soft lighting from sterling candelabra. Surrounding the dining area are fiercely polished antique appointments, and from the shelves various framed and sepia-tinted ancestors watch with certain satisfaction as the Cottar legacy continues in grand style.

Gradually, darkness settles in, and bulleting rain begins to elicit high-pitched trumpets from distant elephant herds. Rasping baboon coughs filter in from a thicket across the river. In an hour these sounds will lull us all to sleep. For now they serve as an exotic backdrop for Chef Joash Omore's vibrant Kenyan feast.

Chef Omore's dishes are mostly vegetarian, reflecting the realities of traditional subsistence economics in Kenya. Back in Nairobi there's a restaurant with a slightly different feel for things. It's called Carnivores. Ordering vegetarian in a place like Carnivores is like, what? Ordering a double espresso at an insomniac's workshop? Aspartame at Hendry County's Sugar Festival? A burger in Bhopal?

In fact, the Carnivores restaurant happens to offer this totally anomalous, weak-kneed option as the final item on an otherwise flesh-centric menu. The problem is, of course, you have to get those weak knees past the lobby, which is dominated by a huge circular charcoal pit where various joints and sides are skewered and roasted on Masai swords—also used to dispatch lions and other Masai. You get the impression that if you carry your Earth First morality into the dining room, you might find your own name on tomorrow's menu board.

On the night I visit, the menu board lists such exotic game as zebra, giraffe, and crocodile. Since hunting was outlawed by the Kenyan government in 1977, you're assured that your zeeb (the local term for zebra) is farm-raised. A strange oxymoron is *domesticated wildlife.*

For novices squeamish about devouring zoo favorites, a

pre-supper cocktail like a *dawa* is the best medicine. *Dawa* is a Swahili word meaning "strong medicine," or something close, and though it's nothing more than a glorified gimlet, the drink does the trick. By the time the waiter begins to slice succulent slivers of flesh from the various haunches, I'm in a kind of primordial, heart-stupid feeding frenzy. The lesson learned, however, is there's a kingdom of flavors and textures available beyond chicken, beef, and pork, especially here in Africa.

SOUTH AFRICA

Continuing education in game can be had at Khaya Nyama, some 2,500 miles to the south. In Zulu, Khaya Nyama means "house of meat," so there's not much gray area in the philosophical direction of this Cape Town restaurant. Set in a sort of DreamWorks version of a bushman's cave, Khaya Nyama owner and super-predator Carl Staude recruits menu fodder from a nearby farm and, typically, harvests the entrées himself. Certainly, he cooks them, and he's as accomplished a chef as he is an outdoorsman. Over a nip of South African cabernet, he introduces his recipe for puff adder with "First, catch your puff adder," then launches into his perspective on unusual proteins: "Warthog is sweeter than pork, but fully interchangeable. Here, we use belly rib marinated in brandy and basted in honey and mustard, which enhances the natural flavors. I never mask what nature intended: Eland, gemsbok, and ostrich each have unique tastes, wild flavors. These distinctions should be savored, not hidden."

Regarding Carnivores and Khaya Nyama, and what we can charitably refer to as the Flintstone Diet, meat-centered lifestyles have passed in and out of vogue since the Paleolithic era. One side argues that 2 million years of evolution can't be wrong, while the other suggests that eating meat—any meat—in today's world is self-indulgent, unnecessary, and ecologically threatening. Well, there are some obvious considerations. First, unlike most of us, our

UGALI

THIS PLAIN POLENTA-STYLE STARCH IS A STAPLE OF THE MASAI PEOPLE. IT IS IDEAL TO ACCOMPANY DISHES THAT HAVE A RICH, MEATY SAUCE, SUCH AS MAHARAGWE YA NASI (PAGE 14).

SERVES 4

2 CUPS WATER
1 CUP WHITE CORNMEAL
SALT AND BLACK PEPPER TO TASTE

Boil the water in a medium saucepan over medium heat. Stir in the cornmeal. Using a whisk, stir continuously until the *ugali* comes together and cooks out the starch, 10 to 15 minutes. Season with salt and pepper.

NOTE: *Ugali* can be served in soft or hard form, just like polenta. To serve it soft, spoon it from the saucepan onto your serving dishes.

To serve *ugali* like hard polenta, spoon it into a mold of your choice, such as a ramekin, and refrigerate until it becomes firm. Once firm, preheat the oven to 350°F. Unmold the *ugali*. Reheat it on a baking sheet in the oven until the center is hot. To test it, place a thermometer into the center. When it reads 145°F., the *ugali* is hot enough to serve.

hunter-gatherer ancestors were trying to put on weight, not take it off. Second, australopithecines tended to die before they would have developed heart disease anyway. And third, meat is a perfectly natural part of the omnivorian diet, and we have as much right to our share as any other predator on the planet. If that sounds like a wimpy and noncommittal response to a complicated question, it shouldn't; rather, it harks back to the simplest of rules: moderation in everything.

Social moderation hit South Africa a little less than a generation ago, and nothing, gratefully, has been the same since. In the early nineties, apartheid was carted down to the trash heap of history. Wandering the streets of today's Cape Town, your impulse is to measure the progress at every intersection and ensure that South Africa's newfound civil rights are not just governmental lip service intended to ramrod commercial products back onto the world's markets. At first I don't know what to think. Strange dialects are drifting from the windows of the trendy restaurants along Long Street, and peeking into several of them, I find that the cooking and cleaning staff is predominantly black, and they're speaking the odd language called Khoisan—the tribal tongue of the local Bushman. In dining rooms of Long Street there's a smattering of dark faces, but the restaurant-goers and café customers are mostly white. Admittedly, it's a little disconcerting to see no blatant evidence of integration in one of Cape Town's most vibrant quarters.

Up the street, however, sits Mama Africa. With its story-high earth-mother sign and the thumping, solidly African sound of drums leaking from the doorway, it's hard to miss. Inside, we're packed sardine tight in a smoke-filled tavern, in the middle of what appears to be an equal blend of races, white, black, and every shade in between, mingling in a circle around the band, which is jamming with nearly unbelievably spice and energy. This is the South Africa I'd hoped for. This is the musical style that inspired Paul Simon's "Graceland," in which he refers to these percussion-heavy, traditional African tunes as "the roots of rhythm."

The roots of rhythm remain, and more than that besides. Recall the protohuman whose tiny skeleton was discovered in Olduvai Gorge. Called "Lucy" by her finders, she is, for all practical considerations, the individual to whom humanity owes its beginnings. She is our Eve, and she belongs to us all: black, white, and every shade in between. She is "Mama Africa." At the café we catch a glimpse of what the future can hold for this vast land, sometimes ignored and often misunderstood, but always at the margin of our consciences. Inside there's a mosaic of colors, faces, and personalities—each unique but all reacting in unison, all listening to the identical beat.

THE PRODUCTION CREW FOR OUR AFRICA EPISODE AFTER LANDING IN THE MASA MARA IN KENYA. FROM LEFT TO RIGHT: CASEY GAMBA (GUIDE), JEFF FISH (CO-EXECUTIVE PRODUCER), BOB BERG (VIDEOPHOTOGRAPHER), ROGER SMITH (AUDIO ENGINEER), VANESSA POMA (ASSOCIATE PRODUCER), CHRIS KASSEL (WRITER), MASAI WARRIOR, ME, MATT PRESTED (ASSOCIATE PRODUCER/CAMERAMAN), JOE VAUGHN (PHOTOGRAPHER), LOCAL SAFARI GUIDE, TERESA ISABELLE (GUIDE).

Tusker Onion Soup

Tusker is an amber Kenyan beer. This adaptation of French onion soup makes the most of the sweet flavor of Tusker beer.

SERVES 4

SOUP

2 WHITE ONIONS, JULIENNED

2 TABLESPOONS UNSALTED BUTTER

12 OUNCES TUSKER BEER OR ANY AMBER BEER

5 CUPS VEAL OR BEEF STOCK

GARNISH

4 BAGUETTE SLICES

2 TABLESPOONS GRATED PARMIGIANO-REGGIANO CHEESE

$1^{1}/_{2}$ TEASPOONS CHOPPED FRESH FLAT-LEAF PARSLEY

SALT AND BLACK PEPPER TO TASTE

FOR THE SOUP: In a 1-gallon stockpot over medium heat, caramelize the onions in the butter slowly. Stir frequently to prevent the onions from burning. When the onions are caramelized, add the beer and reduce the liquid by one-half. Add the stock to the pot and simmer for 8 to 10 minutes.

Preheat the oven to 350°F.

FOR THE GARNISH: While the soup is simmering, make the garnish. Sprinkle the slices of baguette with the grated cheese and toast on a baking sheet in the oven until slightly golden brown, approximately 5 minutes. When the baguettes come out of the oven, sprinkle the parsley over them.

Season the soup with salt and pepper.

Ladle the soup into 4 deep soup bowls and garnish each serving with a piece of the baguette.

Bollas

Bollas are traditional South African pumpkin fritters served with a brown sugar syrup. I first tried these fritters at a restaurant in Cape Town called Mama Africa.

SERVES 6

SYRUP

1/2 CUP (UNPACKED) LIGHT BROWN SUGAR

1/2 CUP WATER

1 TEASPOON CORNSTARCH

DUSTING MIXTURE

1/4 CUP SUGAR

1 1/2 TEASPOONS GROUND CINNAMON

BOLLAS

1 POUND PUMPKIN, PEELED AND DICED

1 LARGE EGG

3/4 CUP CAKE FLOUR

1 TEASPOON BAKING POWDER

1/4 TEASPOON GROUND CINNAMON

1/4 TEASPOON GROUND MACE

VEGETABLE OIL FOR FRYING

FOR THE SYRUP: Combine the brown sugar, water, and cornstarch in a small saucepan over medium heat. Bring to a boil while stirring constantly. Lower the heat and simmer until the sugar is dissolved and the mixture is syrupy in consistency. Set aside on the back of the stove.

FOR THE DUSTING MIXTURE: In a mixing bowl, combine the sugar and cinnamon.

FOR THE BOLLAS: Cook the pumpkin in a stockpot of boiling salted water until tender. Drain the pumpkin and transfer it to a medium mixing bowl. Mash the pumpkin with a fork until smooth and combine it with the egg, flour, baking powder, cinnamon, and mace.

In a frying pan over medium heat, heat about 1/2 inch of vegetable oil to 350°F.

Drop tablespoon-sized spoonfuls of the pumpkin batter into the frying pan. Fry until golden brown on all sides. Drain on paper towels.

Place the bollas in a serving dish. Drizzle with the syrup, dust with the cinnamon sugar, and serve.

BOBOTIE WITH ROTI

THIS DISH COULD CONTEND FOR SOUTH AFRICA'S NATIONAL DISH. BOBOTIE IS A MINCEMEAT CASSEROLE THAT WAS BROUGHT TO THE CAPE MALAY AREA BY THE FIRST DUTCH SETTLERS. TODAY, SOUTH AFRICANS ROLL THE MINCEMEAT IN THE ROTI TO CREATE SALOMI, A POPULAR FAST-FOOD SNACK.

SERVES **8**

ROTI

3 CUPS CAKE FLOUR

1/4 TEASPOON SALT

VEGETABLE OIL

1 1/4 CUPS WATER (AMOUNT MAY VARY SLIGHTLY)

1/4 CUP PLUS 2 TABLESPOONS UNSALTED BUTTER, SOFTENED

ALL-PURPOSE FLOUR FOR DUSTING

BOBOTIE

2 TABLESPOONS UNSALTED BUTTER

2 CUPS DICED WHITE ONIONS

3 GARLIC CLOVES, MINCED

1 1/2 TEASPOONS CURRY POWDER

1 TEASPOON TURMERIC

2 POUNDS GROUND LAMB OR BEEF

1 1/2 CUPS BREAD CRUMBS

1/4 CUP WHOLE MILK

1 LARGE EGG

1/4 CUP RAISINS

1 GRANNY SMITH APPLE, PEELED AND DICED

1/2 CUP CHOPPED DRIED APRICOTS

1 TABLESPOON GRATED LEMON ZEST

2 TABLESPOONS FRESH LEMON JUICE

1/4 CUP SLIVERED ALMONDS, TOASTED

1 1/2 TEASPOONS SALT

1 1/2 TEASPOONS GROUND BLACK PEPPER

3 WHOLE BAY LEAVES

TOPPING

1 CUP WHOLE MILK

1 LARGE EGG

DURING AN EARLY-MORNING SAFARI, STEFANO CHELI EXPLAINS TO ME THAT THE CHEETAH IS A NOMADIC PREDATOR.

FOR THE ROTI: In a mixing bowl, combine the flour and salt. Add ¼ cup of vegetable oil and work it into the flour until the dough is crumbly. Add enough water to make a soft dough.

On a floured surface, roll out the dough to a rectangle about 13 × 18 inches. Spread the softened butter over the dough and roll the dough from one wide end into a log shape. Cover with a towel and let rest for 30 minutes.

Cut the dough into 12 pieces and roll them into small balls. On a floured surface, roll out each ball into a 6-inch circle.

Fill a frying pan with ½ inch of vegetable oil and heat to 350°F. Fry each circle in the hot oil. Turn over when one side is golden brown. When the other side is golden brown, remove the roti from the oil and place on paper towels to drain.

FOR THE BOBOTIE: Preheat the oven to 350°F. In a sauté pan over medium heat, melt the butter and sweat the onions and garlic until translucent.

Add the curry powder and turmeric, and sauté for 1 minute. Remove from the heat and place the mixture in a large mixing bowl. Add the ground meat, bread crumbs, milk, egg, raisins, apple, apricots, lemon zest, lemon juice, almonds, salt, pepper, and bay leaves. Mix thoroughly.

Place in a 9 × 13-inch casserole dish, smooth the top, and cover the dish with aluminum foil. Bake for 1 hour.

FOR THE TOPPING: Thoroughly combine the milk and egg with a fork. Take the casserole from the oven, remove the foil, and pour the topping over the casserole. Increase the oven temperature to 375°F. Place the casserole back in the oven and bake, uncovered, for 15 minutes, or until the top is lightly browned.

Serve the bobotie with the roti.

MOJITO

THIS IS THE PERFECT DRINK FOR A SUMMER COCKTAIL PARTY.

MAKES 2 DRINKS

JUICE OF 4 LIMES
24 FRESH MINT LEAVES
2 TABLESPOONS SUGAR IN THE RAW
2 OUNCES LIGHT RUM
2 OUNCES DARK RUM
8 OUNCES CLUB SODA
ICE

With a mortar and pestle or blender, grind the lime juice with the mint leaves and sugar. Mix the mint mixture with the light rum, dark rum, and club soda. Chill and serve over ice.

Fried Walnut Chicken with Brandy Pawpaw Sauce

The walnuts are a great addition to the breading mixture.

SERVES 4

SAUCE

4 TABLESPOONS UNSALTED BUTTER

1/4 CUP CHOPPED WALNUTS

1/4 CUP (UNPACKED) LIGHT BROWN SUGAR

1 RIPE MANGO, PEELED AND DICED

1 RIPE PAWPAW (PAPAYA), PEELED, SEEDED, AND DICED

1/4 CUP BRANDY

1/2 CUP WATER

2 TABLESPOONS CHOPPED FRESH MINT

CHICKEN

VEGETABLE OIL FOR FRYING

2 CUPS BREAD CRUMBS

1 CUP CHOPPED WALNUTS

2 LARGE EGGS

2 CUPS WHOLE MILK

4 CHICKEN BREASTS, BONELESS, SKINLESS, AND CUT INTO STRIPS

1 1/2 CUPS ALL-PURPOSE FLOUR

FOR THE SAUCE: In a sauté pan over medium heat, melt the butter and lightly sauté the walnuts for 2 to 4 minutes. Stir in the sugar until fully dissolved. Add the mango and pawpaw, and continue to sauté for 3 to 4 minutes. Add the brandy and flame off the alcohol. Add the water and simmer the sauce for 5 minutes. Stir in the mint and cook 1 minute more. Remove the pan from the heat. Place the sauce in a blender and puree until the sauce is smooth. Return the sauce to the pan and keep warm on the back of the stove.

FOR THE CHICKEN: Fill a 1-gallon stockpot 3 inches deep with vegetable oil. Heat the oil over medium heat to 350°F. (If the temperature is lower, the chicken will absorb the oil and become greasy.)

In a medium mixing bowl, mix together the bread crumbs and walnuts.

In a separate bowl, whisk the eggs and milk together to make an egg wash.

Dust the chicken strips with the flour. Dip the strips in the egg wash and then press them into the bread crumb mixture.

Place the chicken strips in the hot oil. When they begin to turn golden brown, use a spoon or tongs to turn them over. When all sides are golden brown, remove and place on paper towels to drain.

Serve the walnut chicken with the brandy pawpaw sauce.

Young Masai children, happy to make our acquaintance.

Spicy Beef Chapatis

Chapatis are an African version of a taco. The bread can be eaten with numerous types of fillings. Beef, chicken, and vegetarian are the most popular.

SERVES 4

CHAPATIS

2 CUPS ALL-PURPOSE FLOUR

1 CUP WATER

PINCH OF SALT

4 TABLESPOONS OLIVE OIL

ALL-PURPOSE FLOUR FOR DUSTING

FILLING

1/2 CUP DICED WHITE ONION

3 GARLIC CLOVES, PEELED AND MINCED

2 TABLESPOONS OLIVE OIL

2 SMALL RED CHILES, MINCED

1 1/2 POUNDS GROUND BEEF

SALT AND BLACK PEPPER TO TASTE

FOR THE CHAPATIS: In a medium mixing bowl, use your hands to combine the flour, water, salt, and 2 tablespoons of olive oil. Mix until well incorporated and a sticky dough forms. Remove the dough from the bowl and place on a floured work surface. Knead for 3 to 5 minutes. Refrigerate for 20 minutes.

Return the dough to the floured work surface and roll into four 6-inch circles.

Place the remaining 2 tablespoons of olive oil in a sauté pan over medium heat and brown both sides of the chapatis. Remove from the pan and keep warm.

FOR THE FILLING: In a hot sauté pan over medium heat, sauté the onion and garlic in the olive oil until the onion is translucent. Add the chiles and sauté for 1 minute. Add the ground beef and continue to sauté until the meat is thoroughly cooked, approximately 10 minutes.

Season the filling with salt and pepper, and serve on a piece of chapati.

Durban Spiced Shrimp, Cape Malay Mashed Potatoes, and Chive Oil

The spice markets of South Africa inspired this recipe. Durban is located on the east coast, and it has been one of the chief ports for spices being brought in from India, Madagascar, and the Philippines.

SERVES **6**
MAKES **3** CUPS OF SPICE

DURBAN SPICE MIX

1/2 CUP HUNGARIAN PAPRIKA

1/2 CUP ANNATTO SEEDS

1/2 CUP SEA SALT

3/4 CUP WHOLE CORIANDER

1/4 CUP GROUND TURMERIC

1/4 CUP CUMIN SEEDS

1 TABLESPOON PLUS 1 TEASPOON WHOLE ZANZIBAR CLOVES

1 TABLESPOON PLUS 1 TEASPOON GROUND NUTMEG

1 TABLESPOON PLUS 1 TEASPOON GROUND CINNAMON

1 1/2 TEASPOONS WHOLE BLACK PEPPERCORNS

3/4 TABLESPOON MELEGUETA PEPPER (ALSO CALLED GRAINS OF PARADISE OR GUINEA PEPPER; BLACK PEPPER CAN BE SUBSTITUTED)

MASHED POTATOES

1 TEASPOON CUMIN SEEDS

1 1/2 TEASPOONS OLIVE OIL

3 GARLIC CLOVES, PEELED

1 CUP WATER

2 POUNDS RUSSET POTATOES

3/4 CUP HEAVY CREAM

2 SMALL RED CHILES, SEEDED AND CHOPPED

1 SMALL GREEN CHILE, SEEDED AND CHOPPED

1/4 POUND (1 STICK) UNSALTED BUTTER, MELTED

SALT AND BLACK PEPPER TO TASTE

CHIVE OIL

1/4 POUND FRESH CHIVES

1 CUP EXTRA-VIRGIN OLIVE OIL

SHRIMP

30 LARGE SHRIMP, PEELED AND DEVEINED, TAIL LEFT ON

1/2 CUP OLIVE OIL

WHOLE CHIVES FOR GARNISH

FOR THE SPICE MIX: In a large mixing bowl, combine all the spices. Grind in a coffee or spice grinder, sift, and set aside. Unused spice mix will last for approximately 6 months if stored in a cool, dark place.

FOR THE MASHED POTATOES: Preheat the oven to 350°F. Toast the cumin seeds on a baking sheet in the oven for 4 to 5 minutes. Grind the toasted cumin seeds and set aside.

Heat the olive oil in a small sauté pan over medium heat. Add the garlic and sauté until golden brown. Add the water and simmer until the garlic is tender. Remove the garlic and puree. Discard the liquid in the pan.

Boil the potatoes in a pot of water until tender. Drain and place in a mixing bowl.

Scald the heavy cream in a saucepan.

Add the red and green chiles, ground cumin, melted butter, pureed garlic, and scalded heavy cream to the mixing bowl with the potatoes. Use the paddle attachment on the mixer to combine until smooth. Season with salt and pepper. Set aside in a warm place.

FOR THE CHIVE OIL: Blanch the chives in a pot of boiling water for 10 to 15 seconds. Plunge the blanched chives in ice water; this preserves the intense green color. In a blender, puree the chives while drizzling in the olive oil. Push the chive oil through a strainer and set aside.

FOR THE SHRIMP: Dredge the shrimp in the Durban spice mix, enough to coat each shrimp. Heat the olive oil in a sauté pan over medium heat. Sear the shrimp in batches until dark brown, 2 to 4 minutes. Do not overcrowd the pan. Turn the shrimp over and repeat. Remove the shrimp from the pan and place on paper towels to drain.

TO ASSEMBLE: Place a spoonful of mashed potatoes in the middle of a plate. Stand 5 shrimp up and around the mashed potatoes. Drizzle chive oil around the plate and garnish with 2 chives. Repeat with the 5 remaining plates.

A VERY PROUD FISHMONGER IN A MARKET IN NAIROBI.

One of my most adventurous moments in Kenya. Roasting catfish over a fire created by two Masai warriors using only two sticks and making it in under a minute. No kidding!

Mozambican Brown Shark

Carl Staude of the restaurant Khaya Nyama, in Cape Town, showed me his favorite way to prepare Mozambican brown shark. The sauce may seem a little unusual, but it really complements the shark. It would also work well with swordfish.

SERVES 4

SAUCE
JUICE OF 1 LEMON
1/2 CUP BRANDY
1 CUP MAYONNAISE
1 TEASPOON CHOPPED FRESH GINGER
1 GARLIC CLOVE, MINCED
FISH SPICE MIX
3 TABLESPOONS SALT
2 TEASPOONS GROUND CORIANDER
2 TEASPOONS GROUND BLACK PEPPER
BROWN SHARK
FOUR 4-OUNCE FILLETS BROWN SHARK, MAKO SHARK, OR
    SWORDFISH
2 TABLESPOONS OLIVE OIL
2 TEASPOONS GROUND CINNAMON
1 1/2 TEASPOONS MINCED GARLIC
GARNISH
2 TABLESPOONS CHOPPED FRESH FLAT-LEAF PARSLEY

FOR THE SAUCE: In a medium mixing bowl, use a whisk to combine the lemon juice, brandy, mayonnaise, ginger, and garlic. Set aside.

FOR THE FISH SPICE: In a medium mixing bowl, combine the salt, coriander, and pepper. Set aside.

FOR THE SHARK: Season each shark fillet on both sides with the fish spice. Heat the olive oil in a sauté pan over medium heat and add the shark fillets. Once each piece is crispy on one side, turn it over. Add the sauce to the pan and begin to reduce. Sprinkle the cinnamon and garlic over the fillets. When the sauce is brown and thick, and the shark is thoroughly cooked, remove the pan from the heat.

Place a shark fillet on each plate and spoon over the brown sauce. Garnish with chopped parsley and serve.

Cape Brandy Pudding

While traveling in Africa, I learned many traditional holiday dishes. This is a South African dessert that Janette Wiehahn of L'Adorie Estate made for me and my crew in Paarl.

SERVES 4

SAUCE

1 TABLESPOON UNSALTED BUTTER, MELTED

1 CUP SUGAR

1/4 TEASPOON SALT

1 CUP PLUS 2 TABLESPOONS WATER

1/2 CUP BRANDY

1 TEASPOON VANILLA EXTRACT

PUDDING

1 TEASPOON BAKING SODA

1/2 POUND DRIED DATES, PITS REMOVED AND DICED

1 CUP BOILING WATER

4 TABLESPOONS UNSALTED BUTTER

1 CUP SUGAR

2 LARGE EGGS

2 CUPS ALL-PURPOSE FLOUR

1 TEASPOON BAKING POWDER

1/2 TEASPOON SALT

1 CUP FINELY CHOPPED WALNUTS

WHIPPED CREAM

FOR THE SAUCE: In a medium saucepan over medium heat, simmer together the butter, sugar, salt, and water for 5 minutes. Add the brandy and vanilla, and simmer an additional minute. Keep warm on the back of the stove.

FOR THE PUDDING: Preheat the oven to 350°F. In a mixing bowl using a large spoon, combine the baking soda, half of the dates, and the boiling water. Let the mixture cool. In a separate mixing bowl, cream together the butter and sugar. Then beat in the eggs. Sift the flour, baking powder, and salt into the butter mixture. Add the remaining dates and the walnuts to the flour and butter mixture. Combine both mixtures thoroughly and transfer to a 9 × 13-inch casserole. Bake for 40 minutes.

Remove the casserole dish from the oven and let cool for 10 minutes. Serve with the whipped cream and brandy sauce.

Fried Pawpaw

Pawpaw is another name for papaya. This batter also works well for frying firm bananas.

SERVES 4

VEGETABLE OIL FOR FRYING

DUSTING MIXTURE

1 1/2 TEASPOONS GROUND CINNAMON

1/4 TEASPOON GROUND CARDAMOM

1/4 CUP SUGAR

BATTER

1 CUP CAKE FLOUR

PINCH OF SALT

1 TABLESPOON SUGAR

1/2 CUP WHOLE MILK

1 TABLESPOON UNSALTED BUTTER, MELTED

2 EGG WHITES

PAWPAW

2 RIPE PAWPAWS (PAPAYAS), PEELED, SEEDED, AND CUT INTO
   CHUNKS

1 1/2 TEASPOONS GROUND CARDAMOM

VANILLA ICE CREAM

Fill a saucepan 2 inches deep with vegetable oil and heat to 350°F.

FOR THE DUSTING MIXTURE: In a mixing bowl, combine the cinnamon, cardamom, and sugar, and set aside.

FOR THE BATTER: In a mixing bowl, combine the flour, salt, and sugar. In a separate bowl, whisk together the milk and butter. Combine the wet and dry ingredients with a whisk to form a smooth batter. If the batter is too thick, add a little more milk.

In a separate mixing bowl, whisk the egg whites to form stiff peaks. Fold the whipped whites into the batter. Be careful not to overmix the batter and deflate the whites.

FOR THE PAWPAW: Season the pawpaw chunks with the cardamom. Dip each chunk of pawpaw into the batter and deep-fry in the vegetable oil a few pieces at a time until crisp and golden brown. Place the fried pawpaws on paper towels to drain. Dust them with the cinnamon sugar mix immediately.

Serve the fried pawpaw chunks with vanilla ice cream.

Almond Kowadjik

This is a South African adaptation of a Malaysian dessert made of almonds, coconut, and rice.

MAKES 20 SQUARES

1/2 CUP GROUND ALMONDS

1/2 CUP DRIED COCONUT

1 CUP LONG-GRAIN RICE

3 CUPS WHOLE MILK

GRATED ZEST OF 2 ORANGES

1/4 TEASPOON SALT

1/4 TEASPOON GROUND CARDAMOM

4 TABLESPOONS UNSALTED BUTTER

1/4 CUP (UNPACKED) LIGHT BROWN SUGAR

Preheat the oven to 350°F.

Toast the almonds and coconut separately on baking sheets in the oven until golden brown. Set aside to cool.

In a saucepan, combine the rice, milk, orange zest, salt, and cardamom. Bring to a simmer over medium heat and cover. Cook until all the milk is absorbed and the rice is soft. It should not have a bite. Remove from the heat and mix in the butter, sugar, almonds, and coconut. Press the mixture into a buttered 9 × 13-inch casserole and chill.

Cut into squares before serving.

A most elegant dinner table. This is the standard fare if you stay at Cottar's 1920s-style safari camp. You really feel like someone living in the Hemingway era when you have dinner there.

A U S T R A L I A

My fascination with the Land Down Under started back in 1987 when I did my first open water dive in the Great Barrier Reef. Since then I've been involved in some extensive adventuring in Oz.

Besides traveling there to produce two half-hour shows for my Food Network series, I spearheaded a successful international chat session with a group of children at Sydney's Tarranga Zoo and another group at the Detroit Zoo *(Zoo to Zoo . . . Kids to Kids)*. The event allowed these fourth and fifth graders, separated by fourteen thousand miles, to exchange ideas and stories, and to learn about animals from each other's corner of the globe.

But, of course, my most memorable Australian experience was the game I played for forty-one days in 2000: *Survivor II: The Australian Outback*. I won't dwell on this; I'll only try to share a little of the wonder I felt, four hundred miles from Cairns, the city where we started our journey, while becoming a true part of a land that had long held me in the grip of a passionate fascination. What follows is a small slice of the wonderful memories I'd already begun to assemble in Australia prior to *Survivor II*.

OUTBACK

Four hours from Port Douglas, just beyond the hump of the Great Dividing Range, the landscape changes from luxuriant beachfront to an endless spread of gum trees and dust the color of dried blood. This reddish universe, which hooks around the Gulf of Carpentaria and becomes gradually drier until it reaches the continent's arid heart, looks unearthly. Seeing a herd of brontosauruses lumbering by would not seem the least bit out of place; in fact, there *are* actual dinosaur tracks to be found in rocks nearby. Anyway, the six-foot flightless emus, native to the area, make a pretty fair substitution.

What I'm looking for is a kangaroo. It's been three days, and I haven't seen a single one. Having naively assumed that Australia was a Jurassic Park of leaping kangaroo herds, I'm beginning to wonder if the whole marsupial thing is just a bizarre Aussie myth, like the one about Vegemite being edible. From the cockpit of his monstrous all-terrain Toyota Troop Carrier, Aussie George assures me, first, that kangaroos are real and, second, that Vegemite, Australia's legendary breakfast spread, is "tip-top tucker." After a flash he adds, "And it's ticker tucker, too." By which he means that Vegemite is not only good stuff but heart-smart as well.

Here's a heads up: Native Australian may take some practice if you're used to English.

Aussie George has been hanging around since Cairns. He's a driver by trade and an all-inclusive tour guide when required. He's probably somewhere in his fifties, brimming with sinew and soul. He favors an Anzac-style Akubra hat, folded up on one side, and an eight-inch knife on his belt. He has "the look"—something raw, rugged, and rascally. It's a look that you suspect was worn by those British convicts exiled here in the seventeenth century. But there's none of the riffraff inside Aussie George, and he shortly becomes an indispensable companion. Quick with wisecracks and tireless in the field, he's also filled with countless magnificent—if largely impossible—tales from his life. Anything you think you've done, Aussie George has done it already, and done it better. If half his stories are true, he's a cross between Evel Knievel, the Incredible Hulk, and Crocodile Dundee.

On we go. Paved road pretty much ends at the town of Laura, although calling Laura a town is a little like calling Benji a pit bull. Laura is a few shabby breeze-block houses

DAMPER

DAMPER IS THE BUSH BREAD OF AUSTRALIA. HERDERS AND COWBOYS IN THE OUTBACK BAKE DAMPER IN CAMP OVENS BURIED IN THE COALS OF THEIR CAMPFIRES.

MAKES 1 LOAF

4 CUPS SIFTED ALL-PURPOSE FLOUR
1 TEASPOON SALT
1½ CUPS WHOLE MILK
UNSALTED BUTTER FOR COATING
ALL-PURPOSE FLOUR FOR DUSTING

Build a campfire.

In a large mixing bowl, combine the flour and salt, and make a well in the middle. Pour the milk into the well and mix until the ingredients come together thoroughly to form a dough.

Grease the inside of an iron camp oven or cast-iron pot with butter and dust it with flour. Place the dough in the oven or pot and score the top of the dough with a knife. Place the lid on the oven or pot and bake the damper in the hot ashes of the campfire for approximately 30 minutes, or until the bread is golden brown.

If you don't want to bake the damper in a campfire, you can bake it in an oven preheated to 400°F. for approximately 30 minutes.

Damper is best served warm with a Vegemite spread and accompanied by lemon myrtle tea.

and a weatherboard pub populated by an ancient logger who has been at the same wobbly perch for much of his seventy years. Five or six bottles of Castlemain into it, the logger is pretty far gone, but we'll trust his directions. We ramble down the Laura River bed, past a pack of swimming, rollicking, laughing local children.

A dirt road straggles off, wending among thick gum trees with waxy-looking leaves. Still no roos, but with increasing frequency the bush along either side of the path is punctuated by strange humpish figures that look like phalanxes of petrified Cousin Its. Closer inspection reveals less Addams Family and more Frank Lloyd Wright: massive termite nests ranging in size from a few inches to ten feet tall, with interiors as complex and utilitarian as an army bunker.

As the bush gets thicker, the two-track becomes rockier, more rutted, nearly impassable. Aussie George, of course, claims to have seen worse on his best day in the bush, but his Troop Carrier creaks and complains like a crotchety old Saratoga. It's a rough ride, but we're here to find a slice of the genuine outback, and in time we emerge from hardy scrub into a vast grassy field dotted with canvas pup tents.

The Jowalbinna Bush Camp sits at the remote end of the historic Cobb & Co. Coach Road that once shuttled miners from Cooktown to the Palmer River goldfields, but which today is nearly forgotten. The area is called Quinkan, and the scenery is savage, gnarled, and beautiful. Sandstone escarpments rise up to march across the horizon, home to some of the world's most significant rock-art sites. Depicted among these primordial abstracts are mythologies and rituals dating back more than forty thousand years.

Shortly after arriving at Jowalbinna, I notice a tall caramel-skinned fellow waiting Godot-like among the tents. His name is Victor Steffensen, and he's a curator of these famous rock-art sites as well as an expert in the techniques that allowed his aboriginal ancestors to survive in this blighted area for millennia.

We're famished after the day's journey, and as the sun begins to settle among the ruddy peaks, Victor leads us on a "walkabout," a search for supper, assembling a shopping

LINDEMANS' WINEMAKER, PATRICK AULD, SHARING A TASTE OF ONE OF HIS VINTAGES WITH ME. KEVIN HEWITT (VIDEOPHOTOGRAPHER) AND MATT PRESTED (ASSOCIATE PRODUCER) CAPTURE THE ACTION.

list's worth of edibles from a landscape that at first appears relentlessly blighted. He winnows fat grubs from fallen trees and, later, strings them on wire and roasts them over coals; they're juicy and have a distinctive peanut flavor. Quandongs are peachlike, if a little more tart, and kakadu plums are a genuine bush delicacy, available commercially in the form of jelly and chutney. Searching for these traditional staples proves grueling, even with an experienced guide. While we work, Victor demonstrates a peculiar "to-go" pick-me-up that has refreshed a hundred thousand generations before us: Plucking a nestful of green ants from a squat boab tree, he shows me how to "bite the bums off" and drink the juice, providing surprisingly good, vaguely lemony nibbles once you ignore the sharp stings the insects deliver to your fingertips. Later, back at camp, he'll crush the remains of the ant nest, leaf and all, into boiling water, creating a fair approximation of lemon tea. Along with the fruit and bugs, a cooler filled with kangaroo steak is delivered to our campfire by jeep, so my first view of these outrageous creatures comes at the tip of a fork.

Lean and mild, kangaroo steak is delicious; and like well-processed venison, it's about as healthy for you as red meat can get. With the sky blaring tones of magenta and gold, we tuck into the tucker, and it proves an exemplary, if unusual, meal—not the sort you'll find in four-star hotels, perhaps, but overhead there are a thousand exotic constellations that serve us even better. A bottle of Lindemans red washes the feast down in rustic style.

So, a word on wine. As food is my ticket to grasping cultures, wine, for me, often illustrates a region's attitude, mood, and general outlook. To understand Australian wines it's best not to approach on bended knee but to think of it as fun. Australian wines have always had the sort of *oomph* that elite winemakers sometimes blend out in favor of austerity and sophistication. Aussie wines are ripe, luscious, and accessible, among the world's most user-friendly. They are ideal choices to stand beside that dynamic Aussie shellfish pair, shrimp and lobster—and, absolutely, that very Sydney-esque specialty, rock oysters.

The best seafood in Australia, including rock oysters, originates at a colorful and vibrant slab of concrete plopped between Blackwattle and Pyrmont Bay. The only working fishermen's market within Australia's billion-dollar seafood industry, the Sydney Fish Market unloads 65 metric tons of fresh catch per day, mostly during its famous crack-of-dawn silent auction, the largest seafood sale in the Southern Hemisphere.

By the time I arrive, it's already winding down, and the weary merchants and gum-booted fishermen are being supplanted by hungry, vibrant tourists eager to enjoy the variety of retail and dining spots that ring the harbor like jewels. The selection is out of this world, and the tuna teriyaki, steamed mud crabs, and delicately sliced sashimi are difficult to pass up, but for the moment I'm on a mission: trawling for rock oysters. I've been told by a number of sources—hotel workers, touristy backpackers, restaurant owners, shopkeepers, and even beachniks surfing the frothy waves of Bondi Beach—that "rocks" are the single food item that's absolutely and unequivocally unique to Sydney, the one delicacy that can't be found anywhere else in the world. In native parlance, homeboys describe them like this: "Oh, I reckon they're grouse, mate, burstin' briny and sweet in perfect bloody proportions . . . an aphrodisiac to die for . . . almost buttery . . ." And the most common adjective of all: "They're creamy, mate, bloomin' creamy!"

Prior to visiting Australia, my oyster experience was respectable, but it hadn't included this mysterious creampuff, the Sydney Rock. Here and abroad I've taste-tested an array of the hard-shelled morsels, including mild Olympias from Puget Sound, medium-bodied Japanese Kumamotos, and California's soft-textured Hog Island variety grown in the warm waters of Sonoma's Tomales Bay. The verbal descriptions that fly among these tastings generally include variations on "briny," "meaty," and "super-sweet," depending on the environment in which the oyster is farmed.

I've even heard Mallard Creek oysters described as tasting like watermelon.

But the consistent Sydney Rock metaphor is "creamy," and it has me hooked, particularly since that's their claim to fame and evidently what distinguishes them within their mollusk macrocosm. So I determine to seek out the best here at the Sydney Fish Market.

Harborside, many of the retail shops offer oysters, spread out raw-bar style on shaved ice beds alongside impeccably fresh octopus, calamari, salmon, snapper, silver perch, clams, and, naturally, Australia's piscatory paragon: whole giant barramundi. But only one establishment offers nothing but oysters, so I figure that's the place for a crash course in Sydney Rocks.

NSW Oyster Distributors is a stripped-down concern offering a staggering diversity of mollusks, the best selection in the market. Everywhere along simple counters is a riot of shells with dozens of hues. Many are the same species of oyster, but each group possesses its own distinct flavor, texture, and subtle nuances. That's because (not

THE SYDNEY OPERA HOUSE AND HARBOR AT NIGHT. SYDNEY IS ONE OF THE MOST BEAUTIFUL CITIES IN THE WORLD.

unlike the soil in which wine grapes are grown) no two oyster beds enjoy identical conditions, from water temperature to mineral and salt content, and even to the menagerie of microscopic marine critters that share their neighborhood. Thus, here at NSW, oysters are not arranged by species but by geographical origin. Names as specific as Port Macquarie, Wallis Lake, Manning River, and Clyde River are often bed-specific and as explanatory to a mollusk master as any Burgundian label is to a wine steward.

A sturdy-looking young lady in a tank top and a five-star smile indicates the array of Sydney Rocks—"beauts," as she calls them in her Aussie slang. Currently, they're fetching $6.00 Australian per dozen. She feigns undiluted shock when I explain that I'm new to the variety on which she has grown up and virtually staked her career. Immediately, she begins to extol them in terms I've come to expect: "Mate, it's the time of year. . . . You won't believe the cream." And, in fact, as I slurp down half a dozen on the spot (raw, on the half shell, no condiments of course—the only way to appreciate an oyster's subtle flavors), I discover the Sydney Rock's promised essence: a sort of succulent, milky, almost gelatinous ooze, a specific mouth feel quite unlike any oyster flesh I'd ever tasted. I prepare to devour six more. I'm clearly intrigued and puzzled, and, cheerfully, the young vendor lays open the cold, hard truth: "It's the semen, mate. Yah, they're loaded up, especially this time of year."

So that's that. My Sydney Rock oyster experience ends mid-swallow. The second half-dozen remain undisturbed on the counter, and I slowly back away, clearing my throat, looking for the exit as the young lady tries to backpedal into an acceptable mental image. "Well, if it's easier for you, think 'reproductive fluid . . .'"

Yeah, right. Brave eating is one thing; this is . . . well . . . something else. I'm sure there's a strong drink to wash away the taste and lots of alternate, distinctly "uncreamy" munchables very close at hand among the bars, stalls, shops, and cafés in the nearby districts of Australia's incomparable Sydney.

Hunter Valley Emu with Red Wine Marinade and Chayote

Emu is the largest bird in Australia. It is high in protein and low in fat. We made this dish with Patrick Auld, the sommelier of Lindemans wineries. The winery is located in Hunter Valley, Australia's answer to Napa Valley, just outside of Sydney. Wattleseed can be purchased from www.cherikoff.com.au. Quince paste can be found at higher-end supermarkets.

SERVES 4

MARINADE

2 CUPS CABERNET WINE

3 CUPS OLIVE OIL

3 TABLESPOONS DRIED BASIL

1 1/2 TEASPOONS DRIED TARRAGON

1 TABLESPOON CHOPPED FRESH SAGE

1 TABLESPOON QUINCE PASTE

1 TABLESPOON GROUND WATTLESEED

1/2 TEASPOON BLACK PEPPER

1 1/2 TEASPOONS SALT

EMU

2 POUNDS EMU ROUND FILLET OR 4 EMU STEAKS

CHAYOTE

2 CHAYOTE SQUASH, PEELED AND JULIENNED

1 TABLESPOON UNSALTED BUTTER

1 1/2 TEASPOONS GROUND WATTLESEED (SEE PAGE 251)

SALT AND BLACK PEPPER TO TASTE

Prepare an outdoor grill.

FOR THE MARINADE: In a large bowl, whisk together all the ingredients. Place the emu fillet or steaks in the marinade for 1 hour. Turn over and marinate for another hour. Remove from the marinade and pat dry with paper towels.

Grill the meat to the desired doneness—medium-rare to medium is suggested. Using a meat thermometer, cook to an internal temperature of 135°F. for medium. Remove the emu from the grill and allow it to rest for 5 minutes to retain the juices.

FOR THE CHAYOTE: Fill a medium saucepan halfway with salted water and bring to a boil. Blanch the chayote in the boiling water for 30 seconds, then remove from the water.

In a medium sauté pan over medium heat, toss the chayote with the butter and wattleseed. Season with salt and pepper.

Slice the emu and serve with the chayote.

GRILLED PRAWNS WITH LEMON ASPEN DIPPING SAUCE

Lemon aspen juice and pepperberries, indigenous to Australia, will add some zip to this dipping sauce. They can be purchased at www.cherikoff.com.au.

SERVES 4

PRAWNS
16 PRAWNS, LARGEST AVAILABLE, PEELED AND DEVEINED
2 TABLESPOONS OLIVE OIL
SALT AND BLACK PEPPER TO TASTE

DIPPING SAUCE
1 1/2 CUPS CHICKEN STOCK
3 TABLESPOONS LEMON ASPEN JUICE
6 PEPPERBERRIES (SEE PAGE 250) OR BLACK PEPPERCORNS
1 TABLESPOON BLUE GUM OR IRONBARK HONEY
3 TABLESPOONS LOW-SODIUM SOY SAUCE

Prepare an outdoor grill.

FOR THE PRAWNS: In a large mixing bowl, toss the prawns with the olive oil and set aside.

FOR THE DIPPING SAUCE: In a small saucepan over medium heat, reduce the stock by one-half. Turn the heat to low. Stir in the lemon aspen juice, pepperberries, honey, and soy sauce, and heat until the honey is dissolved. Remove the pepperberries. Keep the sauce on the back of the stove.

Season the prawns with salt and pepper. Place them on the grill and cook until the flesh is opaque and firm; the length of time depends on the size of the shrimp.

Serve the prawns with the lemon aspen dipping sauce.

ANZAC Biscuits

ANZAC was the name given to the Australian and New Zealand Army Corps soldiers who landed on the Gallipoli Peninsula in the Mediterranean in the early morning hours of April 25, 1915, during World War I. April 15 is the day that unites all of Australia in remembrance and pride for its men and women who fought and died in all its wars. This day is now known as ANZAC Day, and these biscuits are a symbol of that day.

MAKES 30 BISCUITS

1 CUP ALL-PURPOSE FLOUR
1 CUP QUICK OATS
3/4 CUP SHREDDED COCONUT
3/4 CUP (UNPACKED) LIGHT BROWN SUGAR
3/4 TEASPOON BAKING POWDER
1/4 POUND (1 STICK) UNSALTED BUTTER
2 TABLESPOONS LIGHT CORN SYRUP

Preheat the oven to 300°F.

In a medium mixing bowl, combine the flour, oats, coconut, sugar, and baking powder.

In a small saucepan over medium heat, melt the butter and corn syrup together.

Add the wet ingredients to the dry ingredients. Using a large spoon, mix together to form a smooth dough. Roll the dough by hand into 30 small balls. Place the dough balls on a buttered baking sheet 2 to 3 inches apart. Place the sheet in the oven and bake for 15 minutes, or until golden brown.

Remove the baking sheet from the oven. Let the biscuits cool for 5 to 10 minutes before removing them from the baking sheet.

Serve the biscuits at room temperature.

MORETON BAY BUG SALAD WITH MANGO-GINGER DRESSING

A Moreton Bay bug is a crustacean and a close relative of the lobster. Bay bugs do not have any claws but resemble a lobster in flavor and texture. Emma Morley from Quicksilver Diving Services was my divemaster for one of my dives off the Great Barrier Reef. We prepared lunch together on the dive boat, and this is what we came up with.

SERVES 2

SALAD

2 QUARTS WATER

2 TABLESPOONS SALT

1 MORETON BAY BUG OR TWO 6-OUNCE SPINY LOBSTER TAILS

2 CUPS MIXED GREENS

DRESSING

1 RIPE MANGO, PEELED AND DICED

1 1/2 TEASPOONS CHOPPED FRESH GINGER

1 SMALL RED CHILE, CHOPPED

JUICE OF 2 LEMONS

1 CUP EXTRA-VIRGIN OLIVE OIL

SALT AND BLACK PEPPER TO TASTE

FOR THE SALAD: In a 1-gallon stockpot, bring the water and salt to a boil. Add the bay bug to the boiling water and cook for 12 minutes. Remove the bay bug and chill.

Separate the tail from the rest of the bay bug and discard the body. Crack the tail shell, remove the meat, and dice it.

FOR THE DRESSING: In a blender, combine the mango, ginger, chile, and lemon juice. Blend while slowly drizzling in the olive oil. Season with salt and pepper.

In a medium mixing bowl, combine the bay bug meat and spring greens. Drizzle the dressing over the salad and toss to coat thoroughly.

Divide the salad between 2 serving dishes and serve immediately.

Lobster and Mango Salad Martini

This is a recipe I created for my television show. It is a blend of the Great Barrier Reef and the rain forest of northeastern Australia. For a unique presentation, serve this salad in a martini glass.

SERVES 4

HONEY-MUSTARD VINAIGRETTE

1/2 CUP WHITE WINE VINEGAR

1 TABLESPOON HONEY

1 TABLESPOON DIJON MUSTARD

1 CUP OLIVE OIL

3/4 CUP WALNUT OIL

1/2 CUP LOW-FAT YOGURT

SALT AND BLACK PEPPER TO TASTE

SALAD

FOUR 6-OUNCE SPINY LOBSTER TAILS; BOIL FOR 2 MINUTES, REMOVE SHELL, AND DICE MEAT

1 TABLESPOON OLIVE OIL

2 RIPE MANGOES, PEELED AND DICED

1 RED ONION, DICED

1 JALAPEÑO PEPPER, SEEDED AND DICED

4 CELERY STALKS, DICED

1 TABLESPOON CHOPPED FRESH CILANTRO

2 BLOOD ORANGES, SEGMENTED, OR 2 NAVEL ORANGES

1 HEAD ROMAINE LETTUCE, SLICED INTO CHIFFONADE

FOR THE VINAIGRETTE: Place the vinegar, honey, and mustard in a food processor and start to blend. While the blender is running, drizzle in the oils, one at a time, until well blended. Pulse in the yogurt until just incorporated. Season with salt and pepper. Place the vinaigrette in a small container, cover, and refrigerate until ready to use.

FOR THE SALAD: In a sauté pan over medium-high heat, sauté the lobster meat in the olive oil until golden brown, 4 to 6 minutes. In a medium mixing bowl, place the lobster meat, mangoes, onion, jalapeño, celery, cilantro, and oranges, and toss together gently.

Place a portion of lettuce chiffonade in the bottom of 4 martini glasses. Place a spoonful of the lobster-mango mixture on top to fill each glass. Drizzle the vinaigrette on top and serve immediately.

Prawns Wrapped in Paperbark with Pineapple-Ginger Glaze

Paperbark not only acts as a shield from direct heat but also imparts a smoky flavor. I first used paperbark while in Sydney and can't use it enough now.

SERVES 4

PINEAPPLE-GINGER GLAZE

1/2 CUP PINEAPPLE JUICE

1/4 CUP SWEET ORANGE MARMALADE

2 TABLESPOONS LIGHT SOY SAUCE

2 GARLIC CLOVES, MINCED

1 1/2 TEASPOONS MINCED FRESH GINGER

1 1/2 TEASPOONS CHOPPED FRESH FLAT-LEAF PARSLEY

PRAWNS

1 PIECE DAMP PAPERBARK (SEE PAGE 250)

4 PINEAPPLE RINGS FROM THE CAN

2 TABLESPOONS OLIVE OIL

12 LARGE PRAWNS OR 16 MEDIUM SHRIMP, PEELED AND
DEVEINED

Preheat the oven to 350°F.

FOR THE GLAZE: In a small saucepan over low heat, combine the pineapple juice, marmalade, soy sauce, garlic, and ginger. Bring to a simmer for 2 minutes. Stir in the parsley, cool, and set aside on the back of the stove.

FOR THE PRAWNS: Place the damp paperbark on a large baking sheet. Lay the pineapple rings in the center of the paperbark, leaving 3 inches uncovered on each end.

Heat the olive oil in a sauté pan over medium heat. Sear the prawns in the oil on both sides. Do not cook through.

Remove the prawns from the pan. Line them up on top of the pineapple rings. Brush the prawns with some of the glaze. Fold the paperbark around the prawns to form a package and place on a baking sheet. Put in the oven and bake for 10 to 12 minutes.

Remove from the oven and allow to rest for 3 to 4 minutes. Carefully unfold the package and brush a second light layer of glaze on the prawns. Serve hot.

Shrimp on the Barbie

Here is an Australian dish we have come to know, one with simple, great flavor. Everyone has his own version. Here is mine. You can get chili-garlic sauce in any Asian market.

SERVES **4**

MARINADE
1 CUP TERIYAKI SAUCE
½ CUP OLIVE OIL
1 TABLESPOON CHOPPED FRESH GINGER
3 GARLIC CLOVES, CHOPPED
2 TABLESPOONS ORANGE JUICE
2 TABLESPOONS CHILI-GARLIC SAUCE

SHRIMP
16 LARGE SHRIMP, PEELED, DEVEINED, TAIL LEFT ON
SALT AND BLACK PEPPER TO TASTE
16 PINEAPPLE CHUNKS, RIND REMOVED
4 SKEWERS (SEE NOTE)

Heat up the barbie (or prepare an outdoor grill).

FOR THE MARINADE: In a medium mixing bowl, whisk all the ingredients together.

In a glass dish, line up the shrimp, pour the marinade over them, and marinate for 1 hour.

Remove the shrimp from the marinade, discard the leftover marinade, and season the shrimp with salt and pepper.

Skewer the shrimp and pineapple alternately, with 4 pieces of shrimp and 4 chunks of pineapple on each skewer.

Place the skewers on the grill and cook until the shrimp are translucent, 7 to 8 minutes. Be sure to turn the skewers about every 2 minutes to grill each side.

Serve the skewers hot off the barbie.

NOTE: I recommend metal skewers, but if you use wooden ones, be sure to let them soak in water overnight before using to prevent the skewers from burning.

A little "Throw One on the Barbie" at the home of Piers and Suzanne Akerman. We cooked up quite a feast.

Individual Pavlovas

Pavlova is a meringue-based dessert named after the famous Russian ballerina Anna Pavlova. It was prepared for me at the home of Piers and Suzanne Akerman. I had to catch a seaplane to get to their charming home outside of Sydney. There are many different toppings that you can put on your Pavlova. Fruits such as kiwi, oranges, apples, bananas, and apricots can be sliced and used as a topping. Berries also make a wonderful garnish.

SERVES 6

PARCHMENT PAPER

3 EGG WHITES, AT ROOM TEMPERATURE

1/4 TEASPOON CREAM OF TARTAR

1 TEASPOON CORNSTARCH

1 TEASPOON VANILLA EXTRACT

3/4 CUP SUGAR

1 CUP HEAVY CREAM, WHIPPED

2 CUPS VANILLA OR LEMON PUDDING

FRUITS AND BERRIES OF YOUR CHOICE (I PREFER BLUEBERRIES AND SLICED KIWI)

Preheat the oven to 250°F.

Line a large baking sheet with parchment paper. With a pencil trace eighteen 3½-inch circles on the parchment paper. Turn the paper over so the pencil markings show through.

In an electric mixing bowl, using a whip attachment, combine the egg whites, cream of tartar, cornstarch, and vanilla. Beat at high speed until soft peaks begin to form. Add the sugar, 1 tablespoon at a time, and continue beating at high speed until the mixture is thick and glossy.

Spread (or pipe using a pastry bag with a straight tip) ¼ to ½ cup of the meringue mixture over each circle on the baking sheet.

Bake for 1½ hours. Turn the oven off and let the meringues stay in the oven for 30 minutes without opening the door.

Remove the meringue disks from the oven and let cool to room temperature.

Lift the meringues carefully from the parchment.

In a medium mixing bowl, use a rubber spatula to fold the whipped cream into the pudding. Be careful not to overmix, or the whipped cream will lose its airiness.

Place a meringue disk on each of 6 plates. Spoon ¼ cup of the pudding mixture on each meringue disk. Place some sliced fruits and berries over the pudding layer, then another meringue disk, another layer of pudding, and another layer of fruit. Repeat to make 3 layers of each. Serve immediately.

CANADA

OVERHEAD, THE SUN IS STRUGGLING; IT LOOKS AS IF IT MIGHT BE FIZZLING OUT. FROSTY BANKS OF GRAY HAVE BEEN SWEEPING IN ABOVE THE LAURENTIAN MOUNTAINS, WHICH RAMBLE OFF INTO AN ANCIENT MAZE OF LAKES, FORESTS, AND WETLANDS.

QUEBEC The sun looks as though it has about as much steam left as these bluish humps, once grander than the Rockies but worn to molehills by eons of sharp wind and bad weather. By the looks of things, more of the same is in the immediate forecast.

There are spots on earth that frown at the onset of a winter storm. Entire populations exist who curse at the sight of snow. But here in Quebec, in February, the reaction is quite different. For a million revelers who descend upon the provincial metropolis each year, ice is nice. Hail to hail; three cheers for chilblains. Give them a drifting flake or a windchill factor, and these eager souls pack on their parkas, wiggle into their woolens, and leap with *joie de vivre* and *gaieté de coeur*. Forgive the French, but in Quebec, of course, that's how you get things done. And during the tremendous carnival that ignites Canada's old capital each year at this time, it all translates into the same thing: rediscovering the world beyond the triple panes and salvaging one's spirit from the dreary winter doldrums.

The Carnaval de Québec is the largest and friskiest winter festival in the world. It's Mardi Gras with snowblowers, the Tomatino with frost on the vine, Pamplona with fog-snorting bulls. Today is opening day of the forty-eighth annual hullabaloo, and the lobby of the Frontenac hotel is jammed with guests swinging red plastic horns, bleating rude-sounding melodies loud enough to bring down Jericho. Everybody wears an icon of the carnival's ubiquitous mascot, a somewhat creepy-looking snowman called Bonhomme, who resembles a cross between the Stay Puft giant from *Ghostbusters* and an albino Michelin Man. Also in the arms of three out of four parties we encounter in the Frontenac lobby is ski equipment; the nearby Laurentians offer some of the top runs in Canada.

But skiing happens in countless locations across Canada, on hundreds of hillsides in towns without number throughout the winter. Today and for the next seventeen days the real attraction is the *centreville* of historic Quebec City. Its pedigree goes back nearly four hundred years, and to suggest that Quebec City is picturesque is to wildly understate. Studded with wonderful old buildings, striking bastions, winding lanes, and beautiful parks, Quebec City is an unusual and functional blend of nature and structure, Europe and America, past and present. This inherent plurality makes it unique, even in Canada. The province itself, you will recall, has long considered sovereignty on the federal level, coming closest in 1995 when nearly half the population voted to establish nationhood. This drive for independence is considered neither subversive nor treasonous among the Quebecois, but an inevitability. Such thinking takes root in an obvious reality: Quebec is very much a world apart. Canada is bilingual in name alone; in actuality the national identity is written almost exclusively in English. To most Canadians, government-mandated street signs in both French and English are a bit of a joke; it makes you wonder if tailgated motorists are required by law to curse in two languages. Economic and social independence aside, a ferocious defense of spoken French is at the core of Quebec's pro-sovereign arguments. In Quebec, French does more than rule; it dictates. Even at the Frontenac, where the majority of guests are from the United States, we encounter hotel workers who cannot—the cynics say *will not*—speak English.

Which is fine. Le Château Frontenac is also a world apart, and it can do what it pleases as long as it exists. Called

Noted ice climber and new friend, Guy François, prepares to teach me how to ice climb a frozen waterfall.

"the most photographed hotel in the world," it dominates the skyline of old Quebec like the Opera House dominates Sydney. Rising above ancient ramparts—Quebec is the only walled city left in North America—with a commanding view of the St. Lawrence River, it appears to be an ideal site for defense against barbarian hordes. And, in fact, Fort St. Louis once stood on the same precipice and served that very purpose. The luxury hotel followed, designed in the style of a French renaissance château, opening its oaken portals in 1893. It proved to be an immediate international success, having, in the words of architect Bruce Price, "the advantages of bigness."

To be sure, with its turrets, towers, cornices, and copper roofing, the hotel still resembles the imposing medieval fortress it replaced. Contrast the historic Frontenac with Bonhomme's just-built headquarters around the corner. Bonhomme's is a palace in its own right, if a trifle colder and a bit more bohemian. Squatting beneath the Porte St. Louis archway opposite the National Assembly, the indomitable snowman's lair is the traditional first-stop along the carnival route. Opening ceremonies were last night. A gargantuan display of fireworks, mayoral sermons, and plenty of cockle-warming booze, they went on until the wee hours and a few of these early-morning revelers seem the worse for the wear. Subzero temperatures and ferocious winds don't help, and folks are bundled up in more layers than Winona Ryder at a fashion boutique. Still, Bonhomme's own home sports a line of guests ready to explore its chilly innards. Made from five thousand blocks of ice formed into an astonishing two-story castle, it required twenty men a month to construct and contains numerous snowy walkways that feature souvenirs, photos, and interactive games related to the imaginary adventures of Quebec's favorite snow dude.

A bit farther on, the Village M. Christie is spread out beneath a toboggan run and a Les Knuks pavilion, offering a kid-friendly passel of wintry activities, including a massive ice-fishing tank filled with three thousand catchable trout, a nature trail lined with somewhat beat-up taxidermy

specimens, and even a Hydro-Quebec–sponsored heat booth for those who simply want to throw in the towel—or exchange it for a nose warmer. Nearby, I discover a pastry stand featuring a Canadianized version of the deep-fried quick bread popularly known as "elephant ears." In Quebec they're sold under the brand name Queues de Castor (Beaver Tails) and are close cousins to those doughy, supersweet, guilty pleasures made at state fair concessions throughout the United States, though it's safe to say that they resemble a beaver's end as much as they do an elephant's front. The story goes that they were named by *voyageurs,* the hired hands of the early fur trade, who probably had better things to do than think up fancy dessert names. *Voyageurs,* as it happens, lent more than a couple of good, lusty, practical recipes to the elusive beast termed "Canadian cuisine."

So a word on the beast.

Referring to Canadian cuisine during a radio interview in 1957, Colonel Harlan Sanders, the Pol Pot of poultry, bluntly maintained, "There's no such thing." Chances are, he did not have dinner at Aux Anciens Canadiens as I did.

BONHOMME, THE JOVIAL AND GREGARIOUS MASCOT, PREPARING TO ADDRESS THE CROWD.

HAND-CARVED SNOW SCULPTURE
AT THE CARNAVAL DE QUÉBEC.

Cooks in Quebec seem a little overawed by France's kitchen reputation. Many of the chefs in major hotels are imported from France, and many more depend on classical Del Gouy techniques to create their menus. In a city with a thousand restaurants, nearly one in ten lists French as its "style," whereas suspiciously few lay claim to the category Canadian. And as far as I can determine using city guides and word of mouth, only one fully embraces a range of traditional Quebecois specialties: a place called Aux Anciens Canadiens.

Housed within Maison Jacquet, Aux Anciens Canadiens borrows its name from a novel by Philippe-Aubert de Gaspé, a Jacquet resident from 1815 to 1824. It's the oldest house in Quebec City, and with its massive walls, marvelous wainscoting, and recessed, heavy-hewn cupboards, it is a fitting surround for dishes that have been handed down through generations. Five separate dining rooms display the wares of the centuries; in one hang handtools, in another, heirloom china, and in another, antique rifles. The menu of Chef Jean-Michel Camirand draws inspiration from Quebec's innumerable lakes, swift rivers, and vast forests, where the resources, by their nature, can be big and unwieldy. Eel and sturgeon from nearby Ile d'Orléans are smoked in house, and hams are whacked from the hindquarters of caribou and buffalo. Caribou, which migrate in the northern bush country, offer lean, mild, almost sweetish cuts as long as they are not from animals taken for their racks; like any game meat, trophy specimens are old and tough. A favorite of Chef Camirand is caribou stew with blueberries and wine, and he considers a roasted caribou shoulder among the most savory of main courses. Another popular dish, Trapper's Treat, replicates a Lac St. Jean meat pie: flaky pastry bundled around game and root vegetables. It was at one time a long-anticipated repast for returning *voyageurs*. These hearty canoeists carried goods and pelts back and forth from northern Saskatchewan to Quebec, a distance of about three thousand miles. Paddling fifteen hours nonstop and carrying several hundred pounds over portages required a daily calorie intake that was reported to be upward of five thousand. Traditional Quebecois meals do not fit neatly into Deal-a-Meal.

A slightly more refined and delicate dining style can be found back inside the landmark kitchen at Le Château Frontenac, where Chef Jean Soulard holds court—even while making court bouillon—at his four-diamond restaurant, Le Champlain. Soulard is *not* the Canadian Emeril (he's from Roche-sur-Lyon, France, while Emeril has roots in Ontario), but he's the host of a popular television show and the author of several cookbooks, and is no stranger to kicking notches upward. He was the first master chef in Canada and trained at some of the most exclusive kitchens in the world. His menu reflects an eclectic elegance borne of truffles, escargot, and vintage Alsace gewürztraminer—stuff that does not necessarily hail from the local bailiwick. Like all great chefs he has unlimited respect for the best and the freshest of what grows, swims, slithers, or wanders just outside the mullions, but he's a pragmatist. At the core of his cooking is a philosophy that insists "Great cuisine goes beyond recipes." Soulard's nod to the near comes in the form of creative pairings: mussels in Beaupre mead, smoked Gaspesian salmon *mille-feuille,* Laurentian foie gras in porto sauce, and, best of all, desserts and marinades laden with the one ingredient, the single common denominator on which the Frontenac's Soulard and Aux Anciens Canadiens' Camirand unequivocally agree. According to both, if there is a product that Quebec offers the world of gastronomy in unmatched quantities, with unparalleled qualities, it's maple syrup.

The maple tree (both silver and red) gives to Quebec what the Riesling vine gives Germany: the sugary stuff of legend. Seventy percent of the world's maple syrup comes from Quebec, and in terms of complexity, sweetness, and depth of flavor, Quebec's syrup is far and away the best. Credit savage winters, glorious springtime thaws, and a million acres of virgin maple trees teaming to create ideal conditions for the maximum output of rich sap that rises from the roots each spring. Nor is the comparison of Quebec syrup to German wines totally presumptuous:

TWO SLED DOGS READY TO LEAD THEIR TEAM TO VICTORY.

Syrup is graded according to Canadian federal guidelines and must bear a stamp of government certification.

Native Americans, who did not invent the tomahawk (they were manufactured in Europe) or scalping (a bounty-hunting technique used by settlers), were, in fact, up to their sticky elbows in maple syrup long before white people bought into the practice. The Iroquois shared techniques with French settlers, and, shortly, syrup-making became an integral part of colonial life. The original modus operandi called for hacking holes in maple tree trunks, channeling the semisweet sap into a bark trough, and boiling it in a clay pot to evaporate the water. The length of the boil determined the intensity of the result: Short boiling resulted in mild, thin, and delicate syrups; long-term boiling made maple sugar.

Frankly—and gratefully—we haven't come a long way, baby. On the Ile d'Orléans, fifteen minutes from downtown Quebec, I stop by Cabane à Sucre l'En-Tailleur

(Sugar Shack of the Tree Tapper), where for eight generations maple syrup has oozed and where its production is still very much a handcrafted, painstaking, and low-tech operation.

Old Simon, the family patriarch, is a massive red-nosed fellow who has seen four score of mind-numbing winters on the Ile d'Orléans. Emerging from the house in which his ancestors have lived since 1759, he dons a pair of handmade snowshoes and walks me out into a stand of frosty maples. Simon speaks not a word of English, but that's no problem; the maple syrup flowchart is not difficult to follow. With a sort of begrudging acceptance that certain boneheaded mortals can't share simple conversation in French, he uses copious hand gestures to indicate the process of choosing, tapping, and transporting maple water back to the sugar shack. There, during peak season (mid-March), it will be boiled in stages, each one halted at specific temperatures, ranging from 220 degrees for the lightest syrup to 255 degrees, at which point the sap has been reduced to granulated sugar. Simon's years of experience allow him to forgo that newfangled invention, the thermometer, and he prefers to do everything by his senses. All told, 2002's method of maple syrup production resembles that of the prehistoric Iroquois in every detail but the hardware. Stainless steel has replaced bark and terra-cotta, but otherwise there has been no room or any need for improvement.

Later, on the shore opposite Ile d'Orléans, as the snow begins to fall, I have an opportunity to dig my heels into some ice. Beneath the sensational restaurant of Manoir Montmorency, where Chef Marie-Chantal Lepage creates some of the most sumptuous meals in Quebec, there's a three-hundred-foot ice wall that's quite readily climbable given a bit of instruction and a mountain of nerve. To access this dramatic and picturesque area, a half-mile hike to the base of the falls is required, and from there on it's straight up. A sheet of living ice is being constantly replenished and refined by water seeping from the cliff, making this one of the world's premier climbs. With modern gear—front crampons especially—the climb can be done by first-timers in less than an hour, and is worth every nerve-racking, sweat-draining minute.

Meanwhile, back at the Frontenac, the storm comes on full force, whipping down the St. Lawrence Seaway like a marauding army. A blitzkrieg of snow is driven from the cornices and colonnades and gables so ferociously that it looks like a solid cascade. Beyond the window, Jack Frost isn't just nipping at your nose, he's serving it up on a platter.

Are they daunted, these crazy Canadians? Hardly. They're loving it. They thrive on frost, live for shivers, draw sustenance from the very weather that elsewhere closes schools. Far from being postponed, activities appear to be stepped up. Dogsleds are barreling down St. Louis, and on the clogged Bassin Louise, eager teams of canoe racers search for open water and portage over ice floes. And among the spectators, in their Roots sweaters and Cougar boots, there is only one expression gracing whistles—some wet with Canadian Club, granted: smiles.

Maybe they're frozen in place, but, jeez, what's the Quebecois version of hell anyway? South Beach?

TORONTO

Most modern capitals boast of their ethnicity; nearly all contain cultural pockets and diverse populations, each with its own spice box of scrumptious traditions. That's an up-to-the-minute global reality, table stakes (no pun) for curious diners visiting distant shores. However, few cities have, like Toronto, made so complete a transformation in so short a period of time. Twenty-five years ago, decent dining in Canada's largest city was fairly one-note, meaning steak-heavy menus and predictable wine lists. If you went ethnic, you did what was expected of you, seeking institutionalized Italian, Greek, or Chinese landmarks. An oversimplification, perhaps, but the fact remains that today's Toronto hosts a trove of trendy high-style restaurants alongside the old favorites and has attained a status as a dining destination to rival Paris, New York, Sydney, and Hong Kong.

Hogtown in January. Warm spirits, torrid cabarets, incandescent fashions, a sizzling art scene, and everywhere else frigid bleepin' sidewalks. Mealtime, you'll be looking for a place to duck into out of the cold, and in and around greater Toronto there are more than five thousand places from which to choose. That makes my mission to winnow from this earnest body of eateries four or five valedictorians, a task for a very hungry Hercules. I think I'm up to such gastronomic feats, and I spent a week delving into Toronto's food-savvy establishments: reconnoitering the grooviest buzz joints, nosing out the lustiest newcomers, litmus-testing the oldest standbys, leaving no stove unturned. Now, after a Tums and a calorie-burning jog, I am prepared to recommend the following kitchens without hesitation. Some are desperately cool and overcrowded; others are old-guard mini-gems, quite literally, off the eaten track.

All represent Toronto's dining energy at its most satisfying.

Biryani House

Biryani House is one of those tiny, impossibly cheerful little Indian holes-in-the-wall where the fare is so cheap that you're almost scared to peek inside the kitchen—who knows where they might be cutting corners? Nothing sinister happening here, of course, where sensational dishes issue from a spotless and tightly run, if apartment-sized, kitchen—which explains the pricing structure. At noon you can get a multicourse meal for less than six dollars Canadian. And having done more than peek inside Chef Debu's kitchen, and laid some culinary tracks alongside him, I can attest to his impeccable choice of ingredients, his flawless technique, and his expert preparations. Having apprenticed both in Agra and Madras, Chef Debu exploits the radically different cooking styles of each city, blending the explosive fires of rice-based southern cooking with the creamy, buttery, yogurty richness typically found in India's north.

Heady scents of cardamom, saffron, cinnamon—biryani's

symphony of spices—fill the air as Chef Debu bustles about, grinning, stirring, toasting, hauling orders from the tandoori. The restaurant's namesake dish is a sultry layered casserole whose roots go back to Mongolia, but it is a signature dish in northern India, where in its most intricate incarnation it can be garnished with gold leaf. The gold in Chef Debu's biryani comes from lightly roasted spices, a blend of the five "C's" of *garam masala*—cumin, coriander, cinnamon, cardamom, and cloves—as well as a romance of auxiliary flavors, depending on his mood *du jour*.

Chef Debu's immaculate sensibilities show up again and again, in his pepper-packed pappadam, his *saag*—a curried chicken with spinach and chiles—and in the unusual aromatic semolina pudding, in which this hearty grain is blended with saffron and green cardamom powder and served in sweet squares as the final course in his tasting plate. Big flavors, big colors, big hearts, all wedged into a mighty humble location—shoring up the old adage about the kind of stuff that comes in small packages.

Susur

Susur is a stunning set piece, no doubt. Fretted linen, ostrich leather seats, velvet (yeah, velvet) oil paintings. But it's in good company: Chef Susur Lee is a visual feast himself. Strikingly handsome with broad Asian features and a wrist-thick ponytail, he looks as if he should be wearing a cape and swinging a sword like one of those invincible anime warlords with names like Battle Hunter or Super Dimensional Atragon. His absolutely contemporary menu shows the identical adrenaline and confidence, with wild ingredient pairings and unexpected sensory twists. Wasabi winds up moussed; miso gets mustardized; taro gets the same treatment as dauphin potatoes. There are lily bulbs and caramelized pistachios and currant-filled potato souf-flés, and a dozen other *huh?* concoctions that confound their origins and take on guises you never dreamed they had.

"When people come to a restaurant like this, they shouldn't guess the chef's identity." (Here's a hint, then, Chef Susur—possibly don't name your restaurant "Susur.")

"I like it when people think, when they're surprised. My menu is a mix of the world, everything I've discovered on my travels, a blend of the things I like to eat—it's not French, not Chinese, not Canadian."

Well, Susur is Susur; no further equivocation required. So perfectly does Chef Susur find his flavors, tune his harmonies, and balance his portions that if you *must* call this "fusion," you have to call what everybody else does "confusion." Genius—not a word to be used lightly when referring to glorified griddle jockeys—has been affixed to the name of Susur Lee more than a couple of times. As his dining room manager John Lee phrases it, "To describe Susur's dishes is futile—you have to taste them."

Chef Susur, formerly of Lotus, late of a Singapore consulting gig, has hit Toronto like a returning comet—the brightest star in an already hot culinary sky. Lionized when he was chef-owner of the somewhat less ambitious Lotus,

JOHN PORCO OF PORCO BROTHERS TAKES PREPARATION OF HIS PROSCIUTTO SERIOUSLY.

Beef Carpaccio with an Arugula Salad

Chef Felice Vacca of the Italian restaurant Sotto Sotto in Toronto composed this traditional dish. Carpaccio is generally served as an appetizer.

SERVES 2

ONE 8-OUNCE PIECE CENTER-CUT BEEF TENDERLOIN, TRIMMED

1 LEMON

2 TABLESPOONS EXTRA-VIRGIN OLIVE OIL

SEA SALT AND BLACK PEPPER TO TASTE

1/2 CUP TRIMMED ARUGULA

1 TABLESPOON GRATED PARMIGIANO-REGGIANO CHEESE

Wrap the beef tenderloin in plastic wrap to give it a round shape and then put in the freezer for 24 hours.

The following day, slice the meat on a machine very thinly and arrange the slices on 2 plates. Squeeze half of a lemon over the meat. Drizzle 1 tablespoon of olive oil over the meat. Season with salt and pepper.

FOR THE ARUGULA SALAD: In a medium mixing bowl, toss the arugula with the remaining 1 tablespoon of olive oil and squeeze the other half of the lemon into the bowl. Season with salt and pepper.

TO SERVE: Place the arugula salad on the carpaccio and sprinkle the cheese over it.

he has now opened his eponymous eatery in the same neighborhood (King Street West). Tragically hip décor washes the front of the house with incongruity and wit—*Ghostbusters* dolls, for example, against Marcus Design banquettes. But forget the kitsch; it's the kitchen that grabs you. Nearly as big as the dining room, it's dominated by a garrison of custom-designed equipment, including a steamer the size of Ottawa, capable of moist-heat temperatures so hot that they give everyday ingredients unexpected textures and brand-new flavors. Chef Susur directs the scene with formidable organizational skills, learned recently in China, and watching the kitchen perform is akin to hearing the Toronto Philharmonic. Two columns of chefs flank workstations, moving in perfectly timed tandem, dishing out such delights as spiny lobster tail with pan-seared veal sweetbreads; steamed grouper with chorizo in a Thailandaise glaze. The result is transcendental degustation—clean and piercing synergies as Chef Susur helps pave Toronto's culinary highway into the twenty-first century.

Sotto Sotto

Much as you hate to admit it, there's something irresistible about a place that movie stars find irresistible. Why, for example, Kiefer Sutherland should know more about perfectly prepared funghetti trifolati than, say, the dozen or so satisfied-looking, Italian-speaking *paisanos* dotting Sotto Sotto's subterranean dining room is anybody's guess. But given the chance, it's shamefully obvious whose opinion you'd ask. Me, too.

Hefty, happy Chef Felice Vacca, who looks like a celebrity himself—forgive me, John Belushi, wherever you are—punctuates his conversations with Italian jingles and culinary tips: "Boil pasta for eight minutes, not eleven. *Forget* what the directions tell you." And in eight minutes, tossing crisp pancetta with grated pecorino and a couple of raw eggs, he brings together the best *spaghetti alla carbonara* I've ever tasted. Simplicity is the essence of Felice's cooking style, and he's the first to admit it: Cooking should not be fussy.

Felice learned his stuff at the apron strings of Mama Vacca, a former hotel chef in Rome, who still helps out in Sotto Sotto's kitchen, too much a bundle of tenacity and spunk to retire. Together, at my request, they whip up another one of their favorites, *bucatini all'Amatriciana*—a lusty variation on a classic marinara, using thick, tubular Sicilian pasta to sop up the sauce. "This, me and Mama make all the time," Chef Felice points out, adding, with a wink to his matriarch and mentor, "This how I got so chubby." And it's also why the jet set keeps showing up at the cavern doors. There, Sotto Sotto's fifteen minutes of fame (unlike that of some of these Hollywood *pezzovantes*) is still going strong.

PATRIOT

David Chrystian has been at Patriot's helm since 1997 and has brought to the position not so much an obsession with Canadian cooking as a devotion to Canadian produce. This is good. Featured prominently on his menu are Prince Edward Island mussels, Ontario prosciutto, Quebec foie gras, and everywhere the late harvest and fruit wines at which Canadian winemakers excel. His culinary techniques are not campfire and hearth but cordon bleu.

Says Chrystian: "Most schools teach French or Italian or Asian-based cooking, and whether they'll admit it or not, chefs tend to latch onto these techniques early. What makes excellent food American or Canadian—or even Torontoian—are the ingredients that are available locally." As such, he scores massive hits with such preparations as stuffed saddle of rabbit with lentil tourtière; velvet-centered sautéed calf's liver over broccoli puree and sunchoke-and-red-onion stew in black mustard seed sauce; seared Arctic char with multi-mushroom and root vegetable ragout; foie gras with sage-apple fritters in cinnamon honey.

Patriot exists to remind tourists that dining Canadian does not mean flapjacks and walrus steaks, and that real Canadian décor does not rely on knotty pine or blocks of ice. Patriot's trappings are clever and artsy, as suits its location in the uppity section of Bloor Street. The mezzanine is

Fire-Roasted Japanese Striploin

Chef/owner Guy Rubino of rain in Toronto puts together a simple combination of ingredients that will enable you to create a Japanese flavor for your steaks.

SERVES 4

MARINADE

¼ CUP SAKE

4 TEASPOONS RICE WINE VINEGAR

¼ CUP PLUS 2 TABLESPOONS BRANDY

½ CUP SUGAR

¼ CUP BLACK MISO

STRIPLOIN

FOUR 10-OUNCE WELL-MARBLED STRIPLOIN STEAKS (NEW YORK STRIP STEAK OR DELMONICO STEAK), TRIMMED

FOR THE MARINADE: In a large mixing bowl, whisk together all the ingredients.

Place the steaks in a casserole and pour the marinade over them. Cover with plastic wrap. Let the steaks marinate for 30 to 40 minutes in the refrigerator.

Cook the steaks either on a preheated outdoor grill or in an iron skillet on the stovetop to the internal temperature desired.

Allow the steaks to rest for 6 to 7 minutes before slicing.

stylish, sleek, wide open, and tremendously romantic, and the wine list, from which Chrystian's benchmark menu draws its inspiration, contains sixty selections from the country's most celebrated vineyards. The whole experience raises the bar on what can be expected from a nationally themed restaurant in one of the world's premiere chow towns. Eh?

RAIN

Hitting the restaurant rain at five o'clock, you know you've stumbled onto Toronto's hippest party full-swing. "Stumbled," of course, is a relative term; nobody (who's nobody) slithers through the front door without a hard-to-come-by reservation. Once you get in and are standing chic to chic with the cream of the Hogtown cool crop, you know you're about as "in" as you can get.

rain's owners—who eschew capital letters along with most other conventions (appetizers may follow main courses in their free-spirited, convention-shattering style)—are brothers Mike and Guy Rubino, who learned the food game from their folks. Where they came by their artistic acumen is another story. Design is paramount to all things at rain; the luminous interior is a sleek, minimalist concrete-and-stainless rain forest. A slate waterfall falls two stories, offering a burbling reminder of the restaurant's theme; the bar is a frosted focal point, with subtle inner lighting; and the dining area, subdivided by bamboo, is clean and understated.

Guy Rubino invents his menu as he goes; he wanders around farmer's markets and fish stalls each dawn, picking up such culinary rousers as mangosteens (a sweet-pulped fruit beloved by Thai chefs), hairy-rinded, lichee-like rambutans, wolfberries (not a kid's breakfast cereal but a plump, vitamin-packed Asian raisin), shark's fin, salmon, and deliciously rich hamachi—all of which will serve as scaffolding for various soon-to-be-improvised dishes that are, in Guy Rubino's witty and ever-changing world, as hard to predict as the weather. Back in rain's kitchen, Chef Guy's creativity pours forth like water from a downspout. He builds plates of tempura-fried shark's fin, half-shell oysters dotted with jackfruit relish and reconstituted sea-weed, and box-formed sushi as they do it in China. He fills mangosteen shells with house-made fruit jam and salmon tartare (the clean, citrusy mangosteen equalizes the oily fish); he sprinkles finely ground dried shrimp over rare pan-seared beef, lending an ocean tang to the earthy steak; he dices sea cucumber into lobster stock and sprinkles shaved bonito over the luxe and luscious concoction.

Watching him work, you quickly see that his love for contrast and balance parallels that of his utterly cool environment, and you realize why his culinary and philosophical passions lean toward the East. He maintains, "Asians are masters of balance. Sweet things set off sour, crunchiness dresses up softness, colors clash or blend, but always with a certain amazing control. For me, a plate must offer polarities. I'm after new experiences in every dish; eating a course should be like walking down a hall, opening doors as you go. Each door leads to another door, and so on. That's the idea at rain—keep 'em guessing, and you keep 'em interested."

Lacking a dinner reservation or, God forbid, a triple-digit dinner budget, the visual tsunami that is rain should nudge you in for a beverage at the very least. When at rain it pours, required sipping is the martini-esque house cocktail, the pink and ever-healthy "rainfall," heavy on fresh-squeezed fruit juices and antioxidizing doses of Guy Rubino's pet fruit, the wolfberry. Half the place is the bar anyway, and it is probably the best spot in town for beautiful people watching. As such, rain is a ray of sunshine amid a cloudy bistro climate of nearby clubland, a place equally suited to wet your whistle as to whet your appetite.

MISO COD

CHEF/OWNER GUY RUBINO OF RAIN USES THREE TYPES OF MISO TO PREPARE THIS DELICACY WITH BLACK COD. WHEN FINISHED, THE COD HAS A DELICATE TEXTURE AND A RICH FLAVOR.

SERVES 4

MARINADE
1/2 CUP FRESHLY SQUEEZED ORANGE JUICE
1/2 CUP MIRIN
1/2 CUP SAKE
1 CUP SUGAR
1/4 CUP HATCHO MISO
1/4 CUP RED MISO
1/4 CUP SHIRO MISO

COD
FOUR 6-OUNCE BLACK COD OR SEA BASS FILLETS, SKINNED

FOR THE MARINADE: In a medium saucepan over medium heat, bring the orange juice, mirin, sake, and sugar to a boil. Turn the heat to low. Stir in the misos until they are completely dissolved. (Never boil miso, or it will break down.) Pour the marinade into a casserole and refrigerate until cool.

Place the cod in the cooled marinade and let marinate for 2 days. Turn the fillets over twice a day.

You may cook the cod either in the oven or in the broiler. For the oven, preheat to 400°F. Cook the cod for 10 minutes, or until completely cooked. For the broiler, cook for 3 to 5 minutes on each side, or until the cod fillets are thoroughly cooked.

Serve hot.

Caribou with Red Wine Sauce

While in Quebec City, I was looking to find an example of Canadian cuisine. I found it at Aux Anciens Canadiens. This is a classic French "bourguignonne-style" dish traditionally made with beef, but here using caribou to put a Canadian spin on it. Venison or beef can be substituted for caribou, but may not take as long to cook.

SERVES 4

1½ POUNDS CARIBOU SHOULDER MEAT, CUT INTO 1-INCH CUBES

SALT AND BLACK PEPPER TO TASTE

2 TABLESPOONS UNSALTED BUTTER

1 TABLESPOON OLIVE OIL

1 TEASPOON PUREED BASIL

1 CUP DICED WHITE ONIONS

¾ CUP RED WINE

1 CUP HEAVY CREAM

1 CUP VEAL OR BEEF STOCK

½ CUP WATER

1 TABLESPOON ALL-PURPOSE FLOUR

Preheat the oven to 350°F. Season the caribou with salt and pepper.

In a large ovenproof sauté pan over medium heat, heat 1 tablespoon of butter and the olive oil together. Add the caribou to the pan and brown it on all sides. Once the meat has browned, add the basil and onions. Sweat the onions for 3 to 4 minutes. Add the red wine and reduce by one-half. Add the cream, stock, and water. Cover and place the pan in the oven for 1 to 1½ hours, or until the meat is tender. After taking the pan from the oven, remove the caribou meat from the pan.

In a small sauté pan over low heat, melt the remaining 1 tablespoon of butter. Pour the melted butter into a small mixing bowl. Add the flour to the bowl and mix the butter and flour together to form a paste (this is called beurre manié). Whisk the beurre manié into the liquids remaining in the pan. Simmer the sauce for 3 to 5 minutes and season with salt and pepper.

Serve the caribou meat with a portion of the sauce poured on top.

Les Deux Saumons au Beurre de Corégone

Chef Jean Soulard combines the flavors of smoked salmon, fresh salmon, and salmon roe to create this dish.

SERVES 4

GARNISH
2 PLUM TOMATOES, DICED
1 TABLESPOON OLIVE OIL
SALT AND BLACK PEPPER TO TASTE
CORÉGONE BUTTER
½ CUP CLARIFIED BUTTER
1 OUNCE SALMON CAVIAR
LES DEUX SAUMONS
4 OUNCES SMOKED SALMON, SLICED
4 OUNCES FRESH SALMON, SLICED
SALT AND BLACK PEPPER TO TASTE
2 TABLESPOONS CHOPPED FRESH FLAT-LEAF PARSLEY

Preheat the broiler.

FOR THE GARNISH: In a small mixing bowl, combine the tomatoes and olive oil, season with salt and pepper, and refrigerate.

FOR THE CORÉGONE BUTTER: In a small sauté pan over low heat, melt the clarified butter. Allow to cool to room temperature, then stir in the salmon caviar. Set aside. It is very important that the butter not be hot when the salmon caviar is added, so that it does not cook the caviar.

FOR LES DEUX SAUMONS: Cover 4 plates with slices of smoked salmon. Cover the smoked salmon with slices of fresh salmon. Season with salt and pepper.

Place each plate in the broiler for 30 seconds to cook the salmon.

Drizzle the corégone butter over the cooked salmon.

Serve each salmon plate with a spoonful of the tomato mixture. Sprinkle the parsley over each plate and serve warm.

Lac St. Jean Meat Pie

This meat pie is a traditional dish and is also called Trapper's Treat. When the Quebec City area was first founded, it was populated by mostly trappers and hunters working the St. Lawrence River and its tributaries. This meat pie was made when they had a successful hunting day. I had a chance to taste this dish while filming an episode of my show during the Quebec Winter Carnival.

SERVES 6 TO 8

MEAT PIE

1 POUND GROUND BEEF

1 POUND GROUND PORK

1/2 POUND GROUND VENISON

1/2 POUND GROUND CARIBOU

1/2 POUND GROUND ELK

2 CUPS DICED WHITE ONIONS

2 CUPS SHREDDED CARROTS

4 CUPS SHREDDED RUSSET POTATOES

3 WHOLE BAY LEAVES

1 1/2 TEASPOONS DRIED THYME

1 TABLESPOON SALT

1/2 TABLESPOON GROUND BLACK PEPPER

3 1/2 CUPS CHICKEN STOCK

PASTRY DOUGH

3 CUPS SIFTED ALL-PURPOSE FLOUR

2 TEASPOONS SALT

1 CUP SOLID VEGETABLE SHORTENING

2 TABLESPOONS UNSALTED BUTTER

3/4 CUP COLD WATER

EGG WASH

1 LARGE EGG, BEATEN

1 TABLESPOON WHOLE MILK

Preheat the oven to 350°F.

FOR THE MEAT PIE: In a large mixing bowl, combine the meats, vegetables, bay leaves, thyme, and seasoning.

In a large stockpot over medium heat, cook the meat mixture with the stock for 15 minutes, or until the liquid is absorbed.

FOR THE PASTRY DOUGH: In a large mixing bowl, combine the flour and salt. Cut in the shortening and butter with a pastry cutter or 2 knives. Sprinkle in the water a little at a time while continuously mixing. Work the ingredients into a ball, but be careful not to over-work the pastry dough.

Cut the ball of dough into 2 equal pieces and roll out. Put one rolled-out pastry in a buttered 10 × 13-inch casserole.

Spoon the meat mixture onto the rolled pastry and cover with the other rolled-out pastry. Seal the edges and prick the top with a fork to allow the steam to be released during cooking.

FOR THE EGG WASH: In a small mixing bowl, whisk together the egg and milk. With a pastry brush, coat the top pastry dough with the egg wash.

Place the meat pie in the oven and bake for 1 hour, then lower the heat to 200°F. and continue to bake for 30 minutes.

Remove the meat pie from the oven and let rest for 5 minutes.

Serve hot.

Duo of Pan-Seared Foie Gras and Tuna Loin with Porcini and Potato Ragout

Chef David Chrystian of Toronto's Patriot prepared this dish for me. It highlights one of Canada's most prized products, foie gras.

SERVES **2**

RED WINE COMPOUND BUTTER

2 TABLESPOONS UNSALTED BUTTER, SOFTENED

1 1/2 TEASPOONS CABERNET WINE

TUNA AND FOIE GRAS

1 1/2 CUPS VEAL OR CHICKEN STOCK

1 TABLESPOON UNSALTED BUTTER

6 FINGERLING POTATOES, BLANCHED AND QUARTERED

6 RED PEARL ONIONS, BLANCHED AND PEELED

2 MEDIUM PORCINI MUSHROOMS, HALVED, OR CHANTERELLE MUSHROOMS

SALT AND BLACK PEPPER TO TASTE

TWO 3-OUNCE PIECES GRADE A QUEBEC FOIE GRAS, CLEANED, SCORED, AND REFRIGERATED

ONE 8-OUNCE CENTER-CUT TUNA LOIN

1 TABLESPOON OLIVE OIL

2 LOBSTER CLAWS, COOKED AND REMOVED WHOLE FROM SHELL

2 OUNCES LOBSTER MEAT, COOKED AND ROUGHLY CHOPPED

10 HARICOTS VERTS, BLANCHED

1 TEASPOON CHOPPED FRESH THYME

1 TEASPOON SLICED FRESH CHIVES

FOR THE COMPOUND BUTTER: In a small mixing bowl, combine the butter and wine. Once combined, refrigerate for 10 minutes to allow the butter to harden slightly.

FOR THE TUNA AND FOIE GRAS: Preheat the oven to 375°F.

In a small saucepan over medium heat, bring the stock to a simmer and slowly reduce by one-half. Remove from the heat and set aside.

Melt the butter in a sauté pan over medium heat. Add the potatoes, onions, and mushrooms. Sauté until the vegetables are golden brown. Season with salt and pepper, and add the mixture to a casserole. Place the casserole in the oven to roast the potatoes until they are tender.

In a heavy-bottomed skillet over high heat, place both pieces of foie gras, scored side down. Shake the pan to prevent the foie gras from sticking, and after 45 seconds carefully flip the foie gras. The foie gras should be browned on both sides but still firm in the middle. Remove from the pan and set aside on a clean cloth. Drain most of the foie gras fat from the pan and place the pan over medium to high heat.

Season the tuna with salt and pepper, then sear in the foie gras fat for 3 minutes per side. Put the tuna on a baking sheet and place in the oven for 2 to 3 minutes, until medium-rare.

Heat the olive oil in a small sauté pan over medium-high heat. Sear the lobster claws. Once the lobster claws are seared golden brown, remove from the pan and set aside.

In a large saucepan over medium heat, place the potato mixture, lobster meat, haricots verts, thyme, chives, and reduced stock. Simmer for 3 to 5 minutes.

Stir in the compound butter. Season with salt and pepper. This final mushroom and potato dish is called a ragout.

Place the seared liver and lobster claws on a baking sheet and put in the oven to reheat, approximately 2 minutes. Season with salt and pepper.

TO ASSEMBLE: Divide the ragout mixture between 2 plates. Slice the tuna loin into 4 equal pieces. Sandwich one piece of foie gras between the 2 pieces of tuna. Place on the ragout base and garnish with a lobster claw.

FLORIDA

ONCE UPON A TIME, BACK IN THE 1970S, MIAMI'S OCEAN DRIVE WAS SNICKERED AT BY THE UPMARKET CROWD. ELEPHANT'S GRAVEYARD, THEY CALLED IT, REFERRING TO THE ARMADA OF WRECKS DECAYING ALONG THE MIAMI BEACH SHORELINE.

MIAMI

By this they did not mean the cargo ships that had foundered and sunk on nearby reefs, but the native population: ancient retirees wrapped in terry-cloth robes, staring out at the Atlantic from their BarcaLoungers. Never mind that Ocean Drive flanked the largest concentration of the world's hippest architecture: dozens of Tropical Deco hotels built when Al Jolson was a local headliner. Forget that the weather was truly magnificent, the beaches bountiful, the ocean endless. Ocean Drive had become a joke—at its worst an unfashionable God's Waiting Room, and at its best a sort of cornball diorama of a prehistoric era when chubby, tipsy Jackie Gleason was considered cool. To the in-crowd of 1975, with their lamb-chop sideburns, wide neckties, and candy apple Trans Ams, Miami Beach was totally out of synch with fun times and the good life. For that you had to go to California, the Bahamas, or the French Riviera.

And then they woke up. Amid the eye of the hedonistic storm called the 1980s, a prime-time television series introduced a new generation to South Beach's retro-hip pastels and towering neon, as across the fashion universe, lamb chops gave over to morning-after stubble, and Don Johnson T-shirts replaced five-inch cravats. *Miami Vice* was at least partially responsible for a resurgence of investment capital in Miami Beach, and many of the crumbling hotels between

Lenox and the Atlantic underwent renovation. Visionaries and developers came to an inescapable conclusion, not unlike Mel Fisher did at the helm of his salvage boats: There's gold in them there wrecks.

Not only that, but Jackie Gleason *is* cool.

Today, Ocean Drive is enjoying its new-century heyday; it's chic and populated with the roller-blading body-beautiful great-grandchildren of the erstwhile lounge lizards. Trendy retailers such as Versace, Gucci, and Armani are entrenched in storefronts; sidewalk cafés and art galleries abound; and Deco masterpieces such as the Tides Hotel have reemerged to offer world-class amenities and stunning cuisine by such chefs as Roger Ruch. Meanwhile, the reliable Florida sunshine is unaffected, and the strip of sand between Bayshore and South Pointe Beach is once more an upscale playground.

Discovery, boom build, and collapse, then a rapid and successful renaissance—Miami's history is somewhat repetitious that way. The city has reinvented itself more times than Madonna, from the first displacement of Seminole Indians, through the builder's boom of the Roaring Twenties, past the economic collapse of the Depression, into an explosive period of postwar decadence, during which Al Capone supplanted Al Jolson and put the vice into Miami.

In the sixties what might have been a minor blip on the world's radar screen sent an estimated one hundred thousand Cuban expatriates crashing into downtown Miami, restructuring the city's ethnic makeup and changing its political direction to this day. A second wave of refugees in 1980 established Miami as ground zero for Cuban culture in the United States. Today, the neighborhoods that make up Little Havana, spreading out along numerous streets between 12th and 27th Avenues, are generally the first taste of America that new arrivals from Cuba receive.

How "American" is Little Havana? That's debatable. I discover this while traversing Southwest 8th Street in search of a trio of cooks who go under the business title of Three Guys from Miami. Eighth Street, called *Calle Ocho* throughout southeast Florida, is as unabashedly Hispanic as north-of-the-border gets. Not only is Spanish Little Havana's first language, but it's frequently the only language spoken in the shops, fruit stalls, and little walk-up coffee windows that sprinkle the strip. It doesn't take more than a squint against the Floridian glare to imagine that you've been transported to downtown Guadalajara, Bogotá, or any seedy but industrious Latin American commercial zone. Transplanted Cuban stage sets are everywhere: An overheated supermarket window displays exotic fruit like soursop and mamey, while next door Reyes Photography offers repairs and restorations of family photos, displaying a mug shot of an anti-Castro detainee complete with a height chart and prison uniform. Meanwhile, the Dollar Store is having a special on Top Rider cigarettes and Last Supper wall hangings, while Elian Furniture pays homage to Little Havana's most famous former resident, Elian Gonzales. Next to that, a *botanica* caters to aspiring shamans, featuring jinx-removal spray, wax effigies, rusty horseshoes, and bath oil that claims to cure everything from cancer to hiccups. A mile or so farther down, at 16th Avenue, Calle Ocho offers its own version of Hollywood's Walk of Fame, with Hispanic superstars like Gloria Estefan and Sammy Sosa immortalized in pavement blocks. Nearby, Domino Park is undiluted, old-world Havana, filled with gray-haired Latin guys drinking thimble-sized cups of coffee, arguing politics, and click-clacking through absurdly complicated games of dominoes.

Eventually, I find the Three Guys from Miami inside a fabulous pastry shop at the corner of 8th and 27th. Cubans make some of the world's most wonderful pastry, a legacy of the homeland's abundant sugarcane crop. Even so, dessert will come in its time; first, the Three Guys from Miami ('fess-up time: Two of them are from Havana, and the third is from Duluth) are going to prepare a fully loaded Cuban supper for me.

The three guys, brothers-in-law Raúl Musibay, Glenn Lindgren, and Jorge Castillo, are in love with all things Cuban, and collectively they've spent years tasting, cooking, and refining the techniques of the Cuban kitchen. Some of their recipes are family heirlooms; others are borrowed, combined, and spiced-up from those of friends and neighbors. To my great good fortune this wild and gregarious trio has volunteered to show off their skills at Jorge's sumptuous west Miami home. We begin with snookers of rum and tumblers of iced beer, which lubricates the vocal cords and helps on the initial step: a primer course in Cuban cuisine.

At its most authentic, Cuban cooking draws inspiration from the sophistication of classical Spanish cooking and the lyrical flavors of the Caribbean, bearing little resemblance to strip-mall Mexican. Pork, beef, and chicken appear in various guises, frequently barbecued, and generally soused in *mojo,* a marinade built around garlic, onions, oregano, and sour orange. Black beans and rice are an indispensable accompaniment to such main courses and are referred to as *Mojos y Cristanos* (Moors and Christians—Cubans are never above slipping in a little tongue-in-cheek social commentary). Soups and stews are also a Cuban mainstay, often based on an aromatic sauté of garlic, onions, and sundry peppers called *sofrito.* None of these concoctions is particularly exotic for Middle Americans; it's the Cuban sides, the starch and vegetables, that may raise some eyebrows. Yuca, a term used interchangeably with cassava, is a pasty, mild-flavored root that is boiled and served with butter. Boniato, also called Cuban sweet potato, is a white-fleshed tuber and is less sweet and drier in texture than a yam. The mealy malanga is frequently sliced thin and fried as chips. Plantains are multipurpose cooking bananas, waxy and savory; they show up stewed, fried, mashed, frittered, or baked. Regrettably, this starchy quartet—de rigueur at most Cuban sideboards—can be hard to find in the American heartland, and the specific varieties beloved by Cubans rarely appear outside Florida.

Shortly, the Castillo kitchen is aflutter with advisors, as various aunts, moms, and wives show up to offer the Three Guys pointers in this traditionally non-guy occupation. Jorge talks as he cooks, sharing his fascinating story.

YUCA, YUCA, AND MORE YUCA!

CHIMICHURRI

THIS SAUCE IS GREAT SERVED WITH CHURRASCO, GRILLED SKIRT STEAK. IT CAN ALSO BE SERVED WITH GRILLED CHICKEN BREASTS. THIS CUBAN-STYLE CONDIMENT SAUCE IS SO FLAVORFUL, IT MAY BECOME A STAPLE IN YOUR REFRIGERATOR.

SERVES 4

1 LARGE BUNCH FRESH CILANTRO
6 GARLIC CLOVES, PEELED
1/4 CUP RED WINE VINEGAR
2/3 CUP OLIVE OIL
1/2 CUP DICED WHITE ONION
1/2 CUP SEEDED AND DICED RED PEPPERS
1/2 CUP DICED PLUM TOMATOES
1/2 CUP CHOPPED FRESH OREGANO
SALT AND BLACK PEPPER TO TASTE

Place all the ingredients in a blender and puree on high until thoroughly blended. Add more salt, pepper, and vinegar if needed.

Serve over Churrasco (page 114) or on a Sándwich Cubano (page 96).

Twenty years ago he arrived in Florida penniless and barefoot, having lost his shoes during the famous chaotic boat exodus from Mariel Harbor in 1980. Today, he's a successful respiratory therapist living in a ritzy community and sporting a sharp pair of Pradas. He also grills a pretty mean *chorizo,* a spicy sausage on which he gazes throughout his discourse. As he peels yuca, he quips that he himself is a yuca—an acronym for Young Upscale Cuban American. Meanwhile, Glenn gets his *mojo* working, relegating marinated skirt steak to the grill while Raúl refreshes everyone's rum and coke—a *cuba libre* tastes best when made by a liberated Cuban—and mans a small hand press to form cakes from mashed plantain, later to be panfried. The skirt steak dish is called *churrasco.* By tradition, *churrasco* is Argentinean, but tonight the marinade Cubanizes it, especially when it's accompanied by one of Glenn's specialties, *chimichurri* sauce (a piquant meat-dipper made from cilantro, peppers, garlic, and vinegar) and *empanadas,* paprika-kissed meat pastries steamed in corn husks. Everything is served alfresco, on an open terrace, amid the heady fragrance of Jorge's carefully tended poinciana plants and lit (like Betty Grable's 1941 blockbuster) by a *Moon over Miami.*

It's an idyllic suburban setting, and as we eat, Jorge shares a truth about Little Havana's reputation. Despite being synonymous with the pulse of Cuban life in Florida, most successful Cuban immigrants, folks like Jorge and Raúl, have long since packed up and left, moving to affluent suburbs like Westchester, Hialeah, Kendall, and Miami Lakes. Had they gone much farther, these western-moving nomads would have found themselves, quite literally, up to their necks in alligators.

The Florida Everglades is, for wilderness lovers and adventure seekers, the best-kept secret in America's pack of national parks. A rugged semitropical wetland dominated by sawgrass, mangrove, and cypress, the Everglades covers a million and a half acres and includes basically all of southern Florida. When the peninsula emerged from the ocean during the last ice age, most of it remained low, fragile, humid, and supremely damp, and even today no point in the whole of the Everglades is more than eight feet above sea level. The entire park is essentially a free-flowing river, fed by rain and percolating toward the sea at the sluggish rate of three miles per day. Slinking through this primordial tableau are some of Florida's most outrageous citizens: crocodiles, alligators, manatee, and six-foot panthers. For obvious reasons, sightseeing here tends to be done from the back of a peculiar half-skiff and half-plane hybrid known as an airboat.

Which is exactly what I commandeer the following morning. Thirty miles down the Tamiami Trail, another of Florida's outrageous citizens—a hale, mustachioed local called George Kocish—fires up his twelve-foot Hammant aluminum-hulled swamp taxi and pilots me out into the steamy morning in search of a hummock dry enough to set up a field kitchen. We crisscross water trails once used by Miccosukee Indians, flushing explosions of wood stork from golden ponds, sending heron aloft on seven-foot wingspans, dodging gumbo-limbo trees and skimming past body-surfing snapping turtles, all under the scrutiny of various vacationing vultures. This last group, enjoying their final Dade County hurrah, will soon depart for a much-ballyhooed March 15 return to Hinckley, Ohio.

The airboat's high-performance Cadillac V-8 drowns out the native sound track, but once we arrive at our destination and the engine has been killed, marsh music begins to percolate all around us: bass slapping in reedy coverts,

ERGLADES SAFARI

TALK ABOUT FEELING FREE! IF YOU EVER GET THE CHANCE, SOAR ACROSS THE TOP OF THE WATER IN AN AIRBOAT IN THE EVERGLADES.

crickets singing, frogs croaking, bugs trilling, and off in the distance a low and somewhat disconcerting rumble from some swamp behemoth. We're in the middle of nowhere, and this eerie sound, as well as the aboriginal setting, is a fitting backdrop for cooking dinosaur.

Technically, of course, alligator is not dinosaur, but these days it's as close as you're gonna get. The American alligator is a keystone member of the Everglades ecosystem, creating peat in its nesting activities and controlling prey species. Another item from the gator's plus column is borne out as I fire up the cook stove: They're sensational on the dinner plate. Go figure!

Some squeamish gastronomes have an aversion to eating things that can eat them back. Let it be known that alligator flesh is delectable, neither stringy nor strongly flavored when correctly prepared. And lest outcries rise from conservationists—to whose ranks I proudly belong—today I'm using defrosted, vacuum-packed, farm-raised alligator meat from Louisiana. Anyway, the best gator cuts, primarily from the tail end, produce finely grained white meat, low in saturated fat, high in protein, and lend themselves to a variety of sauces and seasonings. Granted, deep-frying alligator counteracts some of the health benefits, but it's quick and results in moist, tender, and flavorful nuggets delicate enough to make converts out of most naysayers. This afternoon my airboat pilot is an easy sell: He's been living in the Everglades all his life, and here, eating gators—along with feeding them, studying them, and managing their habitat—goes with the territory. Between mouthfuls he shares swamp survival lore, demonstrating how to harvest sawgrass shoots from the mildly brackish marsh water. They're crisp and taste like mild scallions; dried, they can be ground into flour. At one time they were a staple in the diet of the Miccosukee tribe.

Far off, the bull alligator's growl fades as the afternoon heats up, transforming our surroundings into a near sauna. Blood-thieving mosquitoes and no-see-ums arrive, thick as, well, thieves. Blasting back toward the dock, we pass a matted stand of trees whose pale spongy bark appears to be peeling off in some kind of arboreal psoriasis. These are melaleucas, and their existence in the Everglades is an ode to mortal greed and lousy luck. Planted to dry up wetland patches wanted for development projects, these myrtles were originally considered a "natural" alternative to levees and canals. They've spread so voraciously, however, that hundreds of thousands of acres have become a virtual melaleuca monoculture, and the Everglades' fragile balance is clearly threatened.

The bright side? Alligators were once hunted to near extinction throughout the Everglades but have made a comeback so remarkable that in some areas they now threaten to overpopulate and are being carefully culled to ensure their optimum survival. Can the same success be guaranteed for their habitat? We hope so. When the village goes, thus go the villagers. With 80 million years of succulent tail evolution behind them, it would be a shame if this was the tail end for Florida gators.

KEY WEST

My buddy, Buddy Owens, and me in front of the original B.O.'s Fish Wagon—only in Key West.

Lots of people who've been there suspect this, but hardly anybody knows it: Key West is a foreign country.

In 1982, reacting to a border blockade of the Florida Keys, Mayor Dennis Wardlow seceded from the Union, declared war on the United States, and then promptly surrendered and demanded foreign aid. Not known for its sense of humor, Washington ignored all this drunken-sounding nonsense and so far has steadfastly refused to drop any CARE packages over the renamed "Conch Republic."

Now for the weird part. Because of some obscure international law referring to "adverse possession between sovereign nations," Key West wins by default. Well, if the international wheels of justice are greased with bourbon, if capitals can be named Margaritaville, and if official costumes can include wet T-shirts, flip-flops, and beer can hats, long may this funky little mouse roar—and pour. One indisputable lesson from this surreal footnote to American history is that Key West has a whole different thing going on.

Take U.S. 1, for instance. A seriously long highway, it begins on a rickety suspension bridge in Fort Kent, Maine, meanders through fifteen states and one federal district, crosses farms, fields, podunkvilles, and megalopoli, never stopping until it bumps into Roosevelt Boulevard in Key West. Looking over the people who have wound up on this little shard of coral at the southernmost tip of Florida, it's clear that a lot of people treat Key West as the end of their road as well. It's as if somebody pulled the plug on the United States, and everything greasy and limp trickled down here. In Key West you don't worry about how you look, what you do, or where you do it. Bellies overhang waistbands unabashedly; senior citizens drink Budweiser from Styrofoam cups at ten o'clock on Tuesday mornings; stores advertise Cuban products as though there's no such thing as a trade embargo. Pick a day, any day, and Old

Town in Key West is like Boston minus the 364 days that *aren't* March 17.

For all intents and purposes, earning a living in this part of town is a Key West afterthought. Like Blanche DuBois in *A Streetcar Named Desire* (written in Key West in the forties), plenty of residents appear to depend on the kindness of strangers. Every night in Mallory Square a congregation gathers to watch the sun melt into the horizon, and, counting on their exuberance and often inebriated generosity, dozens of wacky artists do street shtick for tips. There's the Statue Guy, spray-painted silver from head to toe, whose job description is standing there quietly. There's the Cat Guy, who forces reluctant-looking felines to jump through burning hoops. There's the Pincushion Guy, who allows a nail-studded board to be hammered into his chest. *Cirque du Soleil* it isn't, but it's entertaining, all good fun, and all in keeping with Key West's wise motto, which is, as paraphrased by local restaurant owner Buddy Owens, "If it ain't life threatening, don't sweat it."

Buddy—B.O. to close friends, which is you, me, and everybody else—is true to his word, too. He's bohemia's Grand Poobah, a hearty-partying full-bearded Florida-holic, big enough to knock you on your keister if you act as if you're taking things too seriously. His famous downtown eatery is the litmus test that proves him out. In the first place, naming your restaurant B.O.'s Fish Wagon is a little like naming your perfume Eau de Jockstraps. In the second place, anywhere else in the United States the joint would be condemned, whereas in Key West it's a landmark, a civic anchor, a "destination" restaurant. Seventeen years ago B.O. began modestly, serving hangover food from the bed of his pickup truck, and several zillion M.F. (Mom's Finest) burgers and grouper sandwiches later he's wound up . . . modestly. The original pickup still functions as one of the outside walls; the other three are a hodgepodge of driftwood, sheet metal, and shipping crates. B.O.'s looks like something out of a Max Fleisher cartoon, like a strong sneeze would blow it down. Asked how they lock up after hours, waitress Sam shakes her head at the absurdity of the

B.O.'s CLAMS CASINO

My good ol' buddy Buddy Owens served up this dish out of his fish wagon down by the wharf. If you ever get to Key West, definitely go to B.O.'s and taste this great appetizer recipe at its source.

SERVES 4

16 FRESH LITTLENECK CLAMS

1 TABLESPOON MINCED PEELED SHALLOTS

3 GARLIC CLOVES, PEELED AND MINCED

1/2 CUP DICED PLUM TOMATOES

1 TABLESPOON UNSALTED BUTTER

1/4 CUP KEY LIME JUICE

1 1/2 TEASPOONS CHOPPED FRESH OREGANO

1 TABLESPOON CHOPPED FRESH BASIL

6 TABLESPOONS GRATED PARMESAN CHEESE

Preheat the broiler.

In a steamer, steam the clams until they open. Remove the top shell of the clam and discard it.

In a medium sauté pan over medium heat, sauté the shallots, garlic, and tomatoes in the butter for 3 minutes. Add the key lime juice, oregano, and basil, and continue to cook for 1 minute.

Stuff the tomato mixture into the clams and top with the cheese. Place the stuffed clams under the broiler until the cheese melts and browns.

Serve hot.

notion, shoos away a stray cat and a rooster, and demonstrates by looping a rope across the entrance. Anything ever get stolen? According to Sam, nobody notices. In the background, meanwhile, B.O. is hustling around his postage-stamp-sized kitchen, flipping patties, dropping fry baskets, spewing one quotable quote after another: "Don't know how ya want it, boys, so I'm gonna make it just right," and "Gourmet cookin' in five minutes," and "Hell, I don't know what kind of fish it is. It comes outta the water. You happy?"

And the amazing thing is that amid the piles of junk, the rusting walls, the cat fur, the chicken feathers, and the staff's nonchalance-raised-to-the-power-of-three, everybody is.

Something more deliberate is happening over on Duval, where Mangoes is surfing a peak wave of popularity. The restaurant—possibly the best in town—specializes in the hyper-modern style of island cookery that goes by the cute, catchy, and perfectly appropriate term "Floribbean." Floribbean blends Caribbean colors and flavors with old-school Florida standbys. The result is pure *minceur*—lighter, tastier, and healthier than both. At Mangoes the synergy is managed by Executive Chef Paul Orchard, whose perspicacious palette belies his youth; Chef Paul, in fact, is so young that you're surprised his folks let him stay

RICHARD AND SUANNE HATCH, PROPRIETORS OF BLUE HEAVEN AND LIVING THE KEY WEST DREAM.

up late enough to serve the dinner crowd. Cornerstones of his marvelous menu are yellowtail snapper wreathed in passion fruit *beurre blanc*, Key West pink shrimp seared with a light curry of lemon and sour orange, and his signature mushroom martini: sautéed wild mushrooms served in classic V-shaped stemware. Everything is delivered with humor and style, either in the sumptuous upstairs dining room or on a romantic patio beneath tropical skies.

Falling between Mangoes' grace and B.O.'s grease, Blue Heaven offers love's labor in a supremely casual courtyard along Key West's historic Petronia Street. The story goes that Hemingway used to referee boxing matches beneath the property's almond tree, where the kids of Blue Heaven's founders, Suanne and Richard Hatch, now swing—but, then again, everybody in Key West claims to have a Hemingway connection. What's less disputable is that Ernest himself would have gone nuts over Richard's easy and freewheeling menu, which includes such plump morsels as grouper in lime-honey glaze and tuna with black bean and ginger sauce. Papa missed his chance, but journalist Charles Kuralt claimed that Blue Heaven's scallop sauce "would make cardboard taste good." What a lovely image! Wonder if he tried the pancakes, Richard's true fame claim—the wait for which has folks lined up every morning. Richard's secret? A few ounces of Key West Sunset Ale in every batch, a trick he picked up from a buddy whose brew-sprinkled bread left a lasting impression. Said pancakes are a popular pre-plunge meal for Key West divers: "Sticks with them all day," according to Suanne Hatch. Suanne, who used to do art for the tourists in Mallory Square, is herself a perfect portrait of the Key West dream. Having spent years barely scraping by, operating from a houseboat off Christmas Tree Island, she maintains an almost Zen-like calm amid the storm of customers, seemingly bemused at the trappings of Blue Heaven's phenomenal success—including her newly acquired town house in Paris. Somehow, stretched out on the funky blue picnic table in the courtyard, with sons Ricky and Andy limb-swinging behind her and husband Richard emerging from

RICHARD'S "VERY GOOD" PANCAKES

SINCE THE WORD "EXCELLENT" IS OVERUSED, RICHARD HATCH CHOSE TO CALL THESE "VERY GOOD" PANCAKES. LET ME TELL YOU, THEY ARE EXCELLENT.

SERVES 6

6 CUPS ALL-PURPOSE FLOUR
1/4 CUP BAKING POWDER
3/4 CUP SUGAR
1 TABLESPOON SALT
6 LARGE EGGS
4 CUPS PLUS 1 TABLESPOON WHOLE MILK
2 TABLESPOONS CIDER VINEGAR
6 TABLESPOONS KEY WEST SUNSET ALE OR AMBER BEER
1 TABLESPOON SOUR CREAM
3/4 CUP PEELED AND DICED RIPE MANGO
3/4 CUP FRESH BLUEBERRIES
UNSALTED BUTTER
MAPLE SYRUP

In a large mixing bowl, sift together the flour, baking powder, sugar, and salt. In a separate large mixing bowl, combine the eggs, milk, vinegar, beer, and sour cream. Using a rubber spatula, fold the wet ingredients into the dry ingredients until they are well blended.

Preheat a greased griddle or large skillet. Place a desired amount of batter on the griddle. Add the desired amount of mango and blueberries to the batter. When bubbles begin to appear on the surface, use a spatula to flip the pancake over and finish cooking. Repeat with each pancake.

Serve with butter and maple syrup.

CASA MARINA JERK WET RUB

Chef Kevin Montoya of the Casa Marina Hotel made this jerk wet rub for a 22-pound black grouper caught off the coast of Key West. He rubbed the marinade over the fish, roasted it whole, and served it on a platter at the beach. What an adventurous dish with great flavor and presentation!

MAKES 1 QUART

1/2 CUP GROUND ALLSPICE

1/4 CUP GROUND CINNAMON

1/4 CUP GROUND NUTMEG

1/2 POUND PEELED AND CHOPPED FRESH GINGER

1 LARGE YELLOW ONION, DICED

1/2 CUP MINCED GARLIC

1/2 CUP KEY LIME JUICE

1 CUP OLIVE OIL

1/2 CUP CHOPPED FRESH THYME

ONE 3-OUNCE CAN CHIPOTLE PUREE

1/4 CUP KOSHER SALT

6 CUPS CHOPPED SCALLIONS (WHITE AND GREEN PARTS)

In a blender, puree all the ingredients except the scallions. Once the mixture is smooth, add it to a large mixing bowl and stir in the scallions.

This wet rub is best used with fish or chicken. Rub it on by hand and then roast or bake the fish or meat.

the kitchen with his ponytail and million-dollar grin, she looks as if she'd be just as happy in the houseboat.

Key West's laid-back reputation, its *aura popularis,* is due in part to Jimmy Buffett's spifflicated lament to lost love and compromised sobriety, "Margaritaville." The 1977 dirge doesn't mention Key West by name, but by the time it hit radio's top ten, Jimmy was already an honorary Conch, with a bungalow on Fleming Street, and nobody doubted that the tune's front-porch swing was Buffett's own. Since then, Buffett has sold his digs and moved on, but he left behind a downtown speakeasy, Jimmy Buffett's Margaritaville, where parrotheads flock on principle, lapping tequila at the source and bemoaning real or imagined broken hearts.

Which should not entirely fool you. As a going concern, Key West was not built on giggle water and moping, but on blood, sweat, and fishing tackle. Bluer even than the sky or the ocean are the collars of the indomitable Conch workforce, the native fishermen who discovered first the nearby sponge beds, then the green turtles, then the pink shrimp, and, most recently, thanks to Joe Weiss, proprietor of Miami's incomparable Joe's, the stone crab. These scrumptious crustaceans abound in the shallow waters off Florida's coast, but it wasn't until 1921, when Weiss gave them a kitchen audition, that anyone even realized they were edible. Today, millions of them are lured into baited traps strung along lengths of rope, hauled aboard customized boats, and processed—that is, their legal-sized claws removed and the crabs set free. With apologies to the good-lifers lounging over at Smathers Beach, the work done by stalwart seamen aboard these crabbers is more thankless than any Jimmy Buffett heroine.

I know because I spent a day aboard the *Coral Keys 5*, a 43-foot Torres crabber, manhandling traps alongside First Mate Bennett Orr.

Orr is a genuine one-legged Ahab, a seventeen-year veteran of the briny deeps, who tolerated my presence only with the guarantee that I wouldn't goof off, wouldn't get seasick, and wouldn't get hit in the head with a 35-pound crab trap. Crabbing is a tight business without a huge margin for error either financially or safety-wise.

We set out at dawn, spearing through crystal waters off nearby Marathon Island, arriving at our specified buoy line about an hour later. Stone crab season runs from October through May, and what follows is typical for a crabbing expedition during this period when more than six hundred separate traps can be pulled during the course of a single day.

Styrofoam buoys, color-coded and numbered, are gaffed by a long hook and hauled aboard. The line is wound around a mechanical apparatus that drags the crab trap from the seabed and deposits it on a steel tray at the boat's gunwale. The trap, made of food-grade plastic, is quickly powerwashed, blasting away barnacles and seaweed, and its contents are removed. This includes delights like moldering pig's feet (used as bait), numerous squatters (spiny lobsters, little groupers, and octopuses), and at least one (sometimes more) stone crab. Traps are rebaited and tossed back; on the other side of the gunwale, each crab is measured and graded, and if it's too small, back it goes as well. If not, one or both claws are removed in quick, deft motions before the crab is released. Done properly, the amputation is instantaneous and said to be untraumatic—though nobody I know is taking bets. Still, crabs in the wild release claws naturally when threatened, and in any case, within a year or two the claw will regenerate. Over a lifetime a single male can produce any number of entrées for Joe's crab-crazed customers; they will be dipped in billows of mustard sauce, washed down with a Niagara of wine, and followed by several bazillion slices of what is, in fact, Key West's *genuine* legacy to the culinary universe: key lime pie.

Regarding which Kermit insists, with apologies to *Sesame Street*, "It is *too* easy being green."

Kermit is diminutive and cuddly and somewhat Muppet-like, but he's not a frog: He's Kermit Carpenter, a cool little baker with a cool little shop on the corner of Greene—where else?—and Caroline. Key West Key Lime Shoppe specializes in goodies pressed, squeezed, and other-

KERMIT'S KEY LIME PIE

KERMIT CARPENTER OF KERMIT'S KEY WEST KEY LIME SHOPPE SHARED THIS RECIPE WITH ME. (CHEF KERMIT PREPARES ONE OF THE BEST KEY LIME PIES IN KEY WEST AND HE HAS PLENTY OF COMPETITION. KERMIT'S KEY LIME JUICE CAN BE FOUND AT WWW.KEYLIMESHOP.COM.

MAKES ONE 9-INCH PIE

ONE 14-OUNCE CAN SWEETENED
    CONDENSED MILK

3 EGG YOLKS

1/4 CUP KERMIT'S KEY LIME JUICE

ONE 9-INCH GRAHAM CRACKER PIECRUST

WHIPPED CREAM

Preheat the oven to 300°F.

In the bowl of a mixer using a whip attachment, blend the milk and egg yolks at low speed until smooth. Add the key lime juice and blend for 1 minute. Pour the mixture into the piecrust and bake for 15 minutes.

Remove the pie from the oven and let cool for 15 minutes. Refrigerate for 1 to 2 hours before serving.

Top with whipped cream and serve chilled.

wise extruded from these potent green golf balls: mustard, tea, cookies, salad dressing, fudge, coffee, and, when the mood strikes him, pies. In truth, Kermit's pies are prizes, renowned as the best in Key West, which, with nostalgia for names, makes them the best key lime pies in the universe. Key limes themselves are not native to the island but tagged along with the original wave of settlers, finding the climate as ideal as their hosts. Though most of them are today's lawn ornaments, their kitchen value far outstrips that of their larger "Persian" cousins: Key limes are juicier, tastier, and more tart, thus enhancing various chemical reactions. Traditionally, key lime pies do not require cooking because the acids solidify the filling.

Kermit swears by his ovens, however. His recipe calls for the addition of whipped egg yolks, followed by about fifteen minutes at 300 degrees. The result is a silken texture and a custardlike body, which is what snags him all the awards, especially when combined with the quality and freshness of ingredients. Freshness is key in everything—everything, that is, except key limes. Ah, the nasty little underbelly of the Conch Republic pastry cartels! The scandal! Matt Drudge, take note: Key limes are not grown commercially in Key West, and even if they were, they wouldn't be used by Kermit Carpenter. Kermit prefers concentrated juice, which comes in bottles from Mexico. When he thinks of the number of limes he'd have to squeeze every day to kick out his limey portfolio, he shudders. He makes over one hundred successful products out of key limes—statistics that turn the envious competition green. In the entrepreneurial spirit of America's only Caribbean island, Kermit has figured out how to do more with less.

Jimmy Buffett, Buddy Owens, the silver mime in Mallory Square—all would be proud. Life's too short to worry about squeezing anything but your significant other, and the sunset over the Gulf won't last forever. At the close of the day, Key West is a small town that's a multimillion-dollar industry that's run like a small town. And if you can say that five times fast, it's time for another margarita.

CAPTAIN TONY

OF ALL THE CHARACTERS TO BE FOUND IN KEY WEST (AND THERE ARE A FEW), CAPTAIN TONY TARRACINO IS THE MOST VENERABLE.

Don't take my word for it: The grizzled, hard-nosed, shoot-from-the-hip former Key West mayor has been immortalized in song (Jimmy Buffett's "Last Mango in Paris" was written about him) and film (Stuart Whitman played him in 1978's campy *Kill Castro*). Captain Tony remains, at eighty-five, one of the most popular tourist attractions on the island. Catch him if you can, and this crusty ol' former shrimp boat captain will mesmerize you with tales of Ernest Hemingway, Tennessee Williams, Jerry Jeff Walker, and any of Key West's dozens of well-known figures, most of whom he's hung around with over the fifty-plus years he's lived here. And lest you think any of the tales are tall, all can be verified in the various newspaper articles that line the walls of his famous speakeasy, Captain Tony's Saloon. Captain Tony is the real deal, representative of everything that is Key West: Lose the BS, loosen your collar, have a cocktail, and damn the torpedoes.

Oh, and as a side note, Captain Tony also happens to be my biological father, but that's another story.

HERE I AM SITTING WITH THE INFAMOUS CAPTAIN TONY.

Coconut Bread and Conch Rolls

Henrietta Weaver from The Art of Baking has come up with what she calls "Key West's official bread," coconut bread. This recipe may be turned into loaves or rolled out by hand into the shape of conch shells.

MAKES 30 TO 35 ROLLS OR 10 LOAVES

FILLING FOR CONCH ROLLS

1 CUP GRATED COCONUT IN SYRUP

1 CUP SHREDDED UNSWEETENED COCONUT

COCONUT BREAD OR CONCH ROLLS

2 TABLESPOONS DRY ACTIVE YEAST

1/2 CUP WARM WATER

1/2 CUP SUGAR

2 LARGE EGGS

1 1/2 CUPS WHOLE MILK

1/2 CUP SOLID VEGETABLE SHORTENING

1/2 CUP GRATED COCONUT IN SYRUP

1/2 CUP SHREDDED UNSWEETENED COCONUT

2 TEASPOONS SALT

3 1/2 CUPS ALL-PURPOSE FLOUR

MELTED BUTTER

FOR THE FILLING (needed only for the rolls): In a mixing bowl, combine the coconut in syrup and shredded coconut.

FOR THE BREAD OR ROLLS: In a small mixing bowl, dissolve the yeast in the warm water and let it begin to foam. In a large mixing bowl, use your hands to combine the sugar, eggs, milk, shortening, coconut in syrup, shredded coconut, salt, yeast-water mixture, and half of the flour. Once the ingredients are well incorporated, place the mixture in the bowl of a standing mixer with a dough hook attachment. Gradually add the rest of the flour. When all the flour is mixed in, remove the bowl from the mixer and cover with a cloth. Let rise for 1 1/2 hours. Punch down the dough in the center with your fist and cover the dough again. Let rise for another 30 minutes.

Preheat the oven to 350°F.

Punch down the dough a second time. Cut into 30 to 35 4-ounce balls if making conch rolls or ten 8-ounce balls if making bread.

If making loaves, coat the insides of ten 3 × 6-inch loaf pans with cooking spray. Press a ball of dough into each pan. Let rest for 30 minutes, then bake for 20 minutes, or until golden brown. Brush the tops with butter when you remove the loaves from the oven.

If making conch rolls, roll out the 4-ounce balls into circles, 6 to 8 inches in diameter. Roll up the circles to form a spiral shell and place on a buttered baking sheet. Let rest for 30 minutes.

Baste the outer portion of the rolled-up section of rolls with the coconut in syrup mixture. Bake for 12 minutes, or until lightly golden brown.

Once the rolls are removed from the oven, brush with melted butter.

Conch rolls and coconut bread are best served warm.

TROPICAL PASSION FRUIT MARTINI WITH A WATERMELON ICE POP

If you stay at The Tides in South Beach, try a Tropical Passion Fruit Martini while sitting on the patio overlooking Ocean Boulevard or at the piano bar café in the evening.

MAKES 4 DRINKS

ICE POP
WATERMELON, SEEDS REMOVED AND RIND CUT OFF
4 CINNAMON STICKS
MARTINI
1 CUP VODKA
1 CUP PASSION FRUIT JUICE
4 HIBISCUS FLOWERS

FOR THE ICE POP: In a blender, puree enough watermelon pieces to yield about 1 cup of juice. Strain the juice and then measure. Fill an ice pop tray with the watermelon juice and place in the freezer. When it is halfway frozen, insert the cinnamon as the ice pop sticks. Let it continue to freeze until solid.

FOR THE MARTINI: In a tumbler, shake together the vodka and passion fruit juice with ice. Pour the martini into 4 glasses while straining out the ice. Add a watermelon ice pop and garnish each glass with a hibiscus flower. Serve, enjoy, and relax!

SAUCE BOSS GUMBO

BILL WHARTON, THE SAUCE BOSS, IS BOTH A SUPERB COOK AND A SLIDE GUITARIST. BILL MAKES GUMBO DURING HIS SHOW. HE MADE THIS RECIPE AT HIS SHOW AT TOBACCO ROAD IN MIAMI. THE SAUCE BOSS AND THE INGREDIENTS NOT ONLY PROVIDE EXCELLENT MUSIC FOR THEIR FANS, BUT THEY ALSO FEED THEM GUMBO AFTER EACH SHOW. CHECK OUT HIS SAUCES AND GUMBO RECIPES AT WWW.SAUCEBOSS.COM.

MAKES 1½ GALLONS

1½ CUPS OLIVE OIL

2 CUPS ALL-PURPOSE FLOUR

1 WHOLE COOKED CHICKEN, PREFERABLY POACHED, BONES AND SKIN REMOVED

1 GALLON CHICKEN STOCK

2 WHITE ONIONS, DICED

2 GREEN BELL PEPPERS, SEEDED AND DICED

½ CUP HOT SAUCE (BILL WHARTON'S LIQUID SUMMER HOT SAUCE IS SUGGESTED)

1 POUND SMOKED SAUSAGE, DICED

2 MEDIUM ZUCCHINI, DICED

1 POUND OKRA, STEMS REMOVED, SLICED

1 POUND MEDIUM-SIZED SHRIMP, PEELED AND DEVEINED

2 CUPS SHUCKED OYSTERS

1 POUND COOKED CRAWFISH

SALT AND BLACK PEPPER TO TASTE

1 CUP COOKED LONG-GRAIN RICE PER SERVING

Place the olive oil in a large stockpot over medium heat and stir in the flour. While continuously stirring with a large spoon, cook over high heat until it is brown in color.

Add the cooked chicken, stock, onions, and bell peppers. Bring to a boil, then lower the heat to a simmer. Add the hot sauce, sausage, zucchini, and okra. When the okra is cooked, about 30 minutes, bring the gumbo back to a rolling boil and add the shrimp, oysters, and crawfish. Let boil for 3 minutes to cook the seafood. When the seafood is completely cooked, season with salt and pepper.

Serve the gumbo in a bowl over cooked rice.

Goombay Gumbo Soup

Blue Heaven is one of those restaurants you have to see to believe. Proprietor Richard Hatch shared this recipe with me.

MAKES 1½ GALLONS

ROUX

1¼ CUPS CANOLA OIL

1¼ CUPS ALL-PURPOSE FLOUR

GUMBO

½ CUP MINCED GARLIC

2 TABLESPOONS OLIVE OIL

1½ CUPS DICED CELERY

1½ CUPS DICED RED BELL PEPPERS

1½ CUPS DICED GREEN BELL PEPPERS

2 TABLESPOONS CHOPPED FRESH OREGANO

1½ TEASPOONS DRIED BASIL

1½ TEASPOONS CHOPPED FRESH THYME

8 CUPS CANNED DICED TOMATOES

½ CUP WORCESTERSHIRE SAUCE

2 TABLESPOONS KOSHER SALT

1½ TEASPOONS CRACKED BLACK PEPPER

7 CUPS WATER

1 POUND OKRA, SLICED INTO ¾-INCH PIECES

2 TABLESPOONS GUMBO FILÉ

¼ CUP CHOPPED FRESH BASIL

1 CUP COOKED LONG-GRAIN RICE PER SERVING

FOR THE ROUX: Place the canola oil in a large sauté pan over medium heat and whisk in the flour. Cook while stirring continuously until golden brown. Set aside.

FOR THE GUMBO: In a large stockpot over medium heat, sweat the garlic in the olive oil for 3 to 4 minutes. Add the celery, red and green bell peppers, oregano, dried basil, thyme, tomatoes, Worcestershire sauce, salt, and pepper. Cook for 3 to 4 minutes. Add the water and simmer for 15 to 20 minutes. Stir in the roux. Whisk until it has completely dissolved. Add the okra and continue to simmer another 15 minutes.

Stir in the gumbo filé and fresh basil, and simmer for 3 minutes. Do not let the soup boil once you have added the filé. Adjust the seasoning if necessary. This is best served over long-grain rice.

Sándwich Cubano

The Cuban sandwich was taught to me by the Three Guys from Miami: Jorge Castillo, Raúl Musibay, and Glenn Lindgren, the "honorary" Cuban. Glenn explained to me that the key to the Cuban sandwich is the bread. Only one bread works the best, Cuban bread. If you can't get your hands on any, a fresh loaf of Italian bread can be substituted, one that is crusty on the outside and soft in the center. The same ingredients are used for a smaller sandwich called a "medianoche," meaning "midnight." Its bread is made from sweeter egg dough, and it was originally designed to be a midnight snack.

SERVES 4

1 LOAF CUBAN BREAD

UNSALTED BUTTER, SOFTENED

SLICED DILL PICKLES

1 POUND LECHÓN ASADO (ROASTED CUBAN PORK) OR ROAST
    PORK, SLICED

1 POUND SLICED HAM

1/2 POUND SWISS CHEESE, SLICED

MUSTARD OR MAYONNAISE (OPTIONAL)

Preheat a griddle or large sauté pan and coat with cooking spray.

Cut the bread into 4 sections about 7 to 8 inches long. Turn the sections on their sides and cut lengthwise as you would for a sandwich. Spread butter on the inside of both halves. Add the ingredients in this order: pickles, roasted pork, ham, and cheese. Be generous.

Place the sandwich on the prepared griddle or sauté pan. Add a heavy iron skillet or press on top of the sandwich to flatten it. Try to compress the sandwich to one-third of its original size. Grill the sandwich for 2 to 3 minutes on each side, or until the cheese is melted and the bread is golden brown. Be sure to watch the temperature of the griddle; if it is too hot, the bread will burn.

Garnish with mustard or mayonnaise if desired. Slice the sandwich in half diagonally and serve.

Kenyan Kachumbari

Jamaican Conch Chowder,
garnished with avocado slices

above Key Lime Pie, velvety and rich, from Kermit in Key West

left The infamous Australian Pavlova, with layers of lemon cream, blueberries, and kiwi

right Richard's "Very Good" Pancakes, with blueberries and mango, from Key West's Blue Heaven

A Sándwich Cubano, with ham, roasted Cuban pork, and Swiss cheese, found in Miami

Roasted Corn Salsa, with red bell pepper and chipotle chile,
made by Spencer Moore of Felix's in Cabo San Lucas

left Blackened Shrimp with Mashed Sweet Potatoes and Andouille Cream, made by Antony Field of Bonne Terre Country Inn outside of Memphis on a segment of my show

below The key to this shrimp and andouille sausage gumbo is its nutty brown roux

right Prawns with Pineapple-Ginger Glaze, baked in Australian paperbark

top Freshly made Guacamole

left Cornmeal-Crusted Lake Perch with Young Spinach and Roasted Tomato-Fennel Marinara

right Sopa de Pollo con Tortillas–serrano chiles give this Mexican chicken soup a kick

Motu Picnic Kabobs–bacon-wrapped scallops skewered and grilled with pineapple, mango, red onion, and red pepper

Pumpkin and Butternut
Squash Soup, with
frizzled leeks

Poisson Cru, the unofficial national
food of French Polynesia

Freshly made Mackinac Island fudge

A selection of freshly brewed coffees to be tasted, along with a variety of coffee beans
following page Puget Sound's Dungeness Crab Salad with Avocado, Cucumber, Tomato, and Basil

FRIED EVERGLADES ALLIGATOR

When I was in the Everglades, I made sure that alligator didn't make a recipe out of me. Actually, you don't have to catch an alligator for this recipe. It is available frozen, cleaned, and diced. You can order it directly from www.lilsalseafood.com.

SERVES 4

MARINADE
3 GARLIC CLOVES, PEELED AND FINELY CHOPPED
1 1/2 TEASPOONS DRIED BASIL
1 1/2 TEASPOONS DRIED OREGANO
1 TABLESPOON SALT
1 TEASPOON GROUND BLACK PEPPER
ALLIGATOR
1 1/2 POUNDS ALLIGATOR MEAT, TRIMMED
VEGETABLE OIL FOR FRYING
3 LARGE EGGS
1/4 CUP WHOLE MILK
ALL-PURPOSE FLOUR FOR DREDGING
BREAD CRUMBS FOR BREADING
GARNISH
COCKTAIL SAUCE
1 LIME, SLICED INTO 8 WEDGES

FOR THE MARINADE: In a large mixing bowl, whisk together all the ingredients.

FOR THE ALLIGATOR: Place the alligator meat in the marinade and let it marinate for 2 hours in the refrigerator.

Place the vegetable oil in a 1-gallon stockpot and heat to 350°F.

In a medium mixing bowl, whisk together the eggs and milk (this mixture is called an egg wash). Remove the alligator from the marinade and dredge each piece in the flour. Dip in the egg wash and then roll in the bread crumbs.

Gently drop each piece of breaded alligator into the hot oil. Fry until it is golden brown and floats to the top. Drain on paper towels.

Serve the alligator warm with your favorite cocktail sauce and 2 lime wedges per serving.

Churrasco with Mojo and Fried Plantains

The Three Guys from Miami took a piece of meat that is usually considered a tough cut and turned it into a flavorful meal. An important step to remember is to let the meat rest after grilling. This prevents the juices from leaving the meat when slicing. Slice the meat across the grain so it is tender when eating. Plantains, also called "fufu" in Cuba, are used for a garnish with this dish. The plantain is a variety of banana, and it is also called the "cooking banana."

Grandma Castillo preps plantains for cooking.

SERVES **6**

FRIED PLANTAINS

2 QUARTS VEGETABLE OIL FOR FRYING

3 FIRM PLANTAINS

SALT AND BLACK PEPPER TO TASTE

MOJO

20 GARLIC CLOVES, PEELED

2 TEASPOONS SALT

1½ CUPS SOUR ORANGE JUICE (2 PARTS ORANGE JUICE AND
  1 PART LEMON JUICE)

1 CUP MINCED WHITE ONIONS

1 TEASPOON CHOPPED FRESH OREGANO

1½ CUPS OLIVE OIL

CHURRASCO

3 POUNDS SKIRT STEAK, TRIMMED

FOR THE PLANTAINS: Place the vegetable oil in a 1-gallon stockpot
and heat to 350°F.

Peel the plantains and cut into 1-inch pieces. Fry the pieces in the oil
for 1 minute. Remove from the oil and use a small plate to press
down on the pieces to flatten them. Return the pieces to the frying
oil and continue to fry until golden brown. Remove from the oil,
drain on paper towels, and season with salt and pepper.

FOR THE MOJO: Using a mortar and pestle, mash the garlic and salt
into a paste. Place the mashed garlic in a medium mixing bowl and
stir in the sour orange juice, onion, and oregano. Let the mixture sit
at room temperature for 30 minutes.

Place the olive oil in a medium saucepan over high heat. Remove
from the heat before it begins to smoke. Whisk in the garlic–orange
juice mixture until well blended. Transfer the mojo to a casserole
dish and cool in the refrigerator.

Place the skirt steak in the cooled mojo and marinate for 2 hours.
Turn the skirt steak over once while marinating.

Prepare an outdoor grill.

Remove the skirt steak from the marinade, place on the grill, and
grill to desired doneness. The Three Guys from Miami prefer
medium-rare. Let the skirt steak rest for 5 minutes. Slice thinly
across the grain. Serve with fried plantains and Chimichurri
(page 80).

Jumbo Prawn, Lobster, and Shrimp Cake, and a Gingered Dashi Broth

Chef Roger Ruch at The Tides Hotel guarantees his guests an adventure in dining. This is one of his house specialties.

SERVES 4

DASHI BROTH

1/2 TEASPOON WHOLE CORIANDER SEED

1/2 TEASPOON WHOLE FENNEL SEED

1 1/2 POUNDS CHICKEN LEGS, ROASTED

1/4 POUND CARROTS, CHOPPED

1/4 POUND WHITE ONIONS, CHOPPED

1/4 POUND LEEKS, CHOPPED

2 GARLIC CLOVES, PEELED AND CHOPPED

6 TABLESPOONS WHITE WINE

1/2 CUP PLUS 2 TABLESPOONS SHERRY VINEGAR

5 CUPS CHICKEN STOCK

2 OUNCES LIGHT SOY SAUCE

1 1/2 TEASPOONS MINCED PEELED FRESH GINGER

1 1/2 TEASPOONS CHOPPED FRESH CILANTRO

1 1/2 TEASPOONS SZECHWAN PEPPERCORNS

1/4 CUP VEAL DEMI-GLACE OR 1/2 CUP VEAL STOCK REDUCED BY ONE-HALF

1 FRESH THYME SPRIG

1 TABLESPOON HOISIN SAUCE

1/2 TEASPOON DARK CHILI POWDER

1/2 TEASPOON HUNGARIAN PAPRIKA

1/2 TEASPOON CURRY POWDER

1/2 TEASPOON GROUND CUMIN

1/4 POUND FENNEL, CHOPPED

2 TABLESPOONS DASHI POWDER

CLARIFICATION

3 EGG WHITES

1/2 CUP DICED WHITE ONION

1/4 CUP DICED CELERY

1/4 CUP PEELED AND DICED PARSNIPS

JUICE OF 1 LEMON

1/4 CUP WHITE WINE

LOBSTER AND SHRIMP CAKES

1/4 POUND FLORIDA SPINY LOBSTER MEAT, UNCOOKED AND
  ROUGHLY CHOPPED

1/4 POUND MEDIUM-SIZED SHRIMP, PEELED AND ROUGHLY CHOPPED

11/2 TEASPOONS MINCED GARLIC

2 TEASPOONS FISH SAUCE

1/4 CUP SWEET PEAS

3 TABLESPOONS UNSALTED BUTTER

PRAWNS

4 JUMBO PRAWNS, UNPEELED

SALT AND BLACK PEPPER TO TASTE

2 TABLESPOONS UNSALTED BUTTER

4 SMALL BUNDLES OF PEA SHOOTS

FOR THE DASHI BROTH: In a large stockpot over medium heat, toast the coriander and fennel seeds for 1 minute. Add all the other ingredients and let simmer for 1½ hours. Strain the broth through a chinois or a strainer lined with cheesecloth. Wipe out the pot. Return the clear broth to the stockpot.

TO CLARIFY THE BROTH: Whip the egg whites to soft peaks. Fold in the onion, celery, parsnips, lemon juice, and wine. Add the egg white mixture to the broth and slowly simmer on medium-low heat for 1 hour. Do not boil. Strain the broth again and keep warm.

FOR THE LOBSTER AND SHRIMP CAKES: In a food processor, combine the lobster and shrimp meat, garlic, fish sauce, and peas. Pulse the mixture until it comes together but is still very chunky. Divide the mixture into 4 equal portions, shape into balls, and then flatten with your hand to about 1 inch thick.

In a large sauté pan over medium-high heat, melt the butter and let it get very hot. Add the 4 cakes to the pan and cook until the bottoms are deep golden brown. Flip over and cook the other side to the same color. Place on a baking sheet.

Preheat the oven to 350°F.

FOR THE PRAWNS: Season the prawns with salt and pepper. In a sauté pan over medium heat, sear the prawns in the butter until the shells turn bright red. Turn over and continue to sear until the other side is also bright red. Place on the baking sheet with the lobster and shrimp cakes. Place the baking sheet in the oven and cook for 3 to 4 minutes.

TO SERVE: Place 1 cup of dashi broth in 4 serving bowls. Place a lobster and shrimp cake in the center of each bowl. Place a whole prawn on top of each cake and garnish with pea shoots.

SOUTH

PACIFIC

THE MOST BEAUTIFUL ISLAND ON EARTH? JAMES MICHENER'S FAMOUS DESCRIPTION OF BORA-BORA IS SUBJECT TO CROSS-EXAMINATION BY CHAMPIONS OF MARTINIQUE OR MAJORCA, OR OF GREECE'S SANTORINI, OR OF PORQUEROLLES ON THE RIVIERA.

BORA-BORA

But at five in the morning, with the faintest hint of pastel infusing the cushion of night clouds, with a pellucid lagoon stroked by the sighs of trade winds, with the misty silhouette of mountains beginning to emerge behind the trills of waking rock doves, Bora-Bora is the softest. Fools alone remain asleep when Eden stirs. *Bonitiers,* Polynesian tuna boats, skiff through the Te Ava Nui Pass toward the open ocean. The hillsides are alive with the movement of local women meandering among hibiscus trees, picking baskets of blooms. By degrees the rising sun stokes tropical engines, hot and serene, stripping layers of shadow from the mountainside.

My two children, Josh and Alicia, and I don snorkel gear to explore the quiet lagoon at its most picturesque. Half an hour further along, the clouds wear rosy hems and the lagoon has picked up horizontal flashes from distant breakers. The doves, which the natives in their singsong language call *u 'u aira' o,* have finished chirping and begun earning a living. Land crabs skitter across snowy beaches. A delivery truck rumbles along Bora-Bora's only road, and the sound of crunching gears and the smell of diesel exhaust is grating and inappropriate—Eden's serpent emblazoned with a logo for Twisties Chicken Flavour Chips. But reality settles into paradise along with the workday, and, in truth, it's been a long time since these islands bore the wholly unsullied look of the retouched and color-balanced postcards peeking out from showcases at the resort boutiques.

Of the 130 islands that make up French Polynesia, Bora-Bora is fairly typical. A green hump of volcanic sputum surrounded by a turquoise lagoon and, farther out, by a rosary of coral reefs and small islands called *motus*, Bora-Bora gained its reputation in part from Rodgers and Hammerstein's musical *South Pacific*, loosely based on a James Michener wartime chronicle. In terms of climate and milieu, Bora-Bora is not that much different from its sister islands and has a geological legacy that is nearly identical. Scattered like seeds among nearly 2 million square miles of subequatorial Pacific Ocean, the five archipelagos known collectively as French Polynesia (it's a territory of France, and French is the dominant tongue) were formed as the uppermost peaks of volcanic eruptions that occurred along seabed rifts over 40 million years. Individual age pretty much dictates the structure of each island; low, reef-ringed atolls are what's left after a mountain has entirely eroded beneath the sea's surface, while the younger "high islands," with their central jungle-covered peaks, have not yet reached that stage. Bora-Bora, cresting through a very productive middle age, features the best of both: a lush and alpine mainland, an active reef, and a fish-friendly moat in between. It's this central lagoon, painted baby blue by the combination of shallow, nearly tepid water and a sugary bed of pulverized coral below, that gives the South Sea Islands their idyllic and most striking color patterns.

Bora-Bora is ringed by a coastal road that is well paved and as scenic as it gets. From the northernmost tip, heading south to the island's main community at Viatape, the translucent lagoon washes languidly against beaches and breakwalls to your right, while the small, sporadic settlements on the left clamber into groves of breadfruit trees. Pickings from these horizontal gardens appear on makeshift stands before the gates and *tiare* hedgerows, being offered for sale by heavyset matrons dressed in the filmy, ubiquitous wraparound garment, the *peleo*. Beautiful hand-

COCO BEACHCOMBER

Here is a cool cocktail that will surely warm things up at a summer picnic or pool party.

SERVES 1

- 1 COCONUT, TOP CUT OFF AND COCONUT WATER RESERVED
- 2 SCOOPS COCONUT ICE CREAM
- 2 CUPS PINEAPPLE JUICE
- ¼ CUP LIGHT RUM
- 2 TABLESPOONS CRÈME DE CACAO LIQUEUR
- ICE

In a blender, combine the coconut water, ice cream, pineapple juice, rum, and crème de cacao. Blend until thoroughly mixed. Add ice to the coconut and pour the drink over the ice. Serve chilled.

HUAHINE COCKTAIL

THIS IS THE DRINK YOU ARE GREETED WITH WHEN YOU ARRIVE AT YOUR HOTEL ON THE ISLAND OF BORA-BORA. IT IS ALSO A GREAT WAY TO GREET YOUR GUESTS AT A COCKTAIL PARTY. TRY ADDING A LITTLE VODKA FOR AN EXTRA KICK.

SERVES 4

ICE

1/2 CUP PINEAPPLE JUICE

4 TABLESPOONS ORANGE JUICE WITH PULP

6 CUPS DICED WATERMELON, SEEDS REMOVED

1 DASH BOTTLED STRAWBERRY SYRUP

4 WATERMELON CHUNKS WITH RIND

2 STRAWBERRIES, CUT IN HALF

Fill a blender half full with ice. Add the juices, diced watermelon, and strawberry syrup. Blend until smooth. Pour into a chilled glass. Garnish with a chunk of watermelon and half a strawberry on a toothpick.

made peleos often hang alongside the breadfruit displays, fetching between $10 and $20 apiece.

Breadfruit is one of the mainstays of the rural Polynesian economy, and, of course, this starchy cream-colored orb was the unwitting catalyst for the HMS *Bounty*'s famous mutiny, an incident that in many ways put these islands on the map of Western consciousness. Recall that sapling breadfruit trees, intended to feed slaves in the Caribbean, were the cargo that HMS *Bounty* sought during its now infamous Polynesian sojourn in 1788. To believe the storybook-cum-Hollywood version of the event, Captain Bligh was a cruel martinet whose abuses led heroic First Mate Fletcher Christian to seize control of the merchant ship.

Interpreting historical as opposed to fictional evidence, it seems that the genuine Bligh was not only a fair fellow by his day's standards, but an officer who inspired loyalty from the majority of his crew (only twelve sided with Christian) and went on to become one of the most respected seamen of his generation. Fletcher Christian, on the other hand, appears to have been something of a pouty—and possibly deranged—problem child. In either version, what's clear enough is that Christian's posse found Tahiti's lure irresistible and decided to stay put rather than return to foggy, chilly, socially repressive England. Stay put he did, and his descendants survive to this day on a rocky little outpost called Pitcairn.

Coming, conquering, and deciding to hang around has been a pattern of Polynesian visitors since the first prehistoric mariners stumbled across these gorgeous islands some three thousand years ago. Whether these brave explorers in their double-hulled canoes came from Malaysia, Indonesia, or South America has never been absolutely determined, but wherever their origin, their terminus obviously had a leg up on home. And they've been jumping ship ever since. Paul Gauguin, the French Post-Impressionist, is perhaps the best known of the self-imposed castaways, and it's impossible to view modern Tahitian artwork without seeing his influence. Gauguin certainly talked the talk, but he wound up bouncing back to France two years after his original landing, decrying the "European trivialities" that corrupted the natives. Although he would ultimately return to die in the Marquesas Islands, his search for paradise amid the lilting palms and seductive *wahines* never quite panned out.

Arriving in Viatape (less a city than a warren of huts and shops, but nonetheless Bora-Bora's megalopolis), I'm in search of Patrick, who is to be my host at the day's highlight; a full-blown Tahitian *ahima'a* cookout on a nearby secluded *motu*. We're supposed to meet at seven, but like most Tahitians, Patrick operates on an ambiguous schedule, which means I'll see him when I see him. That's fine; the day is developing into another rapturous South Sea jewel, and the harbor hosts a myriad of sights and characters to occupy me meantime.

Patrick shows up within twenty minutes of our appointment, winning a South Seas punctuality ribbon. Not that there'd be complaints in any case. Ignoring the fact that he twirls a baton (flaming) and wears a skirt (the unisex peleo), Patrick is the embodiment of Polynesian virility, a massive umber-colored, muscle-ripped hunk of manhood. Given a gridiron, he may be able to tackle Randy Moss. Brandishing elaborate tattoos, flipping his jet-black tresses, and tossing chunks of raw fish at reef sharks, the image that is Patrick is wholly self-created. He exists because we want him to exist. It's no surprise that in college he studied marketing. Patrick has an eight-year-old daughter at school in Beverly Hills, California, and when the other little girls—whose fathers probably couldn't tackle *Kate* Moss—start bragging "My dad's a Silicone Valley consultant" or "My dad's a personal injury lawyer," she puts on a smug little grin and replies, "My dad feeds sharks in Bora-Bora."

With the grand bonhomie of a man who knows his worth as a tour guide, a storyteller, and a beefcake specimen, Patrick leads the way to his colorful bark. Also on board are a pair of young *aparima* dancers, two of the famous *wahines* that so captured Paul Gauguin's imagination. Willow-thin and hopelessly beautiful, they are at the very least the feminine equal of Patrick's über-male icon. They sit silently, almost stoically, wearing the peculiar scowl of South Sea

You want fresh—I'll give you fresh! Oh, yeah, these mahi mahi are heavy too!

islanders. They seem neither friendly nor otherwise, but sport a look that floats in sultry seas of self-confidence and indifference—attitudes that have dashed many a Western heart against the island reefs.

We motor through the crystalline lagoon, past the sprinkling of *motu,* or islets, that ring Bora-Bora as though tossed there by centrifugal force. Beneath us, the water is robin's egg blue and so warm that swimming is nearly uncomfortable, but it offers a smorgasbord of delights for snorkelers. Complex coral colonies abound, and tropical fish of every color and description mass beneath the hull, scattering visibly as we zip by. About twenty minutes out we draw up to a palm-shaded beach and are greeted by a quartet of singing musicians, a third dancer, and a tray of cold drinks. A long table sits beachside, draped in palm fronds and hyacinths, and a lean-to covers the smoking *ahi-ma'a* pit. A couple of jovial, sweat-soaked Polynesians—whose physiques appear to be the result of more than a couple of feasts—are tending the fire in preparation for the cookout, which in Tahitian is called a *tama'ara'a.* Everything has been prearranged by Patrick, of course, and it's clear that he should have passed along his business card to Robinson Crusoe's people.

As the ironwood logs smolder to white-hot, I lend a shoulder to the cooks and arrange porous volcanic rocks over the coals, then help fit a metal grate into the pit. Meanwhile, a knot of older women has been dressing a suckling pig, rubbing it down with sea salt, and prepping the foundation of a classic Tahitian barbecue. The piglet is lowered onto the grate and then surrounded with traditional *tama'ara'a* accompaniments: peeled taro root, halved breadfruit, whole plantains. The entire spread is covered in freshly picked banana leaves and a quantity of burlap. Beach sand is shoveled around the edges, forming an oven. Lacking a meat thermometer, the feast will require between two and three hours to cook.

Patrick, meanwhile, has seized a spare guitar and joined the song boys. It's one talent he may need to delete from his résumé, but the easy, mellifluous tunes and the magical

poetry of South Seas lyrics withstand his rhythmic assault. In the foreground, the girls perform the smooth, sensuous *aparima* dances that two centuries back had English missionaries mopping their brows and passing out cease-and-desist orders lest their brethren, the converters, inadvertently become the convertees.

In a while the tug of the magical lagoon becomes irresistible, and Patrick trades the guitar for an Evinrude rudder. Beneath the jagged spires of the mainland, he pilots us to his favorite place for shark spotting. Baiting sharks can be a hit-or-miss proposition in these fish-heavy waters, for nothing here goes hungry for long; but as he throws anchor, the sharks' reliable point team, dozens of silvery stingrays, begin to circle. Despite their ominous appearance, these gentle giants are as tame as lambs at a petting zoo, and soon

IF YOU THINK GETTING FRESH COCONUT IS EASY, THINK AGAIN—AND THERE AREN'T ANY SAFETY NETS, EITHER!

Polynesian Chicken Drumettes

This is a great appetizer or cocktail party snack.

SERVES 4

2 TABLESPOONS PEANUT OIL

20 CHICKEN DRUMETTES (THE WING WITHOUT THE WINGTIP ATTACHED)

1 CUP LIGHT SOY SAUCE

2 CUPS CHICKEN STOCK

3/4 CUP (UNPACKED) LIGHT BROWN SUGAR

1 CUP PINEAPPLE JUICE

3 DRIED BIRD'S-EYE CHILE PEPPERS, CRUSHED

1/4 CUP CREAM SHERRY

1/2 CUP DICED WHITE ONION

2 TEASPOONS MUSTARD POWDER

2 TABLESPOONS CHOPPED PARSLEY

Heat the peanut oil in a sauté pan over medium-high heat. Brown the drumettes.

In a medium sauté pan, whisk together the soy sauce, stock, brown sugar, pineapple juice, chile peppers, cream sherry, onion, and mustard powder. Bring the mixture to a boil, stirring to dissolve the sugar. Add the drumettes and lower the heat to a simmer. Turn each drumette several times to baste them thoroughly. Simmer for 15 to 20 minutes, until the liquid is reduced to a glaze.

When the drumettes are fully cooked, remove the pan from the heat. Sprinkle parsley over the drumettes and serve hot.

My son, Josh, and I take a dip in a freshwater spring and make some new friends.

my kids are over the side and swimming among them. Both relish the games and caresses; the manta rays are tame enough to hold. Patrick remains on the far side of the boat, tossing chum just beyond the stragglers, and in time the sleek russet forms of reef sharks begin to dart to and fro like shadowy sylphs among the cobalt waves. These sharks, some with a black-tipped dorsal fin, are no more than three or four feet in length and pose no real danger to humans, but taking in the full scope of their feeding frenzy is better accomplished from the boat, so the kids and I abandon the playful rays for a vantage point on the boat's prow—at least that's the story I'm sticking to.

Half an hour later we're famished ourselves and motor back to the *motu,* where the rest of the group have begun to peel back the layers of burlap and now-toasted banana leaves. The aromas that escape with the pent-up steam are scrumptious, and the star attraction, the piglet, has reached the falling-from-the-bone stage prized by pork aficionados around the globe. Uncooked, a suckling pig is not a pretty

sight; it looks as if it belongs on the table of a first-year biology student instead of a cutting board. But slow-cooked in an open-air firepit, it becomes something truly transcendent. We dive into juicy, smoky portions, sweet without needing sauce, the orangey rind crisp and rich. The side dishes are not to universal tastes; breadfruit, even when fully cooked, clings stubbornly to a doughy texture that makes you think it needs another fifteen minutes of flame, and eating taro can be likened to eating lukewarm candle wax. Considerably more palatable are the plantains that emerge from the *ahima'a* golden brown and as sweet as caramel. The standout dish is leaf-wrapped Tahitian *poe*, made from cooked pumpkin mashed with tapioca and pineapple juice, and then lashed with coconut and vanilla— a succulent and complex dessert that resembles its bland Hawaiian counterpart in nothing but name.

Tama'ara'a cookouts are reserved for special occasions, generally for holiday dinners, wedding feasts, and family reunions. The swayful songs and sultry dances are all part of the Tahitian package. Most visitors to Polynesia will not get the chance to experience it in its most authentic incarnation. A more accessible dining blowout takes place back on the island, in Bloody Mary's, Bora-Bora's most popular nighttime attraction and a mecca for celebrity watching— anyone from Marlon Brando to Marilyn Chambers.

Bloody Mary's name has nothing to do with the spicy eye-opener or the Tudor Queen but, rather, with a leading character from *South Pacific*. What makes Bloody Mary's Bora-Bora's most well-known restaurant? The dress code perks up Stateside standards, that's for sure. NO SHIRT, NO SHOES, NO SERVICE signs are one thing, but PANTS OPTIONAL? Waiters wear multicolored wraparounds, and everyone's shoes must be checked at the door, the better to experience the dining room floor, comprised of several tons of coral sand. With the encouragement or at least the toleration of management, patrons show up in anything from haute couture to Riviera casual, which means that wearing underwear is not out of the question—though the image of Marlon Brando in skivvies is enough to put anyone off the parrot fish.

MOOREA ISLAND SPINY LOBSTER GLAZE

MOOREA ISLAND HAS THE SWEETEST PINEAPPLE I HAVE TASTED, EVEN SWEETER THAN THE HAWAIIAN KIND. THIS GLAZE WILL BRING OUT THE SWEET FLAVOR OF THE LOBSTER MEAT AND BECOME A SUMMERTIME GRILLING FAVORITE.

SERVES 4

GLAZE

1 CUP COCONUT MILK, SQUEEZED FROM FRESHLY GRATED COCONUT

JUICE OF 1 LIME

1/2 CUP CHOPPED FRESH CILANTRO

1 CUP PINEAPPLE JUICE

1 CUP CHOPPED FRESH PINEAPPLE

1/2 CUP SWEET ORANGE MARMALADE

1/2 TEASPOON CAYENNE PEPPER

1 TEASPOON SALT

LOBSTER

FOUR 6-OUNCE SPINY LOBSTER TAILS, SPLIT IN HALF

Prepare an outdoor grill.

FOR THE GLAZE: In a food processor, blend all the ingredients for 10 to 15 seconds.

Place the lobster tails in a glass dish, meat side up. Pour the glaze over the tails and let marinate in the refrigerator for 20 minutes.

Grill the lobster tails, meat side down, turning as needed to prevent burning. Turn the tails over after 3 to 5 minutes and baste with the glaze. The tails are finished when the meat is firm and opaque, approximately 10 minutes. Serve immediately.

The restaurant, from palm-thatched ceiling to Matira Beach sand, was patterned after the Bastille Day huts that Tahitians build for their annual six-week celebration of the transplanted French holiday. In the original brainstorm, Bloody Mary's was going to appeal chiefly to Tahitians, to whom a year-round Bastille Day hutch would have nostalgic, hungover appeal, but as it happens, the place caught on wildly with outsiders. The concept is straightforward enough: Upon entering, guests are presented with an iced display of locally caught seafood, the better to make an advanced assessment of the kitchen's offerings. By necessity, therefore, the menu is in endless flux, solely dependent on the daily luck of the fishermen. The night we stopped in, unusual selections included duckbill snapper; small, grillable cavally; and a couple of monstrous spiny lobsters, which held court over their less animated brothers. The open kitchen prepared everything to a turn, and as far as I'm concerned, shored up the restaurant's stellar reputation. Alas, that night there was nobody from Hollywood's *who's who* for a *what's what* of second opinions.

TAHITI

The island of Tahiti is the largest landmass in French Polynesia and contains its only city of note, Papeete. Sprawled around a protective harbor on Tahiti's north shore, Papeete is cosmopolitan by the standards of empty ocean, perhaps, but in terms of international appeal, it has a way to go. It's as if they took the world's most exotic location and struggled to denature it. McDonald's, Sony, Coca-Cola—squint, and you could be in Omaha. Neither particularly attractive (native building materials were banned in 1884, so buildings tend to be hard-nosed and without soul, while all but the costliest residences are roofed in corrugated tin) nor exhilarating (South Seas heat and humidity, wonderful on languid beaches, is something else inside close urban confines), Papeete is little more than a barely functional link to modern commerce.

For tourists there's not much in Papeete to oversell. Restaurants tend to be mediocre and overpriced; the streets are crowded and smelly; and shopping is better reserved for wealthy locals. Fashion, in particular, is a day late and a dollar high. Nightlife is relatively lackluster, but this can be attributed to a limited supply and demand. For the most part, visitors don't come to Polynesia looking for a downtown scene, and islanders themselves tend to be sane, sober, and quiet people. There's little crime, not much of a drug problem, and surprisingly little poverty. My Tahitian guide, Carl Emery, put it this way: "We're chickens here— early to bed and early to rise."

In the resultant healthy, wealthy, and wise environment, you'd expect at least a superlative open-air market, and in this regard Papeete gets the highest of marks. The municipal market of Mapuru a Paraita has been one of Papeete's most popular attractions for more than a century. It serves both as an axis from which to launch cottage-industry crafts—hand-carved totems, masks, and beautiful pareos and baskets—and as the nucleus for wholesale and retail fish, meat, produce, and flowers throughout the South Seas. The *Marché*, as it's known, is a hit with foodies and souvenir shoppers in Papeete, though the rest of the city may prove something of a miss.

Thinking to catch the best of the catch, the daily selection of seafood, I arrive at the market at daybreak, only to find that the fish stalls are either unmanned or sparsely stocked. Even among the early-rising Tahitians, I discover, the best seafood shows up around nine. In the interim I ascend to the market's second floor, where the bulk of the handcrafts are located. Among the artwork, of which Polynesians are justifiably proud, I pore over bolts of beautiful fabric and multicolored sarongs; leaf through the traditional Tahitian one-tone paintings done on vegetable paper; and peruse the meticulously woven hats, mats, and baskets made of pandanus leaves. A member of the screw pine family, pandanus is an interesting multipurpose material. The fibrous fronds are used both for weaving and for flavoring food; its nutlike and grassy aroma enhances rice

PRAWNS WITH VANILLA-COCONUT SAUCE

A TAHITIAN NAMED TAPUTU ON THE ISLAND OF MOOREA TAUGHT ME THIS DISH. IT COMBINES THE SUBTLE FLAVOR OF COCONUT MILK WITH TAHITIAN VANILLA.

SERVES 2

1 WHOLE COCONUT

1 TABLESPOON UNSALTED BUTTER

16 MEDIUM-SIZED SHRIMP, PEELED, DEVEINED, AND WITH TAIL ON

1 VANILLA BEAN, SPLIT AND SCRAPED

SALT AND BLACK PEPPER TO TASTE

Split the coconut in half and grate 1 cup of coconut meat. Place the grated coconut in a piece of cheesecloth. Gather up the ends of the cheesecloth and wring out the coconut milk by twisting the cheesecloth over a bowl. You should get about 4 tablespoons of milk. Set aside.

In a medium sauté pan over medium heat, melt the butter. Add the shrimp, vanilla bean (as a garnish), and scrapings. Sauté for 2 to 3 minutes. Add the coconut milk and simmer for 4 to 5 minutes. Season with salt and pepper.

Serve hot.

dishes, especially when combined with the subtle taste and creamy texture of coconut milk.

The coconut palm is the Polynesian staff of life, and just as buffalo served Native Americans, all parts are used. The meat is an essential ingredient in countless island dishes; the husks contribute the raw material for rope, jewelry, and clothing—the ludicrous-looking coconut shell bra included; the trunks are building material; and the fronds are woven into waterproof roofing. The trees are omnipresent throughout the South Pacific, which is not to say that the fruit is easy to come by. On the island of Moorea I had a chance to watch the death-defying harvest technique of one muscled young nut—he required two minutes to complete a hand-over-hand climb to the top of a 60-foot trunk, whereupon, without any safety gear, he cut loose a few husks and then skittered, simianlike, back to earth. Watch a couple of rounds like that, and I challenge you to look upon a humble Mounds bar without a newfound respect.

Downstairs at the market, as the freshest seafood begins to arrive, the coconut stands are going strong. One serves whole green nuts (the "drinking" stage) with the tops whacked off. Ice cold and sipped through a straw, the juice is refreshing and nutritious. As a bonus, the inner flesh—which hasn't yet hardened into the waxy white meat we're used to—can be scooped out and eaten like jelly.

Bananas also occupy a tremendous amount of market real estate, and the varieties available are astonishing. From the lilliputian *rima rima* to the loaflike *homoa,* there are dozens of in-between sizes with flavors ranging from creamy sweet to starchy dry, in such colors as yellow, garnet, orange, green, and blue. Other exotic and, this morning, readily available produce include the grublike, gently perfumed Tahitian ginger; the acidic star-shaped carambola; the astringent quenette—an after-school favorite for Tahitian youngsters; the legendary juice-jammed Polynesian grapefruit, known by the French *pamplemousse;* and the rare but luscious cayenne cherry that makes sensational jams and chutneys. Many fruit stands also push homemade *monoi,* the Tahitian all-purpose aromatherapy body rub made from coconut oil and various natural aromatics. One of the most popular additions is vanilla. Having just spent an evening at a Moorea vanilla plantation, watching the painstaking method of hand-pollination by moonlight, I'm particularly attentive to the spread of beans in the market.

Meanwhile, my ship has come in over in the seafood aisles. Fresh fish is spread out over the iced counters, clear-eyed, multicolored, and delectable. There are red and yellow snappers, mahi mahi, mackerel, fish from the "lowlands" (what the local sea rovers call the shallow waters around atolls) and from the deep blue beyond. Many of these piscine peacocks will be made into the ever-popular island dish called *poisson cru*. A variation on ceviche, poisson cru is made from any firm-textured fish; it is thinly sliced while raw and tossed with scallions, carrots, red pepper, coconut milk, and lime juice. So ubiquitous is poisson cru in Tahiti that it is absolutely standard on the menu of every upscale restaurant and downtown *roulotte* on the island.

A PAPEETE LOCAL PREPARES TAHITIAN FAST FOOD AT A ROULOTTE.

Roulottes, incidentally, represent Tahitian dining in its most unaffected form: fast food unsullied by McFranchises. Dining at a roulotte should comprise at least a couple of meals for every foodie who ventures to Polynesia. Essentially, they are vans converted to mobile kitchens, and about forty of them can be found parked near the waterfront. Each roulotte dispenses an individual specialty—nothing too ambitious: pizza, barbecue, sashimi, chow mein. Since nobody features exactly the same thing, everybody seems to get along. At Chez Mamy they're whacking off slices of baguette; at Chez Therese it's translucent, paper-thin swordfish; while at La Boule Rouge crepes are the ticket, especially the sublime "Tahitian," which is stuffed with coconut, chantilly, and banana, and swimming in velvety blankets of chocolate sauce. A dastardly delight for the senses, no question, in total disregard of rules for sensible living, of cholesterol counts, and of belt sizes.

But, then again, if not in Tahiti—where the tropical siren song has caused responsible men to cash in house, hearth, health, and every future Monday morning at eight A.M.—then where?

FLAMING TORCH JUGGLER PATRICK TAIRUA ALSO HAPPENS TO BE THE BEST GUIDE ANYONE COULD ASK FOR IN BORA-BORA.

MOTU PICNIC KABOBS

"MOTU" MEANS "LITTLE ISLAND" IN THE TAHITIAN LANGUAGE. THE AFTERNOON WE SPENT ON ONE UNINHABITED "MOTU" WILL ALWAYS BE ETCHED IN MY MIND; IT WAS THE MOST ENJOYABLE PICNIC EVER, ESPECIALLY SINCE MY CHILDREN, JOSH AND ALICIA, WERE WITH ME.

SERVES 4

GLAZE

1 CUP PINEAPPLE JUICE

1/4 CUP LIGHT SOY SAUCE

1 TABLESPOON WORCESTERSHIRE SAUCE

1 TABLESPOON DRY SHERRY

1 TABLESPOON CHOPPED ORANGE ZEST

1/2 CUP SWEET ORANGE MARMALADE

1/4 CUP HONEY

JUICE OF 1 LIME

KABOBS

16 SEA SCALLOPS

16 BACON SLICES

EIGHT 8-INCH WOODEN SKEWERS, SOAKED OVERNIGHT IN WATER

1 RED ONION, PEELED AND CUT INTO 8 CHUNKS

1 RIPE MANGO, PEELED, SEEDED, AND CUT INTO 8 PIECES

1 RED BELL PEPPER, STEM, RIBS, AND SEEDS REMOVED, AND CUT INTO 8 PIECES

1/4 PINEAPPLE, RIND REMOVED, CORED, AND CUT INTO 8 PIECES

SALT AND BLACK PEPPER TO TASTE

Prepare an outdoor grill.

FOR THE GLAZE: In a medium saucepan over medium-low heat, whisk the ingredients together. Simmer until reduced by half.

TO ASSEMBLE THE KABOBS: Wrap each scallop with 1 piece of bacon. On each skewer, pierce a piece of red onion and push it to 1/2 inch from the bottom of the skewer. Pierce the scallop through the bacon and push it down to the red onion. Pierce a chunk of mango, a piece of red pepper, one more bacon-wrapped scallop, and finally a chunk of pineapple. Season with salt and pepper.

Place the kabobs on the outdoor grill and brush with the glaze to coat entirely. Cook for 2 minutes, rotate the skewers, and reglaze. Repeat this step two more times. Reglaze, and serve hot.

Poe

"Poe" is closely related to poi in Hawaiian cooking. The difference is that Hawaiian poi is always made with taro root, while Polynesian "poe" can be made with taro root, pumpkin, fruits, or any combination of them. Also, Polynesian "poe" is much sweeter and commonly served as dessert at special ceremonies or for Sunday dinner.

SERVES 12

2 CUPS PEELED, DICED, AND SEEDED RAW PUMPKIN

1 CUP TAPIOCA FLOUR

1 VANILLA BEAN, SPLIT AND SCRAPED

1 CUP PINEAPPLE JUICE

1 COCONUT, SPLIT AND PULP GRATED

1 BANANA LEAF

ONE 6-INCH PIECE SUGARCANE, CUT INTO SMALL PIECES

1/2 CUP COCONUT MILK

Preheat the oven to 300°F.

Place the pumpkin pieces in a medium stockpot over medium heat and cover with water. Bring to a boil, then simmer until the pumpkin is fork-tender. Strain the water from the pumpkin.

In a large mixing bowl, mash together the cooked pumpkin, flour, vanilla bean scrapings, and pineapple juice.

Squeeze the grated coconut over the banana leaf to coat it with the milk. This will help prevent the *poe* from sticking to the leaf. Discard the grated coconut pulp. Fold the leaf to make a pocket. Place the *poe* in the pocket and put in the oven for 2 to 2½ hours.

Using a food processor, puree the sugarcane and then put through a chinois or strainer lined with cheesecloth to remove the water. Discard the pulp.

Unwrap the leaves and scoop the *poe* into a bowl. Fold in the coconut milk and sugarcane water.

Poe is a traditional finger food, so dive in!

Everyday Island Chicken

This recipe was given to me by one of the locals from Bora-Bora. It really captures the flavor of Polynesia.

SERVES 4

GLAZE
2 TABLESPOONS LIGHT SOY SAUCE
1 TABLESPOON (UNPACKED) LIGHT BROWN SUGAR
1 CUP PINEAPPLE JUICE
1/2 TABLESPOON GRATED FRESH GINGER
1 GARLIC CLOVE, MINCED
1/4 CUP HONEY
1 1/2 TEASPOONS CHOPPED ORANGE ZEST

CHICKEN
1 WHOLE CHICKEN, AROUND 3 POUNDS
SALT AND CRACKED BLACK PEPPER TO TASTE
2 TABLESPOONS SHREDDED UNSWEETENED COCONUT

Preheat the oven to 400°F.

FOR THE GLAZE: In a small saucepan over medium heat, whisk together the soy sauce, brown sugar, pineapple juice, ginger, garlic, honey, and orange zest. Reduce the glaze by one-third and then cool to room temperature.

FOR THE CHICKEN: Place the chicken on a wire rack with a drip pan underneath. Season outside and inside the chicken with salt and pepper, and then put in the oven.

Roast the chicken for 15 minutes, then turn the temperature down to 350°F. Roast an additional 20 minutes. Brush the glaze on the chicken and return to the oven for an additional 15 minutes.

Remove from the oven and sprinkle the shredded coconut over the entire chicken. Place back in the oven for 5 minutes, or until the coconut is toasted.

Remove the chicken from the oven and let rest for 5 minutes. Carve and serve.

Roasted Moorea Pineapple with Aged Rum, Coconut Sorbet, and Little Honey Cakes

Chef David Liébaux of the Pearl Beach Resort always uses indigenous ingredients, such as the Moorea pineapple and coconut, in this fabulous dessert.

SERVES 6

LITTLE HONEY CAKES
1/2 POUND (2 STICKS) UNSALTED BUTTER

6 TABLESPOONS POWDERED ALMONDS OR ALMOND FLOUR

2 CUPS SIFTED CONFECTIONER'S SUGAR

3/4 CUP ALL-PURPOSE FLOUR

6 LARGE EGG WHITES

2 TABLESPOONS TAHITIAN HONEY

1 VANILLA BEAN, SPLIT AND SCRAPED

COCONUT SORBET
2 CUPS GRANULATED SUGAR

2 CUPS WATER

1 1/4 POUNDS FRESHLY GRATED COCONUT

2 TABLESPOONS SHREDDED UNSWEETENED COCONUT

PINEAPPLES
4 MOOREA PINEAPPLES, PEELED, CORED, AND SLICED (3 SLICES PER PINEAPPLE), OR 2 HAWAIIAN PINEAPPLES

2 TABLESPOONS UNSALTED BUTTER

GRANULATED SUGAR FOR SPRINKLING

1/2 CUP LIGHT RUM

GARNISH
6 TABLESPOONS SHREDDED COCONUT

FOR THE LITTLE HONEY CAKES: In a medium sauté pan over high heat, cook the butter until browned. Be careful not to burn the butter.

In a large mixing bowl, combine the powdered almonds, confectioner's sugar, and flour. Whisk in the egg whites and honey, then add the scrapings of the vanilla bean to the mixture. Pour in the hot browned butter and blend the batter until smooth. Let the batter rest for 24 hours in the refrigerator.

FOR THE COCONUT SORBET: In a medium saucepan over medium heat, bring the sugar and water to a boil.

In a medium mixing bowl, combine the syrup mixture with the grated and shredded coconut. Cool, then chill. Freeze in an ice-cream machine according to the manufacturer's instructions.

FOR THE PINEAPPLES: In a large sauté pan over medium heat, sauté the pineapple slices in the butter. Sprinkle the pineapple slices with sugar. When the bottoms of the pineapple slices are lightly browned, flip them over and sprinkle them with more sugar. Add the rum to the pan and turn the slices 3 to 4 times to coat them. The pineapples are done when both sides are lightly browned. Set the roasted pineapples aside until needed.

Preheat the oven to 350°F.

Prepare a mini-muffin tin with paper liners or butter the tin and coat with flour. Put the honey cake batter into the tin. Bake for 10 to 15 minutes, or until they are light golden brown.

TO ASSEMBLE THE PLATE: Pile 1 tablespoon of shredded coconut in the center of each plate. Place a scoop of sorbet on the coconut. This will help prevent the sorbet from sliding on the plate. Place 3 honey cakes next to the sorbet. Lay 2 pineapple slices against the sorbet. Garnish with a sprinkling of coconut around the plate.

THE JOURNEY TO THE SOUTH PACIFIC WOULD NOT HAVE BEEN COMPLETE WITHOUT MY TWO FAVORITE TRAVEL COMPANIONS, JOSH AND ALICIA. HERE ON THE ISLAND OF MOOREA WE SAMPLE FRESH PINEAPPLE.

MAHI MAHI WITH MANGO-VANILLA SAUCE

MAHI MAHI APPEARS ON EVERY MENU IN TAHITI AND IS PREPARED IN MANY DIFFERENT WAYS. THIS SIMPLE GRILLING METHOD MAKES ONE OF MY FAVORITE DISHES.

SERVES 4

OLIVE OIL
3 TABLESPOONS MINCED SHALLOTS
1/4 CUP WHITE WINE
1 RIPE MANGO, PEELED, PITTED, AND SLICED
3 TABLESPOONS HEAVY CREAM
1 VANILLA BEAN, SPLIT AND SCRAPED
1 TABLESPOON TOMATO PUREE
SALT AND BLACK PEPPER TO TASTE
FOUR 6-OUNCE MAHI MAHI FILLETS, SKINNED

Prepare an outdoor grill.

Heat 2 tablespoons of olive oil in a medium sauté pan over medium heat. Sauté the shallots until they are translucent. Add the wine and mango. Sauté for 20 seconds. Add the cream and reduce the mixture by one-half.

Add the vanilla bean scrapings to the pan and stir the mixture. Turn the heat to low. Add the tomato puree. Cook for 1 to 2 minutes. Place the sauce in a blender and puree for 1 minute. Beware of steam when pureeing hot liquids.

Pour the sauce through a strainer, return it to the sauté pan, and bring to a simmer. Season with salt and pepper. Keep warm on the back of the stove.

Season each mahi mahi fillet with salt and pepper, and brush with olive oil. Grill the fillets for 1 to 2 minutes, rotate 90 degrees, and grill an additional 3 to 4 minutes. Turn the fillets over and repeat the grilling process. Remove the fillets from the grill.

Serve with the mango-vanilla sauce.

Curried Shrimp with Rima Rima

Rima rima is a variety of banana that grows in French Polynesia. It has a yellow skin and flesh similar to the Cavendish species that is America's favorite, but it is about half the size. The combination of the curry and the coconut milk complements the natural flavor of the shrimp.

SERVES 4

1 CUP BASMATI RICE

1³/₄ CUPS WATER

4 TABLESPOONS UNSALTED BUTTER

2 RIMA RIMAS, PEELED AND CUT IN HALF LENGTHWISE,
   OR 1 CAVENDISH BANANA

24 MEDIUM-SIZED SHRIMP, PEELED AND DEVEINED

SALT AND BLACK PEPPER TO TASTE

2 TABLESPOONS OLIVE OIL

2 GARLIC CLOVES, PEELED AND MINCED

2 TEASPOONS CURRY POWDER

¹/₂ CUP COCONUT MILK

In a 2-quart saucepan over medium heat, combine the rice, water, and 1 tablespoon of butter. Bring to a boil and stir once. Lower the heat, cover, and simmer for 15 minutes. Set aside, covered, on the back of the stove.

In a medium saucepan over medium heat, melt 2 tablespoons of butter and add the rima rima pieces. Brown on all sides and drain on paper towels.

Season the shrimp with salt and pepper.

Heat the olive oil in a large sauté pan over medium heat. Sauté the shrimp for 1 minute and then add the garlic. When the shrimp is cooked halfway, add the curry powder and cook for 2 to 3 minutes while continuously stirring the shrimp. Add the coconut milk and toss to coat the shrimp. When the shrimp is fully cooked, stir in the remaining 1 tablespoon of butter.

Serve with the cooked basmati rice and a piece of caramelized rima rima for garnish.

POISSON CRU

THIS HAS QUICKLY BECOME ONE OF MY FAVORITE DISHES. I HAVE ALWAYS APPRECIATED THE USE OF FRESH LIME JUICE IN MARINATING FISH AND SEAFOOD, SUCH AS IN CEVICHE, AND THE COCONUT MILK ADDS A NEW DIMENSION TO THE DISH. RON SAGE OF PAINAPO BEACH GAVE ME THIS RECIPE.

SERVES 2

1 FRESH WHOLE COCONUT

12 OUNCES TUNA LOIN, DICED

1/2 CUP QUARTERED AND SLICED CUCUMBER

1/2 CUP JULIENNED CARROTS

1/4 CUP JULIENNED RED BELL PEPPER

1/4 CUP JULIENNED YELLOW BELL PEPPER

1/2 CUP DICED PLUM TOMATO

1/2 CUP JULIENNED WHITE ONION

1/4 CUP SLICED SCALLIONS (WHITE AND GREEN PARTS)

SALT TO TASTE

1/4 CUP LIME JUICE

Split the coconut and grate the meat. You should get about 2 loosely packed cups of coconut meat. Set aside.

In a large mixing bowl, combine the tuna, cucumber, carrots, red and yellow peppers, tomato, onion, and scallions. Gently toss the mixture with your hands. Season with salt and lime juice.

Place the grated coconut in a piece of cheesecloth. Gather up the ends of the cheesecloth over a bowl. Wring out the milk from the coconut by twisting the cheesecloth tighter and tighter. Add the coconut milk to the poisson cru and toss gently.

Serve immediately.

Grilled Tuna with Mango-Papaya Salsa

Tuna is abundant in the waters around the South Pacific, and papaya trees are seen throughout the islands. This salsa can also be served with mahi mahi or chicken that has been grilled.

SERVES 2

PAPAYA SALSA

1 PAPAYA, PEELED, SEEDED, AND DICED

1 MANGO, PEELED, SEED REMOVED, AND DICED

1/2 RED BELL PEPPER, DICED

2 TABLESPOONS CHOPPED FRESH CILANTRO

1/2 TEASPOON RED PEPPER FLAKES

1 1/2 TABLESPOONS HONEY

JUICE OF 1 LIME

SALT AND BLACK PEPPER TO TASTE

TUNA

TWO 6-OUNCE TUNA STEAKS

SALT AND BLACK PEPPER TO TASTE

1 1/2 TEASPOONS OLIVE OIL

Prepare an outdoor grill.

FOR THE SALSA: In a large mixing bowl, combine the papaya, mango, red pepper, cilantro, pepper flakes, honey, and lime juice. Season with salt and pepper. Refrigerate until ready to use.

FOR THE TUNA: Season the tuna with salt and pepper. Lightly coat each piece with oil to prevent sticking to the grill grates. Place the tuna on the grill and rotate 90 degrees after 1 minute. Grill an additional 2 minutes, then turn over and repeat the process. Cook to the desired doneness. I recommend medium-rare.

Serve each tuna steak with a scoop of mango-papaya salsa.

JAMAICA

FOOTBALL, FORGET ABOUT IT. DRIVING'S A GAME OF INCHES. GRANTED, IT PRETTY MUCH SUCKS EVERYWHERE, BUT IN THIRD WORLD COUNTRIES LIKE JAMAICA, THE SHEER STOMACH-CHURNING, NEAR-MISS TRAUMA OF GETTING BETWEEN POINTS A AND B TENDS TO MAKE FOR MEMORIES.

Jamaica's traffic record is among the world's worst, a consequence of lousy roads, zero signage, macho drivers, wandering livestock, and a pretty loose attitude toward substance abuse. Fifty-five percent of crash victims in Jamaica test positive for marijuana; that's a factoid. The facts are that within half an hour of landing in Montego Bay, I came upon a rollover accident; twenty minutes after that I saw a motorcyclist hit a cow (both were shaken but neither hurt); and twenty-four hours later, on the outskirts of Ocho Rios, I was among fifty-plus locals who were using a makeshift bamboo crowbar to help free a man whose Toyota had just been sideswiped by a tour bus. Jamaica is a hit to the solar plexus nearly from the moment you step off the plane.

Ricky tells me he has seen two dozen serious car crashes in his lifetime, and he's only twenty-two. He's a Jamaican native and the driver of my rented road-weary Samurai. He caused none of those accidents, by the way; I know because I asked. Gratefully, as the days ahead verify, his driving skills are matched by his ability to anticipate, investigate, and/or extricate us from situations as varied as paramilitary drug searches and voodoo curses. Likewise, Ricky's knowledge of Jamaican culture is extraordinary, a consequence of street smarts and a nose that's always turned to nuance.

Jamaica is the third largest of an island group that is scattered like stepping-stones from western Venezuela nearly to the tip of Florida's peninsula. With English as its official language and slang-heavy "patois" as its common tongue, Jamaica is a member of the Commonwealth referred to as the West Indies. Fringed by snowy beaches, with verdant and fertile mountains forming a bisecting backbone, the island enjoys an extraordinary climate and a wonderful agricultural tradition. So varied and unusual are the foods available here that the average tourist can down any number of meals without tasting a familiar main ingredient.

Take the national fruit, ackee. When mixed with slivers of dried, salted cod, it is omnipresent on the Jamaican breakfast menu. Ackee is one of the culinary consequences of the slave trade; an imported evergreen tree that was shipped in from West Africa, it now grows wild and produces a fist-sized pod that's available in virtually every roadside fruit stand and farmer's market. Ackee pods are red on the outside and, upon maturity, pop open to reveal a glistening trio of patent-leather black seeds. If you don't see the seeds, don't eat the meat, since prior to this natural, sun-prompted split, ackee fruit contains certain amino acids that can kill you. Likewise, the ruddy fibers must be discarded along with the water used to blanch the flesh, since they can cause severe gastrointestinal problems. Ackee appears to be the vegetable kingdom's answer to puffer fish. Risk factors aside, the edible portion is called the aril, which ranges in color from pale beige to sharp yellow and has a texture similar to calf's brain. The similarity in pronunciation between "ackee" and "icky" is reputed to be coincidental, but the fact is, this strange fruit was banned from sale in the United States until very recently.

Ackee is not the only agricultural product of Jamaica with legality issues. Marijuana is readily available everywhere you go. It was once the most profitable cash crop on the island, and no realistic view of the place would be complete without at least a cursory mention. Rastafarians worship it, and if you fail to prompt enterprising souvenir salesmen at roadside stands, they'll frequently bring up the subject. They call it *ganja,* and it comes cheap.

JAMAICAN RUM PUNCH

THIS POPULAR DRINK IS OFFERED THROUGHOUT JAMAICA. THE SAYING GOES "One of sour, two of sweet, three of strong, and four of weak."

MAKES TEN 12 1/2-OUNCE DRINKS

1 1/4 CUPS LIME JUICE (SOUR)

2 1/2 CUPS SIMPLE SYRUP
(A MIXTURE OF 1/2 WATER AND 1/2 SUGAR SIMMERED UNTIL THE SUGAR IS DISSOLVED)

3 3/4 CUPS LIGHT RUM (STRONG)

5 CUPS WATER (WEAK)

ICE

In a large punch bowl, whisk together the lime juice, simple syrup, rum, and water.

Serve over ice.

DIRTY BANANA

JUST WHAT THE DOCTOR ORDERED
FOR AN EVENING COCKTAIL
WITH FRIENDS.

MAKES 2 DRINKS

¼ CUP TIA MARIA COFFEE LIQUEUR

¼ CUP JAMAICAN RUM CREAM OR
   BAILEY'S IRISH CREAM

½ CUP WHOLE MILK

2 TABLESPOONS SIMPLE SYRUP
   (A MIXTURE OF ½ WATER AND
   ½ SUGAR SIMMERED UNTIL THE
   SUGAR IS DISSOLVED)

1 RIPE BANANA

2 CUPS ICE

2 CHUNKS PINEAPPLE FOR GARNISH

In a blender, combine the Tia Maria, rum cream, milk, simple syrup, banana, and ice. Blend until smooth.

Serve in a frosted mug. Garnish each drink with a chunk of pineapple.

Ricky, my driver, claims to be a marijuana teetotaler, and my trust in this is more than wishful thinking, since for the most part Jamaicans will freely admit to growing, selling, possessing, smoking, processing, and exporting ganja if that, in fact, is their thing. Sure it's illegal, like driving sixty-six miles per hour on the freeway is illegal. If it's any consolation, the cannabis industry is currently on the decline, as better, stronger, and cheaper varieties are being developed worldwide. In today's Jamaica, most pot is grown for personal consumption.

That's obvious when Ricky pulls onto the shoulder of the southbound A3, exits, and immediately trips over a four-foot hemp plant growing in the middle of the grassy median. He discreetly ignores it, since it probably belongs to one of the tenants of Faith's Pen, just on the other side of the freeway, which is why we stopped to begin with. Here, an hour below Ocho Rios, more than fifty food shacks stretch along the curvy roadway that backs up against the mountains. It's a can't-miss destination for anybody with half an appetite or interest in real Jamaican cookery. Once *the* pit stop of every human being traveling between Kingston and the north coast, it remains only slightly less popular than it did in the pre-McDonald's era. Evidently, part of its survival is due to the auspices of Guinness beer, whose logo appears beside each stand's professional-looking signboard, with names like Early Bird Shop, Cherry's Spot, The Love Zone, and Shut, Day and Nite—which turns out not to be ironic but simply a business owned by a fellow named Shut. These pretty signs dangle incongruously above absurdly rustic open-fronted shanties where cooking is done over halved oil drums on makeshift legs, and running water trickles in from a huge, circular, concrete "catchment" stamped into the nearby mountainside. Don't say *third world street vendor* and don't think *salmonella*; consider *authentic tastes of the Caribbean*. Natives call this "yard" food—as in "back," not "grave"—and each ramshackle hut guards reputations built over many years. Everybody prepares a particular specialty, and nobody in this tight little food community seems eager for cutthroat competition. There's hot roast corn, escoveitch fish, baked breadfruit, stewed chicken, curried goat, beef patties, cocoa bread, bammy, pepperpot soup, stewed gungo peas and rice, fish tea, peppered shrimp, mackerel rundown, stamp and go.

And, naturally, jerk.

Johnny Cool's kiosk is huddled toward the Kingston side of Faith's Pen and is unremarkable to look upon. It has the same battered drum pan grill, and the same wreaths of sweetish pimento-coal smoke drifting between wooden slats plastered with advertisements for such absurdities as Magnum Tonic Wine with Vigorton, a sort of Jamaican health hooch. No James Beard Awards dangle from Cool's corrugated tin awning, nothing that would identify his spice-saturated slabs, incendiary haunches, and spicy thighs and wings as being the best jerked flesh to be had in Jamaica. Okay, so that's strictly a matter of opinion, but it's the opinion of Chef Walter Staib, who has accompanied us on today's jerk jaunt. And with four decades of restaurant experience under his belt, as well as being the first inductee into the Caribbean Culinary Hall of Fame, his opinion has to be worth something. He shares a little of the history of Johnny Cool, who learned jerking arts from his father, and who shortly steps out from the smoky shadows to greet his biggest fan. Cool is about thirty; he is a five-foot bundle of spunk and vinegar with a sinewy physique that makes him look like a boxer with one vicious low blow.

Walter Staib's story is nearly as wild. Late of the Beaches Resort, this rubicund, hard-drinking, mid-fifties chef, originally from the Black Forest, came to Jamaica— *Chamayka* in his thick *Cherman* accent—in order to learn West Indian culinary techniques at the source. Today, he is probably the island's most authoritative food scholar. He'll ramble on indefinitely about the flavor subtleties between goats that are raised on this sort of grass or that; he'll explain the differences among all thirteen varieties of yams grown here; and he'll lay into any restaurant in town that doesn't buy produce from local farmers. And while Johnny Cool sucks down a tepid Red Stripe and manhandles

ACKEE AND SALTFISH

ACKEE IS A FRUIT THAT MUST BE EATEN RIPE; IT IS POISONOUS BEFORE IT OPENS INTO ITS RIPENED STAGE. ACKEE CAN ALSO BE BOUGHT CANNED, WHICH IS PROBABLY YOUR SAFEST BET.

SERVES 4

1/2 POUND SALTED CODFISH

2 TABLESPOONS OLIVE OIL

1 SMALL WHITE ONION, DICED

1 BUNCH SCALLIONS, DICED

1 TEASPOON CHOPPED GARLIC

1 FRESH THYME SPRIG

1 RED BELL PEPPER, SEEDED AND DICED

1 GREEN BELL PEPPER, SEEDED AND DICED

1 HABANERO PEPPER, CHOPPED

1/2 POUND COOKED ACKEE

SALT AND BLACK PEPPER TO TASTE

In a medium mixing bowl, soak the codfish in cool water for 1 hour to release the salt.

Drain the codfish and place in a medium sauté pan; add water to cover. Bring to a simmer over medium heat and simmer for 15 minutes. Remove the pan from the heat and strain. Remove any bones. Set aside and let cool.

Heat the olive oil in a large skillet over medium heat. Sauté the onion, scallions, and garlic until the onion is translucent. Add the codfish and sauté an additional 5 minutes. Add the thyme and peppers, and sauté 2 minutes more. Add the ackee and sauté for 3 to 5 minutes.

Season with salt and pepper and serve.

BAMMIES

This Jamaican savory item is made from cassava, which is also called yuca. It is an accompaniment for almost every Jamaican meal.

MAKES 6

3 CUPS PEELED AND GRATED CASSAVA
3/4 TEASPOON SALT
2 CUPS WATER
VEGETABLE OIL TO COAT PAN

In a large mixing bowl, use your hands to mix together the cassava and salt. Add the water a little at a time until a dough forms.

Divide the dough into 6 pieces. With your hands, flatten each piece until it is about 6 inches in diameter.

Coat a medium skillet with vegetable oil and put it over medium heat.

Place 1 piece of dough in the skillet. When the bammy's edge starts to pull away from the side of the pan, after approximately 5 minutes, flatten the dough again with a spatula and turn over. Cook for another 5 minutes, until golden brown. Repeat with the remaining 5 pieces of dough, adding more oil to the skillet as needed.

Serve as the starch for an entrée.

chunks of pork and chicken toward favorite spots on the grill, he'll tell you about his hands-down favorite Jamaican meat preparation: *cherk.*

The origin of the term "jerk" is subject to endless myths and mistakes, and it won't be settled here. It's a toss-up as to whether it refers to the process of "jerking" meat from the bone or the thing your central nervous system does when you inhale a spoonful of Scotch bonnet peppers, or if it is a perversion of the Spanish word *charqui,* referring to dried meat. Logic suggests that the last explanation makes the most sense; *charqui* is also where *jerky* comes from. The precise seasonings required to make a jerk marinade or dry rub are likewise open for interpretation, but the main three are pretty standard: chile peppers, allspice berries, and thyme. To that, ginger, cloves, garlic, and onion can be added, depending on your mood and veggie crisper. As for the meat, pork is traditional, but chicken and beef can be substituted. Jerked fish, though found at numerous roadside stands throughout Jamaica, is more a matter of what's available to the cook, since fish tends to be too delicate to benefit from intense spicing and slow cooking. Once the meat has been dry-rubbed and/or marinated overnight, it is, in authentic Jamaican jerk, barbecued leisurely over charcoals made from native hot-burning and aromatic allspice trees. This wood imparts distinct and vital flavors to the final product and, regrettably, can't be replaced without compromising the results. (Allspice, incidentally, which the Jamaicans call *pimento,* is not a mixture of spices but a berry related to black pepper.)

According to Chef Walter, Johnny Cool's status as jerk guru is a combination of many subtle factors: a nearly perfect amalgam of instinct and experience, an absolute affinity with the fire, and an ability to read the effect that various hotspots have on the grilling meat. "Once you have the flavors nailed down," says Staib, "it's all about heat. Pimento wood can burn at up to eight hundred degrees, which gives the meat a good sear and seals in the juices. From there the trick is to regulate the temperature, using water, distance, or, better yet, green pimento leaves in order to avoid scorching."

Chef Walter is no jerk slouch himself, of course, and I have a sneaking suspicion that he might actually prefer his own product. He once marinated an entire ox in the back of a Toyota pickup and cooked it for eighteen hours—he's just too modest to 'fess up.

Though glutted with Johnny's stupendous barbecue, it's hard to resist a nibble of the other offerings to be found up and down the Faith's Pen strip, especially with Chef Walter's expert monologues delving into backgrounds, histories, and general do's and don'ts of the unusual offerings. Escoveitch fish, for one, is the Caribbean cousin to ceviche, the lime-cured seafood dish popular throughout Latin America. To prepare the Jamaican version, firm fish fillets (most often snapper) are floured, deep-fried, and then doused in a pickle sauce blended from vinegar and lime juice. Generally served at room or open-air temperature, escoveitch is popular on breakfast tables alongside hush puppies, which islanders call "festival," or starchy loaves of piping hot bammy bread.

Made from finely grated cassava root, bammy is, like ackee, another slice of life in the Jamaican oughta-go-on-a-fast lane. The root needs to be processed overnight to leach out its natural cyanide-based toxins. Then it is pounded into metal rings and toasted on a flat griddle. Bammies end up being about six inches around and are often dipped in a popular Caribbean bouillabaisse called fish tea. A spokesman for the United Nations Food and Agriculture Organization, who championed the specialty bread back in 1992 when the cassava industry was hurting, maintains, "Nothing goes better with fish than bammy." And maybe he should know: His name is Robert Salmon.

Rundown is another West Indian standby; it is prepared by slow-simmering mackerel steaks in coconut milk along with tomatoes and chile peppers. Stamp and go are cod fritters, so-named because it is supposed to be easy to hop out of your car to snag a bag from a sidewalk higgler on the fly. Pepperpot soup is a savory concoction of corned beef—frequently replaced with goat—coconut milk, and a fragrant spinach-like green called callaloo; it depends on the aggres-

LAURETTA DAVIS PARNTHER PREPARES MACKEREL RUNDOWN AND HUSH PUPPY—LIKE FESTIVALS.

CURRIED GOAT

IF YOU DO NOT HAVE GOAT IN YOUR REFRIGERATOR, SUBSTITUTE LAMB OR PORK.

SERVES 8

1 CUP CURRY POWDER

3 LARGE FRESH THYME SPRIGS

3 SCOTCH BONNET PEPPERS, SEEDED AND FINELY CHOPPED

2 WHITE ONIONS, DICED

1 BUNCH SCALLIONS, DICED

4 POUNDS GOAT MEAT, BONE IN

1/2 CUP CHOPPED GARLIC

1 CARROT, DICED

2 PLUM TOMATOES, DICED

1 POUND RUSSET POTATOES, DICED

1/2 CUP PEELED AND CHOPPED FRESH GINGER

3 QUARTS CHICKEN STOCK

SALT AND BLACK PEPPER TO TASTE

COOKED LONG-GRAIN RICE

In a large mixing bowl, combine the curry, thyme, Scotch bonnet peppers, onions, and scallions. Place the goat meat in a large stockpot. Pour the marinade over the goat meat, cover, and marinate overnight in the refrigerator.

Remove the goat meat from the marinade. Reserve the leftover marinade.

In a hot braising pan over medium heat, brown the goat meat and garlic. Add the carrot, tomatoes, potatoes, ginger, and reserved marinade. Add the stock, salt, and pepper, and stew for approximately 1 hour, until the meat is tender and about to fall off the bone.

This is best served with long-grain rice.

sive little Scotch bonnet pepper for its bite. Pepperpot is a hearty belly warmer, good for what ails ya, and is often used as a remedy for colds. Since it also, reputedly, can contain *ganja* as a flavoring ingredient, it may likewise be good for what jails ya.

Leaving Faith's Pen, heading north, you pass through the sublime and humid splendor of Fern Gully, a reclaimed riverbed that worms through the hills and forests below Ocho Rios. Home to over six hundred varieties of fern, many of which can't be found anywhere else on earth, the lush foliage and towering fig trees form a canopy over the roadway that pulls you into a Jurassic Park environment for three bizarre miles. Lurking along the shelving embankments are peculiar people whom Ricky calls jack-in-the-bushes. Festooned in fern fronds and wearing mysterious masks and massive headdresses, they give the impression of being primordial shamen in the throes of some ritual; in fact, they're ambitious islanders looking for a couple of dollars' worth of photo opportunities.

The Jamaican countryside is surprisingly varied given the size of the place and the homogeneity of the climate. Dramatic waterfalls cascade down sullen valleys; broad beaches dissolve into turquoise water—the sand brilliant white or rugged black, depending on the coast; peach orchards ramble; and cane plantations saturate broad vales. Everything plays against the human factor, which is, virtually without relief, one of wrenching destitution. With the exception of the tourist destinations, Montego Bay, Negril, Ocho Rios, and Port Antonio, the fabric of day-to-day living in Jamaica is so wretched that it's scarcely conceivable to American sensibilities. Ricky has never been more than a hundred miles from Ocho Rios, and his grand goal in life is to move to Pensacola (where he has a cousin) and work in construction. That's it. His fondest dream: humping two-by-fours in the Florida panhandle. The rural South is no Valhalla, obviously, but I tell Ricky he won't believe it when he gets there. As far as I can judge, there isn't a single small town in the entire United States that is as bad as every single small town in Jamaica.

THIS WAS AN OLD ABANDONED CHURCH THAT WAS SUPPOSEDLY HAUNTED. VISITING IT GAVE ME A FEELING OF FOREBODING.

We pull into a ramshackle filling station to top off the Samurai's "quatah tank." An old man in huge, rolled, Mickey Mouse–like dreadlocks hangs in the center island and gapes at the attendant as the gas is pumped. As in most third world countries, there's an unwritten law which states that for every person working, at least one individual has to be standing around watching. The old man adopts the peculiar akimbo position of relaxing Jamaicans, arms jutting oddly from the side. He's wearing a typically colorful shirt and has a face towel jutting from a rear pocket. He's all island. Possibly, his first name ends in "roy" or "ton"; another Jamaica-ism are names like Fitzroy and Everton, or maybe he's a "Trevor," which in the Carib accent sound like *Chebba*. Whatever it is, he probably goes by Reds or Tony or Junior or some other nickname that's totally unrelated to his given one. Ricky's real name, for example, is Roydel.

Tank filled, Ricky/Roydel steers through Cave Valley's blighted buildings and tumbledown shanties and back into the open countryside. It's a heavily agricultural area, and small homesteads litter the hillside like confetti. Here and there, hoeing amid the conical yam frames, are strikingly light-skinned farmers, descendants of German mercenaries who were given land grants following the American War of Independence. Ginger, onions, and chiles thrive throughout this fertile region: This is Pickapeppa country, home to the factory that produces the highly prized pepper sauces. Beyond there are miles of *arabica* coffee groves, which we angle through, stopping briefly to pluck ripe, red, and surprisingly sweet and edible beans. A side trip takes us through the Circle B banana plantation, where owner Bob Miller entertains us with some fascinating tales of the Caribbean fruit trade, and where I'm able to cook some lunch for my famished crew.

JOHNNY COOL MASTERS THE ART OF JERK COOKING.

Finally, we emerge from the tangled highlands to face the broad and steaming sugar plantations of the world-famous Appleton Estate. The "three R's" of Jamaican escapism are reefer, reggae, and rum, and Appleton is responsible only for the third one, thank you very much. The history of rum in the Caribbean is as convoluted and exciting as the career of Captain Morgan, the colorful pirate who had an estate in Port Royal and who wound up with his grinning mug on a trademark. Cheap and ubiquitous, rum is everyman's tipple, and the two- or three-seat roadside rum shop is often a center for community life, where old men gather to play checkers and young men talk about girls and politics. Lord Byron quipped, "There's nought, no doubt, so much the spirit calms as rum and true religion," sounding very much like he'd thrown back a couple of stiff ones before picking up his quill. The Caribbean rum industry developed in conjunction with the sugar plantations, since by definition rum is made from molasses, the thick syrup that's left after sugarcane juice has been boiled into crystallization. The two trades have forged a symbiotic relationship that's made fortunes in the West Indies since the seventeenth century.

Rum making, during which juice is fermented and then distilled, is basically the same process as is used to produce every liquor in the world, from Louis XIII Cognac to *Dukes of Hazzard* moonshine. Raw rum spirit is either sold off immediately as a super-potent Overproof White, Jamaica's most popular rum, or mellowed for years in oak casks, which adds various bouquets and tastes and, inevitably, hefty price tags.

Appleton has been around since 1655, and rum has been made here since the mid-eighteenth century, which makes it the second oldest liquor brand in the world. Nestled in the lush Nassau Valley, with three thousand acres of sugarcane planted on either side of the Black River, Appleton produces rums that are typical of Jamaica's style: fragrant and full-bodied, in part due to the pot still method of distillation, which tends to preserve more of the minerals and other trace elements found in molasses, adding to the rum's ultimate richness.

JERK MARINADE

THIS JAMAICAN MARINADE IS COMMONLY USED ON PORK AND CHICKEN, BUT IT CAN ALSO BE USED ON SEAFOOD. THE INDIGENOUS HABITANTS WHO POPULATED THE ISLAND BEFORE THE EUROPEANS ARRIVED ORIGINATED IT. IT WOULDN'T BE JERK WITHOUT SCOTCH BONNET PEPPERS. CHEF WALTER STAIB OF SANDALS AND BEACHES RESORTS TAUGHT ME HIS VERSION.

MAKES 3 1/2 CUPS

3/4 POUND SCOTCH BONNET PEPPERS, STEMS AND SEEDS REMOVED, AND ROUGHLY CHOPPED

1/2 POUND FRESH THYME, CHOPPED

6 OUNCES FRESHLY GROUND ALLSPICE

1/2 CUP PEELED AND MINCED FRESH GINGER

1 LARGE WHITE ONION, ROUGHLY CHOPPED

4 BUNCHES SCALLIONS, ROUGHLY CHOPPED (GREEN AND WHITE PARTS)

6 GARLIC CLOVES, PEELED AND MINCED

1 TABLESPOON SALT

1 TABLESPOON GROUND BLACK PEPPER

1 CUP LIGHT SOY SAUCE

1/2 CUP OLIVE OIL

In a food processor, puree the Scotch bonnet peppers, thyme, allspice, ginger, onion, scallions, garlic, salt, and pepper. Transfer the mixture to a large mixing bowl. Whisk in the soy sauce and olive oil.

Use immediately, or store the jerk marinade in the refrigerator for up to a week.

Man's exploitation of man plays a significant role in the story of rum and cane plantations, and there's no sugar-coating it. The abolition of slavery was the single greatest watershed event in the history of Jamaica and, indeed, across the Caribbean. Today's West Indian culture, with equal parts Africa and Europe, manifests a successful social transition from bondage to independence, one that has been achieved without widespread racial disharmonies. And it is well reflected in Jamaica's motto: "Out of Many, One People."

Americans, whose own struggle up from slavery has been less smooth, should take note. "Out of Many, One People" ought to be a familiar slogan, being a translation of the motto that appears on the Great Seal of the United States: *E Pluribus Unum.*

COMMON TRANSPORTATION FOR FRESH-CUT BANANAS.

Mannish Water

Mannish Water, or Goat Head Soup, is supposed to be able to fix what ails you. Also, it is said to give the guys a sex-drive boost—you know, a Jamaican Viagra. (Christophene is another name for the squashlike vegetable chayote.

SERVES 5 OR 6

2 POUNDS GOAT HEAD, ORGANS, AND FEET, OR 2 POUNDS LAMB MEAT

1 1/2 GALLONS WATER

5 GREEN BANANAS, SLICED

1 POUND YAMS OR SWEET POTATOES, DICED

1 1/2 CHRISTOPHENES, SEEDS AND SKIN REMOVED, AND CHOPPED

1/2 POUND TARO ROOT, DICED

1/2 POUND CARROTS, DICED

1/2 POUND TURNIPS, PEELED AND DICED

1 SCOTCH BONNET PEPPER OR 2 HABANERO PEPPERS, SEEDED AND CHOPPED

1 1/2 BUNCHES SCALLIONS, CHOPPED (GREEN AND WHITE PARTS)

3 FRESH THYME SPRIGS, CHOPPED

SALT TO TASTE

Chop the meat into small pieces, rinse with cold water, and place in a large stockpot.

Add the water and bring to a boil over medium-high heat. Lower the heat and simmer for 3 hours, until the meat is tender. Add the bananas, yams, christophenes, taro, carrots, turnips, and Scotch bonnet pepper. Simmer until the vegetables are tender.

Stir in the scallions and thyme. Simmer an additional 4 to 5 minutes.

Season with salt and serve.

CONCH CHOWDER

CONCH IS PRIZED FOR ITS BRIGHTLY COLORED SPIRAL SHELL AND ITS LOW-FAT, HIGH-PROTEIN MEAT.

SERVES 6

GARNISH

1 AVOCADO, DICED

2 TABLESPOONS CHOPPED FRESH CILANTRO

1 TABLESPOON FRESH LIME JUICE

SALT AND BLACK PEPPER TO TASTE

CHOWDER

1/2 CUP DICED BACON

1/4 CUP OLIVE OIL

1/2 CUP DICED WHITE ONION

1/2 CUP DICED RED BELL PEPPER

1/2 CUP DICED CELERY

2 TABLESPOONS MINCED GARLIC

2 CUPS CANNED DICED TOMATOES IN JUICE

1 POUND CONCH MEAT, TRIMMED, POUNDED, AND CUT INTO STRIPS

3 CUPS CLAM JUICE

1 CUP TOMATO JUICE

2 CUPS WATER

1 1/2 CUPS DICED AND PEELED RUSSET POTATOES

3 TABLESPOONS TOMATO PUREE

1 TEASPOON GROUND CUMIN

1 WHOLE BAY LEAF

SALT AND BLACK PEPPER TO TASTE

2 TABLESPOONS TABASCO SAUCE

FOR THE GARNISH: Combine the ingredients and refrigerate.

FOR THE CHOWDER: In a sauté pan, render the bacon until crispy. Remove the bacon from the pan and drain on paper towels.

Heat the olive oil in a 1-gallon stockpot over medium heat. Sweat the onion, pepper, celery, and garlic until tender. Add the tomatoes, conch meat, clam juice, tomato juice, water, potatoes, tomato puree, cumin, and bay leaf. Season with salt and pepper. Simmer for 30 to 40 minutes, until the potatoes are tender. Add the Tabasco sauce and bacon during the last 5 minutes of simmering. Adjust the seasoning.

Ladle the chowder into 6 serving bowls and garnish with the avocado mixture.

Festivals

This is a Jamaican hush puppy that is usually served with rice and beans.

MAKES 3 DOZEN

VEGETABLE OIL FOR FRYING

2¼ CUPS ALL-PURPOSE FLOUR

1 CUP PLUS 2 TABLESPOONS YELLOW CORNMEAL

2 TABLESPOONS BAKING POWDER

½ TEASPOON GROUND CINNAMON

1½ TEASPOONS SALT

¼ POUND SUGAR

¼ POUND (1 STICK) SALTED BUTTER, SOFTENED

1 TEASPOON ALMOND EXTRACT

1 TEASPOON VANILLA EXTRACT

1 CUP WHOLE MILK

Fill a medium stockpot 4 inches deep with vegetable oil. Heat the oil to 350°F.

In a medium mixing bowl, combine the flour, cornmeal, baking powder, cinnamon, salt, and sugar. Using your hands, work the butter into the dry mixture until well incorporated.

In a separate medium mixing bowl, whisk together the almond extract, vanilla, and milk. Stir this mixture into the butter mixture to form a stiff batter.

Drop finger-size festivals into the hot oil and fry until golden brown. Remove with a slotted spoon and drain on paper towels.

FRICASSEED CHICKEN AND CHO-CHO

Fricassee is actually a type of braising, where you sauté the meat first and then stew it with vegetables and stock. It is the most popular way to cook in Jamaica. This dish is usually served with Festivals (page 157). Cho-cho is the patois, or slang, for the squashlike vegetable chayote.

SERVES 6

3 POUNDS CHICKEN MEAT, ANY COMBINATION OF LEGS, THIGHS, AND BREASTS

SALT AND BLACK PEPPER TO TASTE

2 TABLESPOONS OLIVE OIL

2 TABLESPOONS UNSALTED BUTTER

1 TABLESPOON MINCED GARLIC

3/4 CUP DICED WHITE ONION

1/2 CUP DICED CELERY

1 CUP DICED CARROTS

3 CUPS CHICKEN STOCK

1 CUP PEELED AND DICED CHAYOTE

1 CUP PEELED AND DICED RUSSET POTATOES

1 TABLESPOON TABASCO SAUCE

1 TABLESPOON TOMATO PASTE

1 1/2 TEASPOONS CHOPPED FRESH THYME

1 SERRANO CHILE, CHOPPED

1/2 CUP SLICED SCALLIONS (GREEN AND WHITE PARTS CUT INTO 1/2-INCH SEGMENTS)

Season the chicken with salt and pepper.

Heat the olive oil in a wide saucepan over medium-high heat. Brown the chicken on all sides. Add the butter, garlic, onion, celery, and carrots. Sauté for 3 to 4 minutes. Add the stock, chayote, potatoes, Tabasco, tomato paste, thyme, and chile. Simmer until the potatoes and chayote are tender, approximately 15 to 20 minutes.

Stir in the scallions and cook for 2 to 3 minutes.

Season with salt and pepper.

This is best served with festivals.

PIG TAILS AND PEAS

If you don't have any pig tails in your refrigerator, you can substitute diced pork loin. You may notice that the recipe is called "pig tails and peas" even though there are no peas. When this recipe originated, the Jamaican people used kidney beans, not peas. No one really knows why this recipe is called "pig tails and peas."

SERVES 6

2 POUNDS PIG TAILS OR PORK LOIN

¼ CUP PLUS 2 TABLESPOONS VEGETABLE OIL

5 CUPS WATER

2 PLUM TOMATOES, CHOPPED

2 WHITE ONIONS, CHOPPED

1 GARLIC CLOVE, PEELED AND CHOPPED

1 FRESH THYME SPRIG

½ HABANERO PEPPER, SEEDED AND MINCED

½ POUND COOKED KIDNEY BEANS

SALT AND BLACK PEPPER TO TASTE

COOKED LONG-GRAIN RICE, 1 CUP PER SERVING

Wash and dry the pig tails and cut into large dice.

Heat ¼ cup of vegetable oil in a large stockpot over medium-high heat. Brown the pig tails. Add 4 cups of water and bring to a boil. Lower the heat to medium and simmer until the pig tails are tender, and then drain and reserve.

Heat the remaining 2 tablespoons of vegetable oil in a 1-gallon stockpot over medium heat. Sauté the tomatoes, onions, garlic, thyme, and pepper for 4 to 5 minutes, stirring frequently. Add the remaining 1 cup of water and the kidney beans. Stir until well combined and lower the heat to medium-low. Cover the stockpot and simmer for 10 minutes, or until the water evaporates. Remove the cover and stir in the cooked pig tails.

Season with salt and pepper.

Serve with rice.

Chef extraordinaire Walter Staib and I display a suckling pig before spit roasting.

MEMPHIS

TAD TWISTS THE GAUDY GULL-WINGED BUMPER OF HIS '55 CADDY INTO A SLOW TURN, NOSING BETWEEN TROLLEY CARS AND INTO THE TRICKLE OF MID-AFTERNOON MAIN STREET TRAFFIC.

A semi-curious teenager in a doo-rag and an oversized Grizzlies coat cranks his head around to glare the classic cruiser down, while across the street an hourly car-wash pogue waves languidly in our direction. Beyond that there isn't much notice taken. For one thing, the car is no auto-show queen, wheeled out once or twice a year for photo ops. It's a battle-scarred workhorse that has seen active duty since it first rolled off the Fleetwood assembly line more than forty years ago—at a price somewhat under four grand, which was top dollar back then. Its once shocking-pink luster has faded to a sort of unhealthy peach, its white sidewalls are dulled with road grime, and the chrome of its famous twin "Dagmar" impact guards hasn't gleamed since Ike was prez.

This is Memphis, where the fifties, with all their civil strife, postwar vibrancy, and prefranchise promise, haven't entirely dissolved into municipal history. Which is not to suggest that Memphis is focused on its rearview mirror. No chance—not with local entrepreneur Jack Belz's recent redevelopment of eight downtown blocks, crowned by his 2-million-square-foot flagship, the Peabody Place Entertainment and Retail Center, and his equally ambitious gentrification of nearby Mud Island. Clearly, Tennessee's "Metropolis on the American Nile" is forging ahead into the twenty-first century with dollar signs blazing. But even

so, hovering behind the barbecue smoke and river haze is the redolence of the true Memphis, the Memphis of yester-year, the Memphis of fig blossoms and boxwoods and sweet tea on the veranda. It's a yearning for heritage, the essence of slow and easy southern gentility, and it makes this, the gateway to the South's delta country, one of the most endearing and enduring cities in the United States. So much does it have to offer, in fact, that you might make it for twenty-four full hours in Memphis without once hear-ing the name Elvis Presley.

PORK DRY RUB

Here is a dry rub that adds plenty of flavor to a pork butt roast or to ribs.

MAKES 2 CUPS

2 TABLESPOONS ONION POWDER

2 TABLESPOONS GARLIC POWDER

2 TABLESPOONS GROUND BLACK PEPPER

1 TABLESPOON MUSTARD POWDER

1½ TABLESPOONS GROUND CORIANDER

2½ TABLESPOONS KOSHER SALT

1 TABLESPOON CAYENNE PEPPER

1 TABLESPOON GROUND CUMIN

½ CUP (UNPACKED) LIGHT BROWN SUGAR

¼ CUP HUNGARIAN PAPRIKA

¼ CUP DARK CHILI POWDER

3 TABLESPOONS CHOPPED LEMON ZEST

In a large mixing bowl, mix together all the ingredients.

THE DRY RUB WILL KEEP FOR UP TO 3 MONTHS WITHOUT THE LEMON ZEST.

Ah, Elvis. Nearly a quarter of a century after his death, Memphis still seems somewhat cowed beneath a pall of mourning. The puffy pompadour, lacquered ducktail, and sensuous pout is omnipresent on billboards, on bus flanks, on business logos, and even in gang graffiti. Rather than the wails of the bereaved, however, this twenty-five-year-long *shiva* seems to resound more with the steady ka-ching of opportunism.

As every Muslim must trek to Mecca once in a lifetime, so every red-blooded, flag-waving, Nehi grape soda–drinking American owes it to him- or herself to make the pilgrimage to Graceland, and thence to delve beyond the renowned sandstone ramparts so heavily autographed by zealots, freaks, fans, and noncommittal passersby that scarcely a tuck-point remains unscathed. A random sampling: "How Great Thou Our" [*sic*]. "Elvis Schmelvis . . . Errol Flynn Is God"—"He's *dead . . . hello!!?*"

Well, Elvis was a character, and Memphis has long been a lodestone for characters of all sorts. From Hernando de Soto (the hyperkinetic Spaniard who's said to have first chummed around with local Chickasaw tribesmen back in 1541) to Father Marquette (the first of the region's legion of Bible-thumpers), to colorful trappers and riverboat gamblers, treasure seekers, hucksters, and charlatans, the typical denizen of southwest Tennessee has tended toward flamboyance. Back in the heyday of nascent Memphis, many of these human powder kegs put down roots in a rollicking downtown strip known as the "Pinch," a district that survives to this day.

Like many inner-city districts, the Pinch has had its ups and downs, and in the wake of so-called white flight and urban blight, it faced much of the previous century as a seedy vista of slums, flophouses, and weedlots. But it has recently been rediscovered and subsequently redefined as hip and trendy (à la Tribeca and SoHo), thanks in large part to the opening of the one building in Memphis more bizarre than Graceland: the aptly if unimaginatively named "Pyramid." Funky-cool restaurants and happening little watering holes have popped up like umbrella mushrooms after a spring shower, and with the ghost of Elvis teasing my tummy, I stop by a corner eatery which I think the King in a midday cholesterol frenzy would surely have approved.

Chucky's Fried Pies is a good example of the sort of hard-core shoestring establishments that freckle that circle of Memphis existing on the periphery of Jack Belz's new-spangled empire. The corner of Watkins and Overton Park is largely residential, a "hood" by anybody's standards; its low-rent clapboard bungalows and eight-hundred-square-foot starter homes are well tended but look somewhat exhausted after the area's lowest point, the crack wars of the late eighties and early nineties. Chucky's exists not for the casual visitor who motors in from St. Louis, Nashville, or Little Rock, or for the high-brow tourist and convention crowd, or even for the homegrown superstars who still call Memphis home—Cybill Shepherd, out in Harbor Town, to name one. In the words of Charles "Chucky" Gammon, founder, co-owner, and cook, Chucky's is for "us," that is, the surrounding neighborhood and its gang of friends, family, and fried-pie loyalists.

Scoot down Overton to North Main, to the far end of the Pinch, and just underneath the I-40 trellis you'll find a similar helping of deeply serious family cooking at Alcenia's. Walking in, you may be somewhat startled when owner B. J. Chester-Tamayo grabs you in a bear hug and plants a wet one on your cheek, saying, "Gimme a li'l lovin', baby," but that's how she's been greeting patrons, cronies, and newcomers alike, since she opened the doors. Like Chucky, B.J. found her inspiration and, in turn, her life's calling in her mother's recipe books. In this case it was baked goods and canned preserves, of which she's justly in-your-face proud. The glass showcase is loaded with Mason jars brimming with home-canned fruits, whose labels range from the commonplace (peaches and raspberries) to the southern (muscadines and figs) to the *very* southern (*scuppernong*, which winds up being a sweet, yellow, and very southern grape variety). And, like Chucky, she found that regular customers who came in for the spectacular selection of sweets were incessant in their requests for a full-blown

PULLED PORK

PULLED PORK IS BEST SERVED AS A SANDWICH ON A SOFT HAMBURGER BUN WITH BBQ SAUCE AND SOME CHOW CHOW.

SERVES 4 TO 6

PORK
4 POUNDS PORK BUTT ROAST
1 CUP PORK DRY RUB (PAGE 164)
4 CUPS MOP SAUCE (PAGE 167)
SANDWICH
4 TO 6 HAMBURGER BUNS
BBQ SAUCE (PAGE 166)
CHOW CHOW (PAGE 172)

Rub the pork butt roast on all sides with the dry rub. Wrap the pork in plastic wrap and refrigerate for 8 hours.

Preheat the oven to 250°F.

Brush the pork with the mop sauce and place on a drip pan over a large baking sheet. Place the sheet in the oven. Brush the pork every 20 to 30 minutes with the mop sauce. Slow-cook the pork to an internal temperature of 160°F.

Remove the pork from the oven and place on a cutting board. Allow to cool for 15 minutes, then shred the pork with a fork into bite-size pieces.

Serve pulled pork on hamburger buns. Slather on the BBQ sauce. Top with chow chow, place top of hamburger bun onto it, and serve.

BBQ Sauce

You can't do the cuisine of Memphis without a good BBQ sauce recipe. I think you will enjoy this one. It's ideal for chicken, ribs, and roast pork loin. The cayenne pepper and Tabasco add a nice little kick.

MAKES 1 QUART

3/4 CUP (UNPACKED) LIGHT BROWN SUGAR

2 TABLESPOONS HUNGARIAN PAPRIKA

3 WHOLE BAY LEAVES

1 TABLESPOON ONION POWDER

1 TABLESPOON GARLIC POWDER

1 TEASPOON CAYENNE PEPPER

1 TABLESPOON TABASCO SAUCE

1 TABLESPOON DARK CHILI POWDER

1 1/2 TEASPOONS GROUND CORIANDER

1/2 CUP WORCESTERSHIRE SAUCE

3/4 CUP CIDER VINEGAR

1/4 CUP TOMATO PUREE

1 CUP KETCHUP

2 CUPS WATER

1/4 CUP FRESH LEMON JUICE

SALT TO TASTE

In a 1-gallon stockpot over medium-low heat, combine all the ingredients. Simmer for 20 to 25 minutes.

Strain the sauce through a fine sieve and then place it back in the pot. Place the pot in a container or a sink filled with ice water. Stir to dissipate the heat.

When the sauce is cool, place it in a plastic container with a lid and refrigerate for up to 2 weeks.

menu. So she conceded, went with popular opinion, and added a roster of crispy critters, fried chicken, fried pork, and fried steak, along with the requisite choice of sides. Reviews have been uniformly raves, proving that some cooks are born great while others have it thrust into their FryDaddys.

Alcenia Chester, eighty-one years of no-nonsense spit and vinegar, has been to the mountain. Born in Meridian, Mississippi, she has seen the worst that America has offered African Americans, and however much her gait has been reined in by age, none of her self-sufficiency is compromised. Offer a supportive hand, and you're likely to lose it. She's dressed in a massive blue housedress, a flour-dusted apron, and a pair of prehistoric bedroom slippers, and looks—forgive me—like a cross between Jacques Cousteau's minisub and a crotchety basset hound. When she pads through the dining room, notice is taken. She's B.J.'s mother, grande dame of Alcenia's, and author of virtually every recipe in the house. She doesn't cook much anymore, so when she makes an appearance, it means one of two things: Either a very special guest is present, or it's tea cake time again. Lest I feel even the slightest tug of self-importance, kindled by the hovering attention and coddling small talk I've shared with B.J. since showing up, Alcenia pads directly by my table and into the kitchen, where she begins to assemble the ingredients for tea cakes. So earth-shaking is this event to the fabric of the cosmos that restaurant employees get on the phone and alert regulars—that's how popular Alcenia's tea cakes are around here.

Of course, we're talking about Memphis cuisine, and when you do that, you begin and end with barbecue. Smoky, slow-cooked, tangy-sauced pork is an emblem of the South, and Memphis, with her characteristic bravado, claims to be the spigot from which the popularity of these succulent dishes flows. In truth, as wonderful as it is, Memphis barbecuing is hardly the last word in technique and flavor, nor is there even a single all-encompassing "Memphis style." Certainly, per capita, there are lots of 'cue joints in town, but no more than in most southern cities, and among purists, the vinegary North Carolina swabs, rich Mississippi dips, and mustard-based sauces of Georgia enjoy a status that's equal to the molasses and tomato spreads of the Bluff City. With Memphis, the barbecue mecca rep is all about marketing. The World Championship Barbecuing Contest, which is to pig flesh what the Super Bowl is to pig skin, is held each May in Memphis, in Tom Lee Park on the banks of the Mississippi River. In its wake, Memphis has crowned itself the barbecue capital of the South—which makes it, by default, the barbecue capital of the world. They get plenty of arguments from their neighbors, in particular from minuscule Lexington, North Carolina, which hosts a similar festival. We'll let the regional champs fight it out in the charcoal-filled trenches, since we're less concerned with braggarts and pretenders and more with the art form of genuine southern barbecue.

So varied are its guises, however, that for purposes of discussion we'll narrow the term "barbecue" to a specific criterion, one with which few dogmatists will argue: Barbecue must be flavored (sauce or dry rub) pork (shoulder, rib, or the whole pig), and slow-cooked (an hour or more per pound) over some sort of smoldering medium. By this definition, then, the true barbecue belt girds an area running from the Mississippi River to the Atlantic Ocean. Despite its popularity, beef-centric, mesquite-flavored Texas barbecue is no more related to authentic Dixie barbecue than is the Yankee's concept, the backyard cookout, with Dad in his "Hot Stuff" apron quick-searing T-bones and hamburgers.

In fact, barbecue is an invention that probably originated in Africa, traveled to the West Indies with the slaves, and drifted up the Mississippi River by the same route. The pig is the staple meat in the South, since it requires no grazing land and can earn a living in the thick forests that punctuate the cultivated acres. Traditional barbecues arose from social gatherings, during which renegade swine were hunted down, butchered, and cooked. Thus, barbecue became a ritual, which it remains to this day.

MOP SAUCE

MOP SAUCE IS A BASTING SAUCE USED THROUGHOUT THE COOKING PROCESS. IT IS GREAT WITH ROASTS. IT CAN ALSO BE USED AS A MARINADE, AND IT WILL NOT BURN ON THE MEAT SINCE IT DOESN'T CONTAIN ANY SUGAR.

MAKES 7 CUPS

2 1/2 CUPS APPLE CIDER

2 CUPS OLIVE OIL

1 CUP CIDER VINEGAR

1/4 POUND (1 STICK) UNSALTED BUTTER

1/4 CUP WORCESTERSHIRE SAUCE

2 TABLESPOONS GROUND BLACK PEPPER

2 TABLESPOONS GARLIC POWDER

2 TABLESPOONS HUNGARIAN PAPRIKA

2 TABLESPOONS CHOPPED FRESH THYME

2 TABLESPOONS KOSHER SALT

2 TABLESPOONS ONION POWDER

1 1/2 TEASPOONS CAYENNE PEPPER

2 TABLESPOONS MUSTARD POWDER

2 TABLESPOONS TABASCO SAUCE

1 TABLESPOON GROUND CORIANDER

In a large mixing bowl, whisk together all the ingredients.

Marinate the meat for 2 to 4 hours in the mop sauce before you cook it.

While cooking the meat, baste it with the mop sauce every time you turn it over. Once the meat is cooked to the desired doneness, remove from the heat source and discard the remaining mop sauce.

ALCENIA'S TEA CAKES

ALCENIA CHESTER OF ALCENIA'S PREPARED THESE FABULOUS TEA CAKES FOR MY MOTHER'S DAY SHOW. HER RESTAURANT IS ONE OF MEMPHIS'S HIDDEN GEMS.

MAKES 25 CAKES

3 CUPS ALL-PURPOSE FLOUR

1/4 TEASPOON BAKING POWDER

3 CUPS SUGAR

3/4 TEASPOON GRATED NUTMEG

3 LARGE EGGS

1/4 CUP WATER

3/4 TABLESPOON LEMON EXTRACT

1/4 POUND (1 STICK) UNSALTED BUTTER, SOFTENED

1/4 CUP SOLID VEGETABLE SHORTENING

Preheat the oven to 300°F.

On a work surface, use your hands to combine the flour, baking powder, sugar, and nutmeg. Make a well in the center.

In a medium mixing bowl, whisk together the eggs, water, and lemon extract.

Pour the wet ingredients into the well and begin to mix together by hand. Add the butter and shortening. Knead together until it forms a dough.

Use your hands to roll the dough into a log. Use a dough cutter or a sharp knife to cut the log into 25 pieces. Slightly flatten each piece with the palm of your hand. Place on a buttered cookie sheet. Bake for 15 to 25 minutes, until golden brown.

Remove the tea cakes from the oven. They are best eaten warm.

For downtown Memphis visitors, the ritual is no longer played out in smoky shacks behind the big house, where men (and *only* men—this is part of the barbecue tradition) swap stories and baste meat while sucking down prodigious quantities of Southern Comfort, but within 'cue joints like Charlie Vergos's famed Rendezvous. Buried below South Second, this sprawling, knickknack-stuffed pork parlor has been slapping slabs before eager patrons for more than fifty years. In the sixties, Elvis had 'Vous (as the locals call it) vittles flown in to tour locations, and mail-order deliveries are still available to anywhere on the globe. When you worm down the ancient staircase to enter the carefully controlled chaos of Rendezvous caverns, the electricity is obvious. There's a speakeasy bar where you can order pitchers of beer (that and sweet tea, a southern standby, appear to be the only available beverages) as you begin the inevitable wait for a table. But, as on every night at Rendezvous, tonight it is a classic "turn 'em and burn 'em" restaurant, cashing in on volume as well as taste, and the wait ends up being about half what the hostess quoted. Once seated, there's an instantaneous greeting from one of the old-school waiters; it consists of a brusque, businesslike "Talk to me." So you talk ribs, full orders or half. Ordering anything else at Rendezvous is borderline heresy, though the chopped pork gets good reviews from an adjacent table. You'll get accompaniments, mustard-based slaw and baked beans, neither of which lives up to the juicy slabs of spice-dusted ribs. Vergos's magical rub is, understandably, kept hush-hush by the kitchen staff, but a fair guess is that it's mostly paprika and cumin, with cayenne tossed in for the kick. The 'Vous serves up crispy tons of these morsels per day.

Isaac Hayes's place is one of the newest additions to the Memphis BBQ pantheon, and it is certainly the most upscale of the bunch. Filling palatial digs within the Peabody Place Entertainment and Retail Center, it is set up like an old-time supper club, with a small stage against the back wall and tiers of tables in concentric half-circles. Isaac himself, complete with wraparound shades and dashiki, showed up the night I was there, and just before the crowd

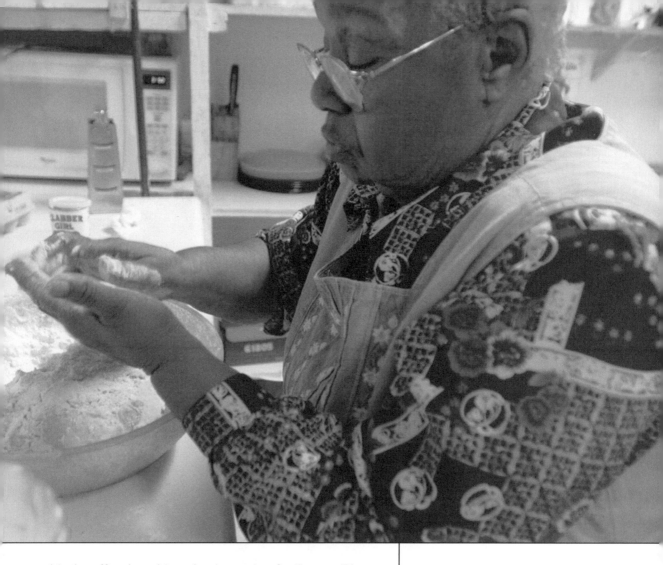

ALCENIA CHESTER MAKING
OLD-FASHIONED TEA CAKES.

hit, he offered me his seductive recipe for Banana Blaze. The barbecue he serves is heavenly—meaty, moist, and sweet. In fact, it's created in collaboration with Famous Dave, Minneapolis's barbecue king, which is a pretty good guarantee that Hayes's diners won't get the shaft. A final but notable note on another morsel from the succulent Memphis foodways, one that comes slashing and bucking and slathering out of the thick mud of the Mississippi River: catfish.

Autumn in the South is pretty good compensation for midsummer. Gone are the bloat and sponginess of thick delta dog days, and the air, in its wake, remains warm without being cloying. Skies are brilliant, nearly haze-free. Mud

THE ONE AND ONLY ISAAC
HAYES. COOKING WITH
HIM WAS A BLAST!

Island, once a rural Memphis satellite, is now a gentrified river park, home to the *Memphis Belle*—World War II's most famous aircraft—and the ultraposh Harbor Town. It sits lazily in the core of the Mississippi current, just opposite the Memphis pyramid, and plays occasional host to U.S.-C.A.T.S., the ever popular United States Catfish Anglers Tournament Series. The series is run by Virgil Dale Agee, a good ol' boy if ever there was one, who also is the only guy you'll ever meet who has got four documented hundred-plus-pound catfish under his angler's belt. Ask Virgil how many folks a 120-pound blue feeds, and he won't miss a beat: "Feeds all of Wardsville, Missouri." That's his hometown and the logical recipient of the massive fish fry that followed his world-record catch. "Butchered him jes' like ya do a hawg. Hung him on hooks and used a chainsaw. Opened up the barn and invited the dadgum town. Had Randy working the fryer, Dave on potatoes. Tasted damn near as good as lobster."

Catfish is mid-America's prime freshwater delight, a mild, clean-tasting, and versatile species. Its legion of fans is growing exponentially now that it has begun to shed its deep-fried image. With apologies to Virgil and his leviathan largesse, the delicate and sweet-flavored flesh of the catfish is better showcased on the grill or in the sauté pan. It lends itself well to subtle seasoning and has a unique texture that perfectly counterpoints a crumb-style crust. Standing by the dock, basking in the clean November sunshine, Virgil Agee holds his scale and waits for the flat-bottomed fishing boats to return with their prizes. It's an uncomfortable wait for Virgil; obviously, he'd rather be out there winning contests, not judging them. Well, it won't be a record-breaking Saturday for anyone, as it happens, but out of the bounty that's hauled to shore I'm able to snag a mess of cats and prepare a quick, impromptu dockside supper for the champs, David Coughlin and Carey Ricketts, and a gang of somewhat crestfallen runners-up.

No meat hooks, no chainsaws, no country barn with an all-you-can-drink Budweiser policy, but there aren't any complaints, either.

Apple BBQ Sauce

This recipe works really well in the fall when you are able to get fresh apple cider.

MAKES 3 1/2 CUPS

2 CUPS APPLE CIDER

1 CUP CIDER VINEGAR

1 CUP APPLE BUTTER

1 CUP APPLESAUCE

1/2 CUP (UNPACKED) LIGHT BROWN SUGAR

1 WHOLE CINNAMON STICK

1/4 CUP WORCESTERSHIRE SAUCE

1 TABLESPOON ONION POWDER

1 1/2 TEASPOONS GARLIC POWDER

1 TEASPOON GROUND CORIANDER

JUICE OF 1 LEMON

SALT AND BLACK PEPPER TO TASTE

In a 1-gallon stockpot over medium heat, combine all the ingredients. Simmer the sauce for 30 minutes.

Remove the cinnamon stick.

Strain the sauce through a fine sieve and then place it back in the pot. Place the pot in a container or a sink filled with ice water. Stir to dissipate the heat.

When the sauce is cool, place it in a plastic container with a lid and refrigerate.

This sauce will last up to 2 weeks when refrigerated.

Chow Chow

Chow chow is a type of southern-style slaw typically used on pulled pork sandwiches.

MAKES 2 QUARTS

VEGETABLES

4 CUPS SHREDDED GREEN CABBAGE

2 CUPS CAULIFLOWER FLORETS

2 CUPS DICED GREEN TOMATOES

1 CUP SLICED WHITE ONIONS

1 CUP SLICED RED ONIONS

2 CUPS JULIENNED RED BELL PEPPERS

1 CUP GRATED CARROTS

3 TABLESPOONS KOSHER SALT

PICKLING LIQUID

$1^1/_2$ TEASPOONS TURMERIC

1 TABLESPOON CORIANDER SEED

1 TABLESPOON WHOLE BLACK PEPPERCORNS

4 WHOLE CLOVES

1 TEASPOON CELERY SEED

2 TEASPOONS DRY MUSTARD

1 TABLESPOON PICKLING SPICE

1 TEASPOON MUSTARD SEED

1 TEASPOON PEELED AND GRATED FRESH GINGER

2 CUPS CIDER VINEGAR

2 CUPS WATER

$1^1/_2$ CUPS SUGAR

FOR THE VEGETABLES: In a mixing bowl, mix together the vegetables. On a large baking sheet, spread out the vegetables and sprinkle them with salt. Cover and refrigerate overnight. The following day, drain the vegetables and discard the liquid.

FOR THE PICKLING LIQUID: Place all the dried spices and ginger on a piece of cheesecloth and tie the corners together to form a bag.

In a 1-gallon stockpot over medium heat, combine the vinegar, water, and sugar. Add the spice bag and simmer for 5 minutes. Add the drained vegetables, bring to a boil, and lower the heat to a simmer. Simmer for 5 to 6 minutes and then remove the spice bag.

Pack the chow chow into sterilized jars and seal with canning lids. Refrigerate until ready to use. Chow chow will keep for 2 to 3 weeks when refrigerated.

FRIED GREEN TOMATOES WITH SOUR CREAM, HORSERADISH, AND YOGURT SAUCE

I HAVE BEEN PREPARING THIS DISH FOR MANY YEARS. HERE IS ONE OF MY FAVORITE SIDE SAUCES TO GO WITH THE FRIED GREEN TOMATOES.

SERVES 2

SAUCE

1/2 CUP SOUR CREAM

1 TABLESPOON HORSERADISH

1/2 CUP LOW-FAT PLAIN YOGURT

JUICE OF 1 LEMON

1/2 CUP CHOPPED FRESH CILANTRO

SALT AND BLACK PEPPER TO TASTE

GREEN TOMATOES

1 GREEN TOMATO

SALT AND BLACK PEPPER TO TASTE

1 LARGE EGG

1/4 CUP WHOLE MILK

1/4 CUP ALL-PURPOSE FLOUR

1/2 CUP YELLOW CORNMEAL

1/4 CUP OLIVE OIL

GARNISH

1 TABLESPOON CHOPPED FRESH CHIVES

FOR THE SAUCE: In a medium mixing bowl, whisk together all the ingredients. Cover and refrigerate until ready to serve.

FOR THE TOMATOES: Cut the tomato into 4 equal slices and season each slice with salt and pepper.

In a medium mixing bowl, beat the egg with the milk until blended.

Spread the flour on 1 plate, and the cornmeal on another. Dredge the tomato slices in the flour. Dip them in the egg mixture and then in the cornmeal.

Heat the olive oil in a large sauté pan over medium heat. Brown each tomato slice well on each side in the oil. Drain on paper towels. Season with salt and pepper.

Serve the fried green tomatoes with the sour cream, horseradish, and yogurt sauce, and garnish with the chives.

MEMPHIS PECAN-CRUSTED CATFISH

I HAD A CHANCE TO COOK FOR ONE OF THE
GREATEST CATFISH FISHERMEN OF OUR TIME, VIRGIL
AGEE. THIS MAN CAUGHT A 120-POUND CATFISH IN
THE MIGHTY MISSISSIPPI RIVER. I CREATED THIS
RECIPE FOR HIS DEBUT ON MY SHOW. HE SEEMED TO
REALLY ENJOY IT AND SAID IT WAS EVEN BETTER
THAN HIS OWN RECIPE.

SERVES 4

SAUCE
2 TABLESPOONS OLIVE OIL
2 GARLIC CLOVES, PEELED AND MINCED
2 CUPS CANNED, DICED TOMATOES
1 TABLESPOON CHOPPED FRESH SAGE
SALT AND BLACK PEPPER TO TASTE

CATFISH
1 CUP CHOPPED PECANS
1/2 CUP YELLOW CORNMEAL
1/2 CUP ALL-PURPOSE FLOUR
3 TABLESPOONS CHOPPED FRESH FLAT-LEAF PARSLEY
FOUR 8-OUNCE CATFISH FILLETS, SKINNED, TRIMMED, AND
    PINBONED
SALT AND BLACK PEPPER TO TASTE
1/4 CUP OLIVE OIL

MUSTARD GREENS
1/2 CUP OLIVE OIL
1 POUND MUSTARD GREENS, CHOPPED
1/2 CUP WATER
SALT AND BLACK PEPPER TO TASTE

Preheat the oven to 350°F.

FOR THE SAUCE: Heat the olive oil in a medium sauté pan over
medium heat. Sauté the garlic for 1 minute. Add the tomatoes and
cook for 5 minutes. Add the sage and cook 2 minutes more. Season
with salt and pepper. Keep warm on the back of the stove.

FOR THE CATFISH: In a wide shallow bowl, mix together the pecans,
cornmeal, flour, and parsley. Season each catfish fillet with salt and
pepper. Dredge each fillet in the breading mixture.

Heat the olive oil in a large sauté pan over medium heat. Sauté the catfish fillets, skin side up, until the coating begins to brown, then turn over and brown the other side. Place the fillets on a large baking sheet, then put in the oven for 3 to 5 minutes to finish cooking them.

FOR THE MUSTARD GREENS: Heat the olive oil in a large sauté pan over medium heat. Sauté the mustard greens for 3 minutes. Add the water and braise the greens until tender. Season with salt and pepper.

TO ASSEMBLE: Spoon some sauce on 4 plates. Place a catfish fillet on top of the sauce, then add the braised mustard greens.

Serve hot.

TWO VERY PLEASED
CATFISH ANGLERS.

Blackened Shrimp with Mashed Sweet Potatoes and Andouille Cream

Chef Antony Field at Bonne Terre Country Inn and Café created this dish for our crew when we were on location shooting my television show. This entire dish is great, but I could eat the sweet potatoes by themselves.

SERVES 4

MASHED SWEET POTATOES

1 1/2 POUNDS SWEET POTATOES, PEELED AND DICED

1 1/2 POUNDS YUKON GOLD POTATOES, PEELED AND DICED

1 TABLESPOON HONEY

1/4 POUND (1 STICK) UNSALTED BUTTER, SOFTENED

1/2 TEASPOON GROUND CINNAMON

SALT AND BLACK PEPPER TO TASTE

ANDOUILLE CREAM

1 TABLESPOON OLIVE OIL

1 TABLESPOON MINCED GARLIC

2 TABLESPOONS MINCED SHALLOTS

2 TABLESPOONS DICED CELERY

1/2 CUP WHITE WINE

1/4 POUND ANDOUILLE SAUSAGE, DICED

1 FRESH THYME SPRIG

1 CUP HEAVY CREAM

1 TEASPOON CAJUN SEASONING

2 TABLESPOONS UNSALTED BUTTER

SALT AND BLACK PEPPER TO TASTE

1 TABLESPOON CHOPPED FRESH FLAT-LEAF PARSLEY

BLACKENED SHRIMP

12 MEDIUM-SIZED SHRIMP, PEELED, TAIL ON, AND BUTTERFLIED

BLACKENING SPICE FOR COATING

SALT AND BLACK PEPPER TO TASTE

1/2 CUP OLIVE OIL

FOR THE MASHED SWEET POTATOES: In a 1-gallon stockpot, cover the sweet potatoes with water. Bring to a boil; cook until fork-tender. Drain.

Meanwhile, in a separate 1-gallon stockpot, cover the Yukon Gold potatoes with water. Bring to a boil; cook until fork-tender. Drain.

Place the hot sweet potatoes and hot Yukon Gold potatoes in one of the pots. Add the honey, butter, and cinnamon. Mash together. Season with salt and pepper. Keep warm on the back of the stove.

FOR THE ANDOUILLE CREAM: Heat the olive oil in a large sauté pan over medium heat. Sweat the garlic and shallots in the oil for 2 to 3 minutes. Add the celery and sauté for 1 minute. Add the wine, sausage, and thyme. Reduce the wine by one-half. Add the cream and reduce the mixture by one-half again. Stir in the Cajun seasoning, butter, salt, and pepper, and cook for 1 minute. Stir in the parsley. Keep warm on the back of the stove. Remove the thyme sprig before serving.

FOR THE SHRIMP: Dredge the shrimp in the blackening spice. Season each side of the shrimp with salt and pepper.

Heat the olive oil in a sauté pan over medium-high heat. Pan-sear the shrimp, being sure not to burn the blackening spice, or it will turn very bitter in taste.

TO ASSEMBLE: Spoon the potatoes in the center of each serving plate. Stand 3 shrimp on the potatoes, with the tails pointing up. Spoon a portion of the Andouille cream over the shrimp and potatoes. Serve hot.

PASSERSBY ARE SERENADED BY THE SWEET SOUNDS OF THE TRUMPET FROM A STREET MUSICIAN IN DOWNTOWN MEMPHIS.

FRIED OKRA WITH BUTTERMILK DIPPING SAUCE

OKRA WOULD NEVER HAVE MADE IT TO AMERICAN SOIL IF IT WEREN'T FOR THE INGENUITY OF AFRICAN SLAVES BROUGHT OVER ON SHIPS. THEY SMUGGLED THE SEEDS INTO THIS COUNTRY AND PLANTED THEM ON THEIR PLOTS. OKRA IS COMMONLY USED IN GUMBOS, BUT IT IS ALSO WONDERFUL ON ITS OWN.

SERVES 4

SAUCE

1 GARLIC CLOVE, PEELED AND MINCED

1/2 CUP BUTTERMILK

JUICE OF 1 LIME

1 TABLESPOON CHOPPED FRESH CILANTRO

1 TABLESPOON CHOPPED FRESH CHIVES

3/4 CUP LOW-FAT MAYONNAISE

SALT AND BLACK PEPPER TO TASTE

OKRA

1 1/2 CUPS ALL-PURPOSE FLOUR

2 LARGE EGGS

1 TEASPOON SALT

1/2 TEASPOON GROUND BLACK PEPPER

1 CUP WATER

VEGETABLE OIL FOR FRYING

16 OKRA, CLEANED, TRIMMED, AND SPLIT IN HALF

FOR THE SAUCE: In a medium mixing bowl, whisk all the ingredients together. Cover and refrigerate.

FOR THE OKRA: In a medium mixing bowl, whisk together the flour, eggs, salt, pepper, and water. Cover the batter and let it rest for 1 hour in the refrigerator.

Fill a 1-gallon stockpot 4 inches deep with vegetable oil. Heat the oil to 350°F.

Dip the okra in the batter and put them directly into the fryer. When the okra floats to the surface and is golden brown, remove from the fryer and drain on paper towels. Season with salt and pepper.

Serve the fried okra with the buttermilk dipping sauce.

Banana Blaze

It was a pleasure to cook with Isaac Hayes at his restaurant, Isaac Hayes Music • Food • Passion. He explained to me that when you make this dessert for your significant other, not only will the bananas be blazing, but she will be, too! You can tell that Isaac is a real ladies' man.

SERVES 4

2 TABLESPOONS UNSALTED BUTTER

2 BANANAS, SPLIT LENGTHWISE AND CUT IN HALF

1/2 CUP MAPLE SYRUP

1 CUP RAISINS

1 1/2 TEASPOONS GROUND NUTMEG

1 TABLESPOON GROUND CINNAMON

1 CUP COGNAC

4 SCOOPS VANILLA ICE CREAM

1 CUP CHOPPED TOASTED PECANS

1 CUP SHREDDED COCONUT

WHIPPED CREAM FOR GARNISH

Coat a sauté pan with cooking spray and heat over medium heat. Add the butter to the pan, and when it is hot, add the bananas. Sear them on both sides.

Add the maple syrup and reduce by one-half. Add the raisins, nutmeg, and cinnamon. Cook for 1 minute. Add the cognac and carefully flame off the alcohol.

Spoon the blazed bananas into 4 serving bowls. Place a scoop of ice cream on each serving.

Sprinkle the pecans and shredded coconut over each scoop of ice cream. Spoon the remaining sauce on top. Place a spoonful of whipped cream on top of everything and enjoy!

FRIED SWEET POTATO PIE

Charles Gammon of Chucky's Fried Pies showed me another way to prepare a pie, by deep-frying. Other fillings may be substituted for the sweet potato, such as apple, cherry, and peach. Just make the filling the same way you would for a traditional pie.

MAKES 10 PIES

DOUGH
2 CUPS SELF-RISING FLOUR OR ALL-PURPOSE FLOUR
1 1/2 TEASPOONS SALT
4 TABLESPOONS SUGAR
1/4 POUND (1 STICK) MARGARINE, MELTED
1/8 TO 1/4 CUP COLD WATER

FILLING
3 POUNDS SWEET POTATOES, PEELED AND DICED LARGE
1/4 POUND (1 STICK) MARGARINE
3 TABLESPOONS VANILLA EXTRACT
1 1/2 CUPS SUGAR
GROUND CINNAMON TO TASTE
GROUND NUTMEG TO TASTE

FOR FRYING
1 QUART VEGETABLE OIL

FOR THE DOUGH: On a clean work surface, combine the flour, salt, and sugar. Cut in the margarine to create a coarse cornmeal texture. Work in the water until the dough is tacky.

Roll the dough into a ball, then cut it into 10 equal pieces. Using a floured rolling pin, roll each piece of dough out on a floured surface to a diameter of 6 inches and about 1/8 inch thick. Set aside.

FOR THE FILLING: In a medium stockpot, cover the sweet potatoes with water and bring to a boil. Cook until fork-tender. Drain well.

In a food processor, combine the hot sweet potatoes, margarine, vanilla, and sugar. Process until smooth. Season with cinnamon and nutmeg.

In a 1-gallon stockpot, heat 1 quart of vegetable oil to 350°F.

TO ASSEMBLE: Put ¼ cup of filling in the center of a dough circle. Fold the dough over the filling and seal the edges with water. Crimp the edges with a fork to close completely. Repeat with the remaining dough and filling.

Once the oil has reached 350°F., place a pie in the oil. Cook for 7 to 8 minutes, until it has a golden brown color. Drain on paper towels to absorb any excess oil. Repeat with the remaining pies.

These pies are best served warm.

FRIED PIES? DID YOU SAY FRIED PIES? WOW, SO GOOD YOU HAVE TO EAT TWO! CHARLES "CHUCKY" GAMMON SHOWED ME HOW THEY ARE DONE.

MEXICO

The panorama is distinct and metaphorical, the overview striking. From an airplane window, Guadalajara looks like a lifeboat being tossed and tumbled on a sandy sea.

Because it sits amid desert country, where urban infrastructures such as water pipes, electricity, and gas lines fail, the city simply stops. From above, any suburban activity looks as if it has been lopped off with a machete.

It's a visual dichotomy that in many ways defines Mexico: the cosmopolitan bustle that takes place on concrete set against a lonely dusty spread of soil and cactus. Old and new, blood and steel, tradition and progress.

Ironic, really. For ten days I've been tracking friend and fellow Detroiter Martina Guzman as she makes a pilgrimage to the small alpine village of Jesús Maria where her grandmother lives and where the annual Parade of Absent Children symbolically repatriates those Mexicans who have moved elsewhere. Along the road, *her* road, I've met chefs and cowboys, candy makers and music makers, spit-polished mayors, and *campesinos* smelling of loam, leather, and horse sweat. And even while feeling like an impossible outsider, struggling with language, customs, and proprieties, I found this severe and fascinating country seeping into my system, establishing itself inextricably. I was being "Mexico-ed." Martina nods at the notion. "You'll be back," she promises. And sure enough, within a year I am— tearing up the Baja backroads on a dirt bike alongside my buddy Chris Haines.

Further ironies: Even as a just-arrived stranger in a

strange land, I'm struck with a certain sense of the familiar. Jalisco state (of which Guadalajara is the capital) is a travel poster of Old Mexico. Agave fields spread beneath cloudless vistas, splashy fiestas unfold in colonial villages, and dusty roads amble off into the broad, striated mountainsides. Jalisco is the birthplace of those most picturesque of Mexican clichés: tequila, mariachi, and rodeo. And Mexican cuisine, with traditions going back nearly three thousand years, traces countless roots through these savage geological vistas.

GUADALAJARA

This city is a treasure trove for the culinary traveler. Adventure beckons, and my primary goal upon landing and wrangling a rented car is to hit Guadalajara's famous Mercado Libertad.

Wending through the urban sprawl of Guadalajara is a trip. The smog settles in like a shroud, saturating the air with acrid saffron-colored haze. It sinks into your lungs like bronchitis, making you feel as though you've smoked a No. 5 stogie or inhaled a string of pulverized chile peppers. Deep within the bowels of Mercado Libertad, of course, you're protected from these sharp urban spewings. Here, the fire in your lungs is, in fact, pulverized chile peppers.

Mercado Libertad, on Avenue Javier Mina, is a sprawling multilevel coliseum filled with a cultural smorgasbord, from the everyday to the exotic: outlandish fish, workaday supper chickens, cow haunches, sheep offal, produce, folksy crafts, kitchen things, knock-off designer clothes. The wares are so numerous and so substandard that the area, formerly called San Juan de Dios, is currently known as Taiwan de Dios.

Every imaginable breed of chile can be found here: fresh, fried, pickled, dried, roasted, toasted, jellied, jammed, powdered, pulverized, hung, and strung; serranos, jalapeños, anchos, habaneros, cayennes, rocotillos, poblanos, and any number of designer peppers, the Cartiers of

Casadores Veracruz Sauce

Chef Ricardo of the Casadores Hotel in Arandas made this sauce for a snapper dish he made for me. This sauce is commonly found in restaurants along the coast of the Gulf of Mexico, particularly in the city of Veracruz.

MAKES 1 QUART

1/4 CUP OLIVE OIL

1 CUP DICED WHITE ONIONS

2 GARLIC CLOVES, PEELED AND CHOPPED

1 GREEN BELL PEPPER, DICED

2 CUPS DICED PLUM TOMATOES

2 WHOLE BAY LEAVES

1 CUP PITTED GREEN OLIVES

1 CUP WATER

SALT AND BLACK PEPPER TO TASTE

Heat the olive oil in a 2-quart saucepan over medium heat. Add the onions, garlic, and green pepper, and cook for 2 minutes. Add the tomatoes, bay leaves, and olives. Cook 5 minutes more.

Add the water and let simmer for 10 minutes.

Season with salt and pepper. Remove the bay leaves.

This is best served over grilled fish or seafood, such as snapper or shrimp.

capsicums—mirasols, sudans, Jamaica colimas. In Mexico, chile is serious business; as a general rule, these fiery pods tend to be the cornerstone of Mexican cookery. Chile peppers represent the color, the *calor,* the potency, and in many ways the soul of the Hispanic kitchen. Here in downtown Guadalajara, Mercado Libertad has been operating for dozens of decades, and while the union locals' signs are new—along with the shoddy blue jeans, ersatz Nikes, and backward baseball caps on teenage vendors—the chile stalls are primordial.

The demeanor at the market is universally upbeat, and crowds are omnipresent. All nationalities are represented; Mercado Libertad is, after all, a tourist attraction. But Guadalajara residents themselves manifest an interesting racial fusion; among locals you can find undiluted Aztec faces, unchanged since their representation on pre-Columbian murals, and in numbers equally abundant, tall, emerald-eyed, and honey-haired natives whose now-distant European ancestry is still very near the surface.

Meanwhile, boothkeepers of every description hustle about in aprons stained from their various fortes, and like the chile vendor who is crooning in a stage-quality tenor,

"*Es mi razon por existe*" (This is my reason for being), there is considerable excitement and satisfaction in their expressions; they're laughing, chatting, hollering, and hawking while flipping pasty pans of *tostada* dough, baking tortillas, filling *molcajete* (pig-shaped bowls made from volcanic rock), and frying meat in massive, woklike *casuelas*. Outside the century-old walls of Mercado Libertad, modern Guadalajara continues to choke on its own fumes; modernity has dragged this once-charming provincial town into Mexico's fastest growing industrial juggernaut.

Fortunately, some things cannot be sprawled into oblivion, and inside the market, whiffs of the past remain—in the faces, in the customs, in the commodities, in the curiosities—stubborn, earnest, and enchanting.

ARANDAS

I clamber into my newly acquired four-door Tsuru and, snagging directions from an amiable English-speaking policeman, head beyond the city limits. The next stop is Arandas, halfway to our destination of Jesús Maria and hometown of Don Felipe.

Don Felipe is the patriarch of El Tesoro and probably the last of the old-school tequila makers. Throughout the journey Martina is tremendously hyped, anxious to meet him, though her interest is decidedly not tequila. A rumor has been floating around her family for eons about her grandmother (a former El Tesoro fieldhand) and the old rascally Don himself. Moonlit liaisons are hinted at. Ardor among the agave is the common whisper. Maybe there's more to this story. This was back in Jalisco's most passionate era, the years following the famous Cristero wars that inspired Graham Greene's novel *The Power and the Glory*. Despite countless trips to Jesús Maria, this will be Martina's first opportunity to meet the old Don face-to-face.

Arandas is seventy miles northeast of Guadalajara. A smog-free zone. This is tequila country, a patchwork of dry gulches, saw-toothed mountains, skulls, bones, thirsty

GUACAMOLE

GUACAMOLE ORIGINATED IN THE
AZTEC WORLD. ITS NAME IS A
COMBINATION OF WORDS FROM
THE NAHUATL LANGUAGE,
"AHUACATLE" (AVOCADO) AND
"MOLLI" (MIXTURE). ITS USES
VARY FROM BEING A GREAT DIP
FOR TORTILLA CHIPS TO A
REFRESHING CONDIMENT FOR
ENCHILADAS OR CHICKEN
SANDWICHES.

MAKES 3 CUPS

4 RIPE AVOCADOS, PEELED AND SEED
   REMOVED

1/2 WHITE ONION, DICED

1 BEEFSTEAK TOMATO, DICED

JUICE OF 1 LIME

1/2 JALAPEÑO PEPPER, SEEDED AND
   DICED SMALL

2 TABLESPOONS CHOPPED FRESH
   CILANTRO

SALT TO TASTE

Mash the avocados in a medium mixing
bowl. Add the onion, tomato, lime juice,
jalapeño, and cilantro. Season with salt.
Refrigerate for 15 minutes.

Serve before the avocado begins to oxidize
and turn brown.

burros, crossroads, and pale blue agave fields wandering into the slopes of the Los Altos highlands.

Tequila country has been cranking out Mexico's most famous beverage since the mid-sixteenth century, though it's likely that native Mexicans have been fermenting the sap of the agave plant for thousands of years. El Tesoro is a fitting house to represent Los Altos's renegade tequila reputation, since it has so far managed to resist the lure—and, in some ways, the sensibility—of hauling itself into a world filled with electricity. That's attributed to the cantankerous penny-pinching of the Don, who is clearly a legendary figure in this hot and flyblown village. Dozens of grinning townsfolk gather to witness the meeting as Don Felipe—who admits to seventy-three, but who must be closer to eighty-seven—strides elegantly from the nail-studded doorway of his colonial house, waving lustily to the group of onlookers. The whole affair takes on the pomp of a papal audience.

Arandas is a long way from the dusty country town called Tequila, and Don Felipe's "hombre-powered" distillery is a long way from the antiseptic modernity of the tequila superpowers whose names are more familiar: El Toro, Sauza, and Jose Cuervo. This diminishes not an ounce of the pride Felipe evidences in his hand-crafted liquor. He insists on leading the way to his quaint distillery, over roads that have not met their match since Ho Chi Minh was making trails. He personally conducts the tour, which involves multiflight stair romps and climbs through piles of recently harvested agave *piñas,* the beachball-sized core of the plant, tequila's source.

The essentials of tequila making are easily absorbed. Once stripped of its outer leaves, the heart of the agave plant resembles a gigantic pineapple. The antiquated courtyard of the El Tesoro distillery is piled high with these peculiar objects, which at this stage have neither taste nor smell. The pile is diminished by slow degrees as three grizzled and serious old-timers hack them in half, one by one, with well-worn axes and load them into brick ovens. The cooking stage lasts about half a day and brings out all the essential sugars in the plant. A strong-smelling mash of brown pulp and fiber is left behind, which workers chew like candy. I'm handed a piece, and the gang waits eagerly for my opinion. Well, there's a juicy sort of agreeableness to a piece of cooked agave, a taste that ranges between cherry-rum pipe tobacco and an overcooked yam, but, clearly, Godiva chocolate is in no immediate danger.

From the ovens, bucketloads of mash are hand-pressed; a millstone as big as a full-blown Harley, operated by four sturdy individuals, squeezes the precious juice into wooden kegs. This sap is then allowed to ferment in the open air for a couple of days. The barrels sit amid the husks of ancient machinery, roiling with the vigor of a witch's cauldron. The smell emanating from the yeasty brew is thick and malty and sweet. Nevertheless, at no point so far has anything even resembling a drinkable beverage been produced. That's because the true art of tequila making is in the process of distilling: the delicate extraction of alcohol and essential flavors, while the bulk of the fermented sap, including toxins, is left behind.

The term "still," recognizable from rural American folklore, refers to distilling equipment. Distilling involves heating the agave "beer" to evaporate the strong stuff through a series of copper tubes, then chilling the steam until it recondenses. The crystal-clear product, which can be sampled as it drips from the still's business end, is raw and as harsh as rocket fuel. If consumed at this point—and plenty do because it's cheap—it produces the identical grief, but little of the sophistication, of the final product.

Good tequila undergoes several further refinements, including redistillation to remove more impurities and slow aging to mellow the youthful exuberance of the liquor. After a couple of months it reaches a stage where it can truly be considered a beverage of distinction and delight, though the best is aged for years in oaken casks. The price of a bottle rises accordingly.

In a certain sense, touring a by-hand tequila distillery is viewing an art form as it dies. Even Don Felipe is being forced to expand, update, and invest. Currently, the distill-

CEVICHE

Ceviche is a staple in many Mexican restaurants. Chef Osman Gomez of the Hotel Finisterra passed this recipe on to me. Actually, an interpreter passed it on to me, since Chef Osman doesn't speak a word of English.

SERVES 4

CEVICHE

1 POUND SEA BASS, CUT INTO 1-INCH DICE

1 CUP FRESH LIME JUICE

1 1/2 TEASPOONS MINCED GARLIC

1/2 CUP DICED RED ONION

1 CUP DICED PLUM TOMATOES

4 SERRANO CHILES, SEEDS AND RIBS REMOVED, AND MINCED

1/2 CUP CHOPPED FRESH CILANTRO

1 CUP PEELED AND DICED CUCUMBER

1 TEASPOON CHOPPED FRESH OREGANO

SALT TO TASTE

GARNISH

1 AVOCADO, PEELED, SEED REMOVED, AND SLICED

In a nonreactive dish, such as a glass bowl, toss the sea bass, lime juice, and garlic together. Let the bass marinate for 30 minutes in the refrigerator.

After it has finished marinating, add the remaining ingredients to the sea bass. Refrigerate for another 15 minutes.

Garnish each serving with slices of avocado.

ing process is wedged into a corner of his factory, while all around, construction crews are engaged in growing the business—literally. Like many Mexican "buildings in transition," the whole place looks as if it's collapsing when in fact it is being put together. Don Felipe is adding capacity: blasting out cavernous cellars and introducing a former taboo—stainless steel—to his operation. The challenge, of course, will be to preserve the pioneer perfection of the handmade while accepting the inevitability of progress.

And as Don Felipe has demonstrated, that's not necessarily a simple task.

Meanwhile, Martina spends a number of clandestine moments in the Don's company. His tongue has clearly been loosened by liberal samples of raw liquor, which he drinks from a bull's horn. Their rapid-fire, high-powered conversations are lost on those of us with grade-school-level Spanish, but it's clear that the old fellow is delighted to recount his memories to this young, curious, and attractive senorita. Never mind the details, it's obvious that Don Felipe's hormones are still packing a punch as strong as his tequila.

JESÚS MARIA

The next morning we arrive in Jesús Maria, where skies are luminous, sharp blue and cloudless. The town won't see a raindrop until June. It's perched on the lip of a high-plateau zone called the Altos de Jalisco, a poetic and postcard-perfect *pueblo* with grilled windows and storybook balconies strung with the strikingly vibrant bougainvillea vines that seem to suspend Mexico within eternal springtime. It's picturesque terrain, but hardly sleepy, especially this week. This is fiesta week, an annual tradition that celebrates patron saints and combines piety, revelry, and coming-of-age rituals.

Additionally, tradition requires that the "absent children" of the region—those who were born here but now live elsewhere—put in an appearance during the grand parade that caps the celebration. As such, Martina's journey home each January is part of a massive influx as nearly three thousand absent children return, a large, bilingual horde absorbed by sinuous sidestreets and dusty alleys, inside the houses of aunts, uncles, and grandparents. Martina's grandmother (Maria del Refugio Hernandez de Guzman) has occupied the same rambling, one-story, whitewashed house for fifty years. Married at seventeen and widowed shortly thereafter, she spent the lion's share of those fifty years raising pigs and goats, picking agave, and helping out with Don Felipe's tequila operations. She lost a brother in the Cristero revolution, and another to pneumonia, but her remaining siblings gather on a threadbare couch this happy morning and chatter like schoolkids.

Martina's fiesta preparations begin moments after we arrive, and the house is a cyclone of energy. Besides Martina, sisters Brenda, Chris, and Maria have come from the States, tugging along nieces, nephews, and cousins. By late afternoon the parade has begun on a swell of high ground where the balconies sag with bright, eager, brown spectators. The bishop comes first, riding point inside a polished Massey Ferguson tractor, carrying a banner reading CRISTO AYER, MAÑANA, Y SIEMPRE (Jesus Yesterday, Tomorrow, and Forever). It's a leftover from New Year's Eve. But don't miss the significance that Y2K had on such hyper-Catholics; for them, 2000 was a milestone anniversary of Christ's birth, not an excuse to sell generators and computer software. The parade is filled with quaint and joyous expressions like this one, plus mock Madonnas, Passion play characters, kids in nun costumes, legends of local significance, deathbed conversions, revolutionary martyrs.

Last comes the absent children, single file, men to the left, women to the right, clustered by family. They've all purchased special, oversized, cream-colored candles from eager entrepreneurs, and they'll donate them to the church at the end of their march. Men in shiny suits and Stetsons carry their candles over their shoulders like clubs or weapons. The girls, in huge heels, new nylons, and evening

TEQUILA SHRIMP

THIS FINE CREATION DEPENDS ON THE AVOCADO TO HELP CREATE A SAUCELIKE TEXTURE AND IMPART ITS FLAVOR ONCE IT IS ADDED TO THE HOT SAUTÉED DISH. IT IS IMPORTANT THAT THE AVOCADO BE FIRM AND NOT OVERRIPE.

SERVES 4

2 TABLESPOONS OLIVE OIL

1 WHITE ONION, DICED

3 GARLIC CLOVES, PEELED AND MINCED

10 SHRIMP, PEELED, DEVEINED, AND SPLIT IN HALF

1/4 CUP TEQUILA

3 PLUM TOMATOES, DICED

JUICE OF 2 LIMES

1 TABLESPOON CHOPPED FRESH CILANTRO

1 AVOCADO, PEELED, PITTED, AND DICED

SALT AND BLACK PEPPER TO TASTE

Heat the olive oil in a medium sauté pan over medium heat. Add the onion and garlic, and sauté until they are translucent, 3 to 4 minutes. Add the shrimp and continue to sauté for 3 to 4 minutes. Stir in the tequila and carefully flame off the alcohol. Add the tomatoes and sauté another 3 to 4 minutes. Add the lime juice when the shrimp are cooked halfway. During the last minute of cooking, fold in the cilantro and avocado. Cook 1 minute more.

Season with salt and pepper.

Serve hot.

YOUNG MEXICAN CHARROS (COWBOYS) WATCHING THE ANNUAL PARADE PASS BY.

dresses, clutch them to their breasts like babies. Martina's group comes about the midpoint of the parade. For the remainder of the week they'll be drinking, partying, attending cockfights, and tearing up the countryside. Today, they're drawn, scrubbed, and attentive. There are things in life that you take seriously.

Mass follows, and an evening of sound and color, during which the streets of Jesús Maria are locked in a spasm of activity. Lights are strung between trees and lampposts, and street musicians play the old classic mariachi hits, many of which had their origins at rural fairs like this one. A fireworks display at ten signals the climactic conclusion of the fiesta, and from there, everyone returns to the homes of friends and relatives to eat, drink, and reminisce.

Maria del Refugio Hernandez de Guzman's table is heavy with her particular brand of family heirlooms: the various recipes that have been handed down and passed along, probably since Cortez was jousting with the Aztecs. "Food is an enormous part of our gatherings," Martina confides as her aunts bustle about the kitchen, sautéing chorizo sausages as plump as bananas, spooning out bowls of crusty fried beans, and spreading platters high with *queso de puerco,* the Mexican version of headcheese. "It's the soul of happiness."

But only a part. Traditions of food and comfort evolve in concert, like the dance of these sisters, moving from stove to counter to table for the billionth time. You assign it to simple familiarity, recognition of one another's quirks, spaces, and habits. But something deeper than that is at work. Watch the sawed-off generation, the chattering little pre-teens who've come down from their snowy Detroit-centered universe only this morning. They're slipping among these stolid elders, brushing skirts, dodging shins, skittering with a practiced grace. Around them there are low murmurs of conversation, both Spanish and English; there are babes at breasts, nursing in stoic silence. They move with a flawless grace, and it cannot have been practiced.

The soul of happiness—anywhere, but especially here, today, in Jesús Maria—is goals shared, common blood. Today, to the Guzmans, family means both reunion and redemption.

BAJA

I'm a guy who grew up with dirt bikes. Small wonder the lure of Mexico's wild Baja Peninsula was irresistible to me. So there I was, enjoying a snow-white beach in Jamaica, when I tripped over one of those obscure little ads that appear in the rear of adventure magazines, the ones that outline trips you may dream of but hardly ever work up the steam to take.

Well, Chris Haines's Motorcycle Baja Adventure leaped out at me and immediately inspired me to take a fateful leap off my rear and toward the telephone. I remembered reading about Chris Haines, a Baja 1000 racer, and a trip he arranged for Lyle Lovett several years back, and I wondered if he could set up something similar for me. What I

ROASTED CORN SALSA

SPENCER MOORE OF FELIX'S IN CABO SAN LUCAS SHARED THIS RECIPE WITH ME. HIS RESTAURANT FEATURES MORE THAN TWENTY SALSAS MADE FRESH EVERY DAY. AT FELIX'S YOU WILL DEFINITELY HAVE AN ADVENTURE IN EATING.

MAKES 3 CUPS

2 EARS OF CORN

1 RED BELL PEPPER

2 GARLIC CLOVES, PEELED AND MINCED

1 CHIPOTLE CHILE, DICED

1 TABLESPOON CHOPPED FRESH CILANTRO

SALT AND BLACK PEPPER TO TASTE

Prepare an outdoor grill.

Shuck the corn and remove any silk, then place the corn on the grill. Grill each side until golden brown, then let cool.

Roast the red pepper on the grill until it is charred on all sides. Then place the pepper in a towel or a covered container to let it steam. Remove it when it is cool. Peel the charred skin off the pepper, remove the stem and seeds, and dice the flesh.

Cut the kernels from the corn cobs.

In a medium mixing bowl, combine the corn, roasted pepper, garlic, chipotle, and cilantro. Season with salt and pepper

Serve the salsa with tortillas or as a topping for tacos.

EARLY MORNING IN BAJA— GETTING THE BIKES WARMED UP.

imagined was a trip where I could ride the dirt in and out of the towns of Baja all the way down to Cabo San Lucas and sample the foods along the way. The arrangements were handled almost immediately, and Chris seemed nearly as excited as I was. The plan called for landing me in La Paz on the east side of the peninsula and then riding the dirt along the coast—just Chris, me, and the scenery. As departure time came closer, reality began to set in. Here I was, a regular guy, getting a chance to ride side by side with a guy who won the Baja 1000 eight out of eighteen times—2001 being the most recent.

At fifty-one years of age, Chris Haines is the portrait of

health. His love for the Baja is obvious. Besides the annual road race he has fifteen years of Baja motorcycle adventures under his belt. His first trip, arranged for Formula One racer Danny Sullivan and his buddies, immediately put Chris and this particular gig on the map. With four used bikes and a trailer, Haines was successful in showing the crew a whole other side of speed.

You may well ask what possesses a person to want to ride hundreds of miles on rough terrain at speeds that can easily send you home in search of a specialty surgeon. I'll tell you in a word: the rush. Not many adventures give you the feeling you get with 600 cc's or 4-stroke power between your legs, especially if you have the Sea of Cortez on one side and Chris Haines on the other, and you're peeling away open road as your bike purrs like a cheetah preparing to make a kill.

The stories that Chris shares along the way are every bit as exciting as the rides. At the end of a long day, with a blazing sun sinking below the Sea of Cortez, nothing beats the yarns of an old road pro, sending you off to dreamland dog tired but eager for another day's ride. Seeing Baja from the back of a dirt bike gives you a feel for the flavor of the country like nothing else. From the small fishing camps to the villages and roadside stands, this is a taste of the real Baja. Be forewarned: Chris is a kind of celebrity to the locals; they often cheer him as he passes through. It's pretty amazing to see him lay one-wheel rubber down two full city blocks while a crowd and a local policeman stand by and applaud.

I learned more about riding during that week with Chris than I have in all my years on dirt bikes combined. There were a few close calls, which only spiced up the adventure. Best of all, I now count Chris Haines, a true gentleman and one of history's most notable Baja racers, a good friend.

SALSA MEXICANA

THIS SALSA IS NAMED MEXICANA BECAUSE IT CONTAINS THE THREE COLORS OF THE MEXICAN FLAG: TOMATOES FOR RED, ONIONS FOR WHITE, AND JALAPEÑO FOR GREEN.

MAKES 3 CUPS

4 PLUM TOMATOES, DICED

1/2 WHITE ONION, DICED

1 JALAPEÑO PEPPER, SEEDS REMOVED (OR NOT IF YOU WANT A LITTLE EXTRA KICK)

2 TABLESPOONS CHOPPED FRESH CILANTRO

JUICE OF 1 LIME

1 TEASPOON MINCED GARLIC

1/2 CUP OLIVE OIL

1/2 TEASPOON GROUND CUMIN

SALT TO TASTE

Combine all the ingredients in a medium mixing bowl.

Serve with tortilla chips or as a condiment for meat dishes.

Baja Beach Lobster and Sole Tacos with Tequila-Lime Salsa

I concocted this recipe on the Baja Peninsula while on a beach on the Sea of Cortez. I was riding with dirt bike champion Chris Haines. This was the perfect lunch on a sunny black sand beach! The lobster and sole came right out of the boat as the local fishermen pulled up to the beach.

SERVES 4

TEQUILA-LIME SALSA

1/4 CUP TEQUILA

1/2 EAR OF CORN, GRILLED AND KERNELS CUT FROM COB

1 AVOCADO, DICED

JUICE OF 3 LIMES

1/2 CUP DICED PLUM TOMATOES

1/4 CUP DICED WHITE ONION

1/2 JALAPEÑO PEPPER, SEEDED AND MINCED

1 TABLESPOON CHOPPED FRESH CILANTRO

SEA SALT TO TASTE

TACOS

1 POUND SOLE FILLETS, SKINNED

SEA SALT TO TASTE

4 TABLESPOONS OLIVE OIL

FOUR 8-INCH FLOUR TORTILLAS, GRILLED

4 LARGE ICEBERG LETTUCE LEAVES

ONE 2-POUND SPINY LOBSTER, BOILED, MEAT REMOVED, AND CHOPPED

2 TABLESPOONS CHOPPED FRESH EPAZOTE OR FRESH CILANTRO

2 TABLESPOONS MINCED SERRANO CHILES

1 PLUM TOMATO, SLICED INTO RINGS

1/2 CUP SCALLIONS, CUT THIN ON THE BIAS (GREEN AND WHITE PARTS)

FOR THE SALSA: In a large mixing bowl, combine all the ingredients. Cover and refrigerate for 30 minutes before using to allow the flavors to blend.

FOR THE TACOS: Prepare an outdoor grill.

Season the sole fillets with sea salt, brush with olive oil, and place on the grill. Grill for 3 to 4 minutes, then turn over and grill an addi-

It doesn't get any better than this! Fresh grilled lobster after several hours of riding through the Baja Peninsula with Baja 1000 racing champion Chris Haines.

tional 2 to 3 minutes, or until they begin to flake. Remove from the grill.

Lay out the grilled tortillas. Place a lettuce leaf on top of each tortilla. Add the grilled sole, followed by the lobster. Sprinkle with epazote and serrano chiles. Add the plum tomato rings and scallions. Spoon the tequila-lime salsa over each taco. Fold the leaves around the filling and roll the tortilla.

Serve warm.

Spicy Carrots

These pickled carrots are used as a condiment in almost every Mexican restaurant. Spencer Moore of Felix's in Cabo San Lucas shared his restaurant's recipe with me. If you would like to try one of Spencer's other salsa and condiment recipes, visit his website: www.felixcabosanlucas.com.

MAKES 1 QUART

12 CARROTS, PEELED AND SLICED IN
    1/4-INCH DISKS
6 JALAPEÑO PEPPERS, SEEDED AND THINLY SLICED
2 WHITE ONIONS, JULIENNED
2 WHOLE BAY LEAVES
2 CUPS WATER
1 CUP WHITE WINE VINEGAR
1 1/2 TEASPOONS DRIED OREGANO

In a 2-quart nonreactive pot, combine all the ingredients except the oregano. If there is not enough liquid to cover the carrots, add more at a ratio of 1 part vinegar and 2 parts water. Bring to a boil and then turn the heat to low and simmer for 3 to 4 minutes. Turn off the heat and stir in the oregano. Cover the pot and let steep for 20 minutes.

Store, covered, in the refrigerator. The longer the carrots sit refrigerated, the hotter they become in flavor.

Sopa de Pollo con Tortillas

This translates as "chicken soup with tor-tillas." A flavorful soup that is great for when you have a cold, it is also light enough to serve during the summer.

MAKES 2 QUARTS

GARNISH
VEGETABLE OIL FOR FRYING
SIX 6-INCH FLOUR TORTILLAS, JULIENNED
SALT AND BLACK PEPPER TO TASTE
SOUP
4 TABLESPOONS OLIVE OIL
3 POUNDS CHICKEN LEGS AND THIGHS
2 QUARTS CHICKEN STOCK
1 WHITE ONION, DICED
1 CELERY STALK, DICED
2 CARROTS, DICED
2 GARLIC CLOVES, MINCED
2 SERRANO CHILES, DICED
2 CUPS DICED PLUM TOMATOES
1/2 CUP CHOPPED FRESH CILANTRO
SALT AND BLACK PEPPER TO TASTE

FOR THE GARNISH: Fill a 1-gallon stockpot 2 inches deep with vegetable oil. Heat the oil to 350°F. Add the julienned tortilla strips. When the tortilla strips are golden brown, remove them and place on paper towels to absorb the excess oil. Season with salt and pepper.

FOR THE SOUP: Heat 2 tablespoons of olive oil in a 1-gallon stockpot over medium heat. Brown the chicken legs and thighs. Add the stock and simmer until the chicken is cooked, about 40 minutes. Once the chicken is cooked, remove it from the pot and let cool.

Heat the remaining 2 tablespoons of olive oil in a skillet over medium-high heat. Sauté the onion, celery, carrots, garlic, and chiles for 5 minutes. Add the tomatoes and sauté another 5 minutes. Add this mixture to the stock and let simmer for 10 minutes.

Meanwhile, remove the skin and bones from the chicken and shred the meat. Stir the chicken and cilantro into the soup. Simmer an additional 5 minutes. Season with salt and pepper. Ladle the soup into serving bowls. Top each serving with fried tortilla strips.

Caldo Verde

This hearty soup has the rich flavors of Mexico. Hope you enjoy it!

SERVES 4 TO 6

GARNISH

1 BAGUETTE

1 WHOLE GARLIC BULB, ROASTED

1 TABLESPOON CHOPPED FRESH FLAT-LEAF PARSLEY

SOUP

2 TABLESPOONS OLIVE OIL

1/2 POUND CHORIZO SAUSAGE, CASING REMOVED

1 CUP DICED WHITE ONIONS

2 GARLIC CLOVES, PEELED AND MINCED

6 RED-SKINNED POTATOES, DICED MEDIUM

8 CUPS CHICKEN STOCK

2 CUPS SWISS CHARD, CUT INTO THIN STRIPS

1/2 CUP COOKED GARBANZO BEANS, RINSED

SALT AND BLACK PEPPER TO TASTE

FOR THE GARNISH: Slice the baguette into 1/2-inch-thick pieces. Cut the garlic bulb in half and squeeze out the cloves. Spread the garlic on the baguette.

FOR THE SOUP: Heat the olive oil in a 1-gallon stockpot over medium-high heat. Add the sausage and sauté for 5 to 6 minutes until thoroughly cooked. Add the onions and garlic, and continue to sauté for 3 to 4 minutes. Add the potatoes and stock, and cook until the potatoes are tender.

Add the Swiss chard and cook another 3 to 4 minutes. Add the garbanzo beans and cook 3 to 4 minutes more. Season with salt and pepper. Ladle the soup into serving bowls. Sprinkle the chopped parsley over the soup, and garnish with a piece of roasted garlic baguette. Serve hot.

Beef Tips Mexicana

This is a classic Mexican dish that you will find in many restaurants in central Mexico.

SERVES 4

1/2 CUP OLIVE OIL

1 WHITE ONION, DICED

2 SERRANO CHILES, MINCED

2 GARLIC CLOVES, PEELED AND CHOPPED

2 CUPS DICED PLUM TOMATOES

1 1/2 POUNDS BEEF TENDERLOIN, DICED AND BROWNED

3 CUPS TOMATO SAUCE

1/2 CUP CHOPPED FRESH CILANTRO

SALT AND BLACK PEPPER TO TASTE

COOKED LONG-GRAIN RICE, ABOUT
   3/4 CUP PER SERVING

Heat the olive oil in a large saucepan over medium heat. Add the onions, chiles, and garlic, and sauté until tender, 4 to 5 minutes. Add the diced tomatoes and browned beef. Sauté for 3 to 4 minutes. Add the tomato sauce and let simmer for 10 minutes.

Stir in the cilantro and season with salt and pepper. Serve over rice.

Sopa de Mariscos

This is Spanish for "seafood soup." Baja menus are all about seafood, and who can blame them? With the Sea of Cortez on the east side of the peninsula and the Pacific Ocean on the west side, Baja has many types of seafood to choose from.

SERVES 8

3 TABLESPOONS OLIVE OIL

1 CUP DICED WHITE ONIONS

1 TABLESPOON MINCED GARLIC

1 CUP DICED CARROTS

3 TO 4 SMALL GREEN CHILES, SEEDED AND THINLY SLICED

1 CUP DICED CELERY

1 1/2 CUPS DICED PLUM TOMATOES

1 POUND MEDIUM-SIZED SHRIMP, PEELED, DEVEINED, AND SPLIT
   IN HALF

How's this for an early-morning catch? This fish will end up in the market and be sold just a few hours later.

1 POUND SEA BASS, DICED

½ POUND SQUID, BODY CUT INTO RINGS AND LEGS CUT IN HALF

1 POUND CONCH, POUNDED AND CUT IN STRIPS

2 QUARTS FISH STOCK

1 QUART CLAM JUICE

2 CUPS TOMATO JUICE

SALT AND BLACK PEPPER TO TASTE

2 TABLESPOONS CHOPPED FRESH CILANTRO

Heat the olive oil in a 2-gallon stockpot over medium heat. Sauté the onions, garlic, carrots, chiles, and celery for 4 to 5 minutes. Add the tomatoes, shrimp, sea bass, squid, and conch. Sauté 3 to 4 minutes more. Add the stock, clam juice, and tomato juice. Simmer for 15 minutes.

Season with salt and pepper. Ladle the soup into 8 serving bowls. Sprinkle some cilantro over each serving.

MICHIGAN

THERE'S AN OLD JOKE ABOUT MICHIGAN'S TWO SEASONS, WINTER AND THE FOURTH OF JULY. OR ARE THEY WINTER AND A COUPLE OF WEEKS OF LOUSY SLEDDING? OR MAYBE THERE ARE FOUR: ALMOST WINTER, WINTER, STILL WINTER, AND CONSTRUCTION. Whatever the punch line, don't believe a word of it. Michigan's winter woes are shamelessly exaggerated, and, in any case, they're but a frosty finale to the greatest seasonal performance on any wooded stage in the country. In northern Michigan, fall colors begin to tickle the hardwood leaves around mid-September, moving downstate at a rate of about a hundred miles a week, peaking about a month later. Color tours are autumn's cheapest thrill, when millions of citizens stuff the Thermal Shield picnic cooler with Jif sandwiches and Faygo pop, strap themselves into the family Caravan, and strike out for the wild red yonder simply to admire foliage. Lacking a University of Michigan game on TV, I'm right there in the middle of the convoy.

So what am I doing looking down when everybody else is looking up? Scrounging among yesterday's fallen leaves when overhead, today's leaves scream for attention? The squat, damp, ugly answer is fungus. The Great Lakes area is home to more than two thousand species of fungi, and gathering edible varieties—something like 5 percent—at their source, the forest floor, is a phenomenal way to spend a crisp fall afternoon. As in any autumn wildlife hunt, you'll find that the thrill of the chase, the exercise, the inherent danger, and the delicious end results are all part of the mushrooming program, called "'shrooming" in local terminology. Morels may be the standard by which

Michigan mushrooms are judged, but they're spring sprouters, and mushroom lovers will tell you that autumn in the Midwest produces a wider, more colorful variety. One such pro, Royal Olsen, comes along on today's hunt.

And make no mistake: If you're not a botanist, you'll probably need an expert's input when mushroom hunting. Mycophobia means "fear of mushrooms," and it's founded in some pretty gruesome history. The simple truth is that a wild mushroom can take you down. No matter how much you think you know about them, no matter how much "this one looks like the one in the book," no matter how many years you've been picking, it doesn't take but a single goof to send you to the emergency room—or the morgue. Royal puts it succinctly: "There are old 'shroomers and there are bold 'shroomers, but there are no old, bold 'shroomers."

He shares a one-sentence rule: There are no one-sentence rules. Edible wild mushrooms often have look-alike cousins that are toxic, and old wives' tales are only as good as the old wives; one can only hope that they practiced what they preached. In any event, caution is the best rule of thumb. That said, we're shortly perched over a stout, short-stemmed specimen with a broad reddish central cap: an

'SHROOMING WITH MUSHROOM AFICIONADO ROYAL OLSEN.

Winesap Apple Pesto Chicken Salad

The combination of apples, chicken, and pesto really works. When I had my gourmet deli, this dish was one of my customers' favorites.

SERVES 4

THREE 7 TO 8 OUNCE CHICKEN BREASTS, GRILLED AND JULIENNED

1/2 CUP JULIENNED RED BELL PEPPER

1/2 CUP JULIENNED RED ONION

2 WINESAP APPLES, PEELED, CORED, AND SLICED

1/4 CUP LOW-FAT MAYONNAISE

1/4 CUP PESTO

SALT AND BLACK PEPPER TO TASTE

1 HEAD BIBB LETTUCE

1 BELGIAN ENDIVE

1/2 CUP CHOPPED AND TOASTED PECANS

In a large mixing bowl, combine the chicken, red pepper, red onion, and apples.

In a small mixing bowl, whisk together the mayonnaise and pesto.

Fold the pesto mayonnaise into the chicken mixture and mix well. Season with salt and pepper.

Line 4 serving plates with the lettuce and Belgian endive leaves. Spoon the chicken salad on top. Sprinkle with chopped pecans. Serve immediately.

orange latex milky. It is so named because when bruised, it oozes a brilliantly colored liquid. The flesh of the orange latex milky is firm and somewhat granular in texture, and when doused in olive oil, it makes an ideal candidate for the grill. We quickly add a number of these to the basket, along with hefty handfuls of blewits, a remarkable purplish mushroom that grows in circular patterns. These are the "fairy rings" of folktales—actually the imprints of long-dead tree trunks. Blewits are known for their distinct concentrated aroma that changes with the soil structure and are wonderful sautéed; once cooked, they lend themselves to pickling and can be frozen with good results. An additional bonus is the blewit's striking color, an almost haunting azure that is retained throughout cooking and allows a chef to construct some unique chromatic combinations.

On the return trip, laden with the nucleus of a wild mushroom risotto, we're fortunate to come across a spread of wild leeks—called ramps by some—another gift of the Michigan wilderness. Though these onionlike shoots are most often sought in early spring, when the leaves and flowers are consumed as a local delicacy, the bulb itself remains harvestable until winter. At this time of year the leek's roots are intensely flavored but tough. They'll require long, slow cooking to soften them up, and as such, make a perfect addition to our risotto. The leeks will lend a spicy spunk to the earthy flavors of the wild mushrooms. Those flavors are to me the essence of autumn.

The nectar of autumn is another story. In Michigan, no color tour is complete without a stop at one of the state's nearly one hundred working cider mills and a draft of freshly pressed apple juice. The town of Fenton sports a mill that has been turning out this seasonal squeeze, this amber ambrosia, since the middle of the nineteenth century. The second stop of my fall circuit finds me at historical Parshallville Cider Mill, where the passion for perfecting cider, under the care of owner Mike Haynes, is as fresh as the fruit. Today's cider unites Jonathan and Ida Red, two varieties familiar to apple lovers in the Midwest. The Jonathan apple contributes an aromatic and sugary tang to the union, while Ida Red's dowry is tartness; it's one of the most acidic apples grown, and it's a good keeper—under controlled conditions. An Ida's flavor sharpens and intensifies over a couple of months. When they come into season, Mark likes to add McIntosh, which lends a spicy perfume, the Delicious sisters, Red and Golden, which offer super-sweet juiciness, and Winesap, which came by its name as a result of a winelike aftertaste, adding depth and volume to the body of the cider.

Since different orchards produce different apples, and since those ripen to peakness in their own time throughout the growing season, it's fair to suggest that no blend of cider is ever exactly the same. That, I've found, is one of the consummate pleasures of mill-hopping.

Outside, the towering hardwoods take on the tint of early afternoon. Back on the road I make a sharp detour north, heading for the confluence of Michigan's two nearest neighbors, Lake Michigan and Lake Huron. The pleasures of a state almost completely surrounded by water are not, of course, strictly terrestrial.

For those lacking a worldview or an atlas, Michigan is a pair of twin peninsulas joined at the Mackinac Bridge. Mackinac Island sparkles just below this hinge, slightly off center on the Huron side, a unique destination that has served as a backdrop for several Hollywood period films, most notably 1980's *Somewhere in Time.* Caught in a sort of tourist-focused time warp, Mackinac Island prohibits motorized vehicles, inviting visitors to rely on horses, bicycles, and their shoe soles while offering vibrant visions of the Midwest's romantic Victorian era. Quaint shopping districts line Main Street, and on the island's eight-mile circuit, numerous Greek Revival–style homes, built by fur barons and their ilk, stand in solemn homage to conspicuous consumption. Coupled with breathtaking rockscapes and broad lake vistas, Mackinac Island's unfettered lifestyle attracts hundreds of thousands of visitors every year. Today, I'll be one of them. However, prior to hopping the ferry at Mackinaw City, I have a date with a local beauty, a nineteenth-century shipwreck. I rendezvous with charter

THE "CATCH" OF THE DAY IS ORANGE LATEX MILKY 'SHROOMS.

operator Larry, and within an hour we're four miles south of Mackinaw City, looking to sniff out the wreck of the *William H. Barnum*, which capsized a hundred years ago— with no loss of life, gratefully. The *Barnum* lies in about seventy feet of water, a mile or so off shore.

Larry is a knowledgeable captain, but the dive proves intense, with tricky currents that presage the season's heavy weather. With visibility limited to about ten feet, even with the potent beam of my Super-8 utility light, I descend on a buoy mooring, reveling in the feeling of weightlessness and adjusting to the murk and the chill. Eerie outlines begin to emerge after ten minutes or so, and plumes of silt explode with any aggressive motion. The *Barnum* sits upright, her ribs festooned in grayish barnacles. Like most wooden ships that have foundered in these clear, cold northern waters, she is in a remarkable state of preservation. Wooden bow decking, fixtures, boilers, and props are suspended in cryonic perfection, looking much the same today as in that wretched April in 1894 when the *Barnum* went down.

With all due respect to the memories haunting this maritime mausoleum, suppertime approaches, and as I delve near the galley, I realize that my dive will offer an unexpected bonus, a culinary lagniappe. Prowling the surface of the machinery are hundreds of ferocious olive green crayfish. The meat of this bold little crustacean is sweeter than that of its high-priced cousin, the lobster, and actually stands up better to elaborate sauces. A deft scurry amid the ghostly beams before surfacing, and I have the makings of a sensational meal, to be prepared on the shores of Mackinac; it will be lubricated with one of the beautiful Rieslings grown and produced on nearby Leelanau Peninsula, and followed by the hedonistic, molar-crumbling confection for which the island is justly world famous.

Fudge was introduced to Mackinac Island between seventy-five and a hundred years ago, depending on whom you ask. Its genesis notwithstanding, fudge has been a massive summertime hit, blending an image of handmade quality with connotations of Fourth of July bandshells, small-town vacations, and youthful indulgence. Trusting

today's testimonials, the fudge phenomenon is linked inextricably with Mackinac's corporate culture, and a souvenir slice is as indispensable to visitors as a flask of water is at Lourdes. Up and down the commercial drag, the scent of chocolate and roasting nuts drifts from candy shops as craftsmen throw and toss creamy batches of chocolate rum, vanilla pecan, triple chip, or maple to the delight of drooling pilgrims. The island's major candy makers jockey for position among these passionate throngs, and each claims to set the best fudge in the Milky Way. Naturally, when dealing with a product so voluptuous, sensual, and, frankly, six-ingredient basic, brand loyalty can easily be forgiven.

For what it's worth, at least when this autumn afternoon began to fade, my sweet-tooth led me to Ryba's Fudge Shop, where sugar-smith Ed is skittering around a squeaky clean kitchen. Ed is part of the team that has been whipping

AT RYBA'S FUDGE SHOP ON MACKINAC ISLAND, YOU GET TO WATCH THEM CREATE FRESH FUDGE ON HUGE MARBLE SLABS.

up Ryba's fudge on Mackinac for three generations, and he hasn't lost his taste for the stuff. He eats it every day. His favorite? None of these hifalutin' bells and whistles for Ed—no dried cherries, coconut sprinkles, or amaretto flavorings. He prefers plain ol' chocolate, thank you very much. So that's exactly the batch that I ask him to prepare.

With the practiced hand of an artist, he first combines the sacred six—sugar, corn syrup, shortening, salt, cream, and chocolate—in precise proportions, and over a slow fire he raises the mixture to 232 degrees, stirring steadily to avoid crystallization. What is created is called, in the trade, a "slurry" and is the fudge's "backbone," the balance of sugars, fats, and proteins that will set as a solid when cooled. As an aside, this is the point where most home fudge makers fail, using poor ingredients, miscalculated temperatures, or lousy equipment. For best results, copper, which responds quickly to temperature changes and distributes heat efficiently, is the kettle material of choice.

Once the slurry is completed, Ed pours it onto Ryba's thousand-pound marble slab and begins to paddle, push, and otherwise harass it into a smooth and creamy magma. The marble, meanwhile, tempers the mixture, cooling it evenly. Once creamed, the fudge is formed into a table-length loaf. Ed, even with my eager if somewhat clumsy help, knocks out the twenty-five-pound batch in about twenty minutes.

Twenty-five pounds of chocolate fudge will last the average consumer until Chernobyl is once again inhabitable. For a working chef driving through the crisp Michigan wilderness, heading back downstate with a hyperkinetic crew of assistants, it might hold out for the rest of the night.

Smoked Whitefish and Crayfish Salad

This dish was created after scuba diving with some buddies in October in the Straits of Mackinac. Our goal was to dive on an old wreck, the schooner "Sandusky," which went down in 1890, and pluck some crayfish off its intact hull. Thanks, Larry, James, Bill, and the other Larry.

SERVES 4

20 HARICOTS VERTS, TRIMMED

2 TABLESPOONS RED WINE VINEGAR

1 TABLESPOON HORSERADISH

1/4 CUP DICED RED ONION

1 TABLESPOON CHOPPED FRESH DILL

1/2 CUP LOW-FAT SOUR CREAM

1/2 CUP NONFAT YOGURT

SALT AND BLACK PEPPER TO TASTE

1/2 CUP DICED CELERY

1 CUP PEELED AND SLICED ENGLISH CUCUMBERS (SLICE INTO HALF MOONS)

1 CUP FLAKED SMOKED WHITEFISH

24 CRAYFISH TAILS, COOKED

3/4 CUP CHOPPED MIXED GREENS

Blanch the haricots verts in boiling salted water for 20 seconds. Remove and add them to ice water to preserve their coloring and prevent further cooking.

In a medium mixing bowl, whisk together the red wine vinegar, horseradish, onion, dill, sour cream, and yogurt. Season with salt and pepper. Refrigerate.

In a separate medium mixing bowl, combine the celery, cucumbers, haricots verts, whitefish, and crayfish tails.

Combine the 2 bowls and fold in the mixed greens. Season again with salt and pepper if needed. Serve immediately.

Michigan Autumn Salad with Baked Chèvre Medallions and an Elderberry Vinaigrette

The mild-flavored almond-crusted medallions of goat cheese pair well with the sweetness of elderberry preserves. You want to use a Montrachet-style chèvre in this recipe because it has a mild flavor and also bakes well.

SERVES 4

VINAIGRETTE

1 TABLESPOON ELDERBERRY PRESERVES (PREFERABLY AMERICAN SPOON FOODS)

1/4 CUP RED WINE VINEGAR

1/2 TEASPOON DIJON MUSTARD

2 TABLESPOONS WATER

1/2 CUP OLIVE OIL

SALT AND CRACKED BLACK PEPPER TO TASTE

SALAD

1 GARLIC BULB

8 SLICES BAGUETTE

1/2 POUND CHÈVRE CHEESE

1 CUP TOASTED ALMOND SLICES

4 CUPS BABY MIXED GREENS

8 LEAVES BELGIAN ENDIVE, JULIENNED

1 GRANNY SMITH APPLE, HALVED, CORED, AND THINLY SLICED

1 CUP DRIED CHERRIES

FOR THE VINAIGRETTE: In a blender, combine the preserves, red wine vinegar, mustard, and water. Blend until the ingredients are well incorporated. Slowly drizzle in the olive oil while blending. Season with the salt and pepper. Refrigerate.

FOR THE SALAD: Preheat the oven to 350°F.

Place the garlic bulb in the oven on a baking sheet. Roast the garlic for 25 to 30 minutes, until the cloves are soft. Remove from the oven and peel away the skin to remove the roasted cloves.

Place the baguette slices in the oven on a baking sheet until they are toasted. Remove from the oven and spread a thin coating of roasted garlic on the slices. Set aside.

Lower the oven temperature to 225°F. Divide the chèvre into 8 pieces and form each piece by hand into a medallion. Hold each medallion in your hand and gently press toasted almond slices on all sides of it.

Place the medallions and baguette slices on a baking sheet and place in the oven. Bake for 2 to 3 minutes.

While the medallions are in the oven, toss together the baby greens and elderberry vinaigrette in a medium mixing bowl. Use only enough dressing to coat the leaves.

Remove the medallions and baguette slices from the oven and let cool for 2 minutes.

Portion the greens on 4 plates.

Top the greens with the endive, apple, and dried cherries. Garnish with 2 warm chèvre medallions and 2 warm baguette slices.

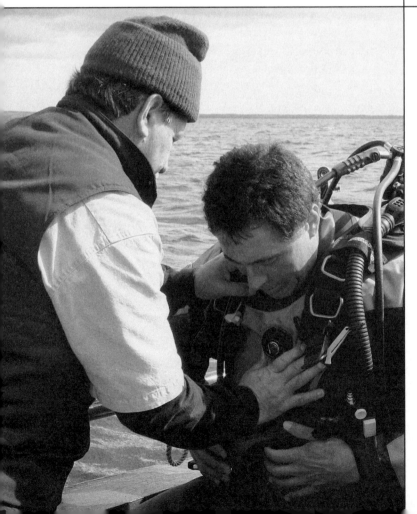

PREPARING FOR AN ICY UNDERWATER SEARCH FOR CRAYFISH, WHICH WE USED WHILE FILMING AN EPISODE OF KEITH FAMIE'S ADVENTURES.

Pumpkin and Butternut Squash Soup

This is my favorite autumn harvest soup. For many years it put many smiles on the faces of my customers at my former restaurant, Les Auteurs.

SERVES **4**

FRIZZLED LEEKS

VEGETABLE OIL FOR FRYING

2 LEEKS, CUT INTO THIN STRIPS

3 TABLESPOONS WATER

YELLOW CORNMEAL FOR DUSTING

SALT AND BLACK PEPPER TO TASTE

SOUP

1½ POUNDS BUTTERNUT SQUASH, HALVED AND SEEDED

1½ POUNDS SMALL COOKING PUMPKIN, HALVED AND SEEDED

6 TABLESPOONS UNSALTED BUTTER

SALT AND BLACK PEPPER TO TASTE

1 SHALLOT, MINCED

½ WHITE ONION, DICED

2 CARROTS, DICED

2 CELERY STALKS, DICED

2 QUARTS CHICKEN STOCK

¼ TEASPOON GROUND ALLSPICE

¼ TEASPOON CHOPPED ORANGE ZEST

GARNISH

1 TABLESPOON CHOPPED FRESH FLAT-LEAF PARSLEY

FOR THE FRIZZLED LEEKS: In a 1-gallon pot, add 2 inches of oil. Heat the oil to 350°F.

Place the leeks in a medium mixing bowl. Drizzle water over the leeks and then coat lightly with the cornmeal. Fry the leeks in the oil until golden brown.

Remove the leeks from the oil and drain on paper towels. Season with salt and pepper.

FOR THE SOUP: Preheat the oven to 350°F.

Place the squash and pumpkin halves on a baking sheet, cut sides up. Scatter 2 tablespoons of butter over the squash and pumpkin, and season with salt and pepper. Bake for 45 minutes, or until the flesh is soft.

Remove the squash and pumpkin from the oven and allow to cool. Remove the skins.

In a large stockpot over medium heat, sauté the shallot and onion in 2 tablespoons of butter until translucent. Add the carrots and celery, and sauté an additional 10 minutes. Add the stock and simmer for 10 minutes. Add the squash, pumpkin, allspice, and orange zest, and simmer 10 minutes more.

In a food processor or using an immersion blender, puree the soup. Add 2 tablespoons of butter during the blending process. Strain the soup through a fine sieve, then return it to the stockpot. Bring to a simmer. Season with salt and pepper.

Ladle the soup into 4 serving bowls. Garnish each serving with frizzled leeks and chopped parsley.

Cornmeal-Crusted Lake Perch with Young Spinach and Roasted Tomato-Fennel Marinara

Growing up in Michigan surrounded by the Great Lakes, I have had my share of lake perch dishes over the years, but this has to be my favorite. The roasted tomato-fennel marinara is also ideal as a pasta sauce.

SERVES 4

MARINARA

1 FENNEL BULB

SALT AND BLACK PEPPER TO TASTE

¼ CUP OLIVE OIL

6 PLUM TOMATOES, DICED

1 WHITE ONION, DICED

1 GARLIC CLOVE, PEELED AND MINCED

1 CUP TOMATO JUICE

½ CUP WATER

2 TABLESPOONS WHOLE-GRAIN MUSTARD

1½ TEASPOONS CHOPPED FRESH BASIL

PERCH

2 POUNDS LAKE PERCH FILLETS, TRIMMED AND PINBONED

SALT AND BLACK PEPPER TO TASTE

YELLOW CORNMEAL FOR DUSTING

ALL-PURPOSE FLOUR FOR DREDGING

1 CUP CANOLA OIL

SPINACH

¼ CUP OLIVE OIL

2 GARLIC CLOVES, PEELED AND MINCED

2 POUNDS BABY SPINACH

SALT AND BLACK PEPPER TO TASTE

GARNISH

4 FRESH BASIL SPRIGS

FOR THE MARINARA: Preheat the oven to 350°F.

Cut the fennel bulb in half. Season with salt and pepper. Place the fennel on a baking sheet, brush lightly with olive oil, and roast until tender, about 30 to 40 minutes. Remove from the oven, let cool to room temperature, and dice.

Heat the remaining olive oil in a medium saucepan over medium heat. Sauté the tomatoes, onion, and garlic for 3 minutes. Add the fennel, tomato juice, water, and mustard. Continue to cook for 3 minutes. Stir in the basil. Remove from the heat and puree in a blender. Return to the saucepan and season with salt and pepper. Keep warm on the back of the stove.

FOR THE PERCH: Lay out the fillets on paper towels. Season each side with salt and pepper. Dredge the fillets in equal parts of cornmeal and flour.

In a large sauté pan over medium-high heat, heat the canola oil until it is hot enough for frying. Fry the fillets, skin side up, until golden brown. Turn over and continue to cook until golden brown. Drain on paper towels.

FOR THE SPINACH: Heat the olive oil in a large sauté pan over medium heat. Add the garlic and sauté until caramelized. Add the spinach and sauté just until the spinach is wilted. Season with salt and pepper.

TO ASSEMBLE: Spoon the roasted tomato-fennel marinara onto 4 plates. Finish by dividing the perch and spinach among the plates. Garnish with a sprig of basil. Serve hot.

Au Sable River Rainbow Trout in a Pouch

There are many great trout streams in Michigan, and this is a perfect recipe for the campfire during a fishing trip. The steam created in the aluminum pouch cooks the trout and vegetables, and combines the flavors really well.

SERVES **4**

¼ CUP OLIVE OIL

FOUR 6-OUNCE FILLETS RAINBOW TROUT, TRIMMED

SALT AND BLACK PEPPER TO TASTE

12 RAMPS, CLEANED AND TRIMMED, OR 1 CUP DICED LEEKS

1 CUP SLICED BUTTON MUSHROOMS

1 CUP DICED PLUM TOMATOES

4 FRESH THYME SPRIGS

4 TABLESPOONS UNSALTED BUTTER

½ CUP WHITE WINE

2 TABLESPOONS CHOPPED FRESH FLAT-LEAF PARSLEY

If camping, make a campfire. If preparing at home, preheat the oven to 400°F.

Tear off 4 pieces of aluminum foil, large enough to make a pouch for each trout fillet. Brush the foil with olive oil to prevent sticking. Place each trout fillet in the center of a piece of foil. Brush each fillet with olive oil and season with salt and pepper.

Place on top of each trout fillet a layer of ramps, mushrooms, and tomatoes. Season again lightly with salt and pepper. Finish with a thyme sprig and 1 tablespoon of butter.

Begin to fold the aluminum foil to form a pouch. Before sealing, add 2 tablespoons of wine to each pouch. Seal the pouches and place on the hot campfire coals or on a baking sheet in the oven. Cook for 20 to 25 minutes.

Unfold the pouches, being careful to avoid the hot steam that is released.

Garnish each serving with parsley and serve hot.

Medallions of Venison with Wild Ramp Risotto and Demi-Glace

Michigan has long been a great state for hunting. Here is a recipe for those deer-hunting guys and gals. Veal or beef tenderloin can also be used in this recipe.

SERVES 4

DEMI-GLACE

¼ CUP DICED WHITE ONION

2 TABLESPOONS UNSALTED BUTTER

½ CUP DICED PLUM TOMATOES

½ CUP PORT WINE

2 CUPS VEAL STOCK

1 FRESH THYME SPRIG

SALT AND BLACK PEPPER TO TASTE

RISOTTO

½ CUP MOREL MUSHROOMS

2 TABLESPOONS UNSALTED BUTTER

12 WILD RAMPS, CLEANED AND CHOPPED, OR ¾ CUP DICED
   LEEKS

¼ CUP CREAM SHERRY

1 CUP ARBORIO RICE

4 CUPS CHICKEN STOCK

SALT AND BLACK PEPPER TO TASTE

¼ CUP GRATED PARMIGIANO-REGGIANO CHEESE

VENISON

EIGHT 3-OUNCE VENISON MEDALLIONS

SALT AND BLACK PEPPER TO TASTE

2 TABLESPOONS UNSALTED BUTTER

FOR THE DEMI-GLACE: In a medium saucepan over medium heat, sweat the onion in 1 tablespoon of butter. Add the tomatoes when the onion is translucent. Sauté for 3 minutes. Add the port and reduce by one-half. Add the veal stock and thyme. Simmer slowly until reduced by one-half, about 20 to 25 minutes.

Whisk in the remaining tablespoon of cold butter. Season with salt and pepper. Strain through a fine sieve and keep warm on the back of the stove.

(recipe continues)

FOR THE RISOTTO: In a large sauté pan over medium heat, sauté the morels in the butter for 3 to 5 minutes. Add the ramps and sauté until wilted, about 1 minute. Add the cream sherry, flame off the alcohol, and reduce by one-half. Add the rice and sauté for 1 minute. Add the chicken stock in 3 stages while continually stirring the risotto with a wooden spoon. When the rice has absorbed the first stage of liquid, add the second, and so on. When all the chicken stock has been absorbed, season the risotto with salt and pepper and stir in the cheese.

If the rice still has a bite to it, add more chicken stock. Once the rice is finished, keep warm on the back of the stove.

FOR THE VENISON: Preheat the oven to 350°F.

Season each medallion with salt and pepper.

In a large sauté pan over medium heat, sear the medallions on each side in the butter. Place the medallions in an ovenproof dish and cook to the desired internal temperature. I suggest medium-rare. Let the medallions rest for 5 minutes before serving.

Serve 2 venison medallions per person, along with a portion of wild ramp risotto and demi-glace.

"Cousin Jacks" Pasties

Cornish miners, known as "Cousin Jacks," brought these meat pies to the Upper Peninsula in the 1850s when the copper and iron mines were first opened. The men warmed their pies on a mining shovel held over their head lamp candles while in the mines.

SERVES 6

EGG WASH
1 LARGE EGG
2 TABLESPOONS WHOLE MILK
DOUGH
3 CUPS ALL-PURPOSE FLOUR
2 TEASPOONS SALT
1 CUP SOLID VEGETABLE SHORTENING
2 TABLESPOONS UNSALTED BUTTER
3/4 CUP COLD WATER

MEAT FILLING

1½ POUNDS GROUND BEEF

2½ CUPS SHREDDED RUSSET POTATOES

1 CUP DICED WHITE ONIONS

1 CUP PEELED AND SHREDDED RUTABAGA

1 CUP SHREDDED CARROTS

4 TABLESPOONS WORCESTERSHIRE SAUCE

1½ TABLESPOONS SALT

2 TEASPOONS GROUND BLACK PEPPER

2 TABLESPOONS UNSALTED BUTTER

FOR THE EGG WASH: In a small mixing bowl, whisk together the egg and milk.

FOR THE DOUGH: On a clean work surface, sift the flour and salt together. Cut in the shortening and butter with a pastry cutter or 2 knives. Add the water and work by hand until the dough pulls together. Form the dough into a ball and let it rest for 30 minutes.

While the dough is resting, prepare the meat filling.

In a large mixing bowl, combine all the ingredients but the butter. Mixing by hand works best. Divide the filling into 6 portions, which should amount to about 1 cup per serving.

Preheat the oven to 400°F.

TO ASSEMBLE THE PASTIES: Divide the dough into 6 equal pieces. On a floured surface, use a rolling pin to roll out each piece into a circle about 7 inches in diameter.

Place the filling in the center of the dough circle. Place 1 teaspoon of butter on top of each portion of filling and seal the edges by applying water with your finger. Use a fork to crimp the edges. Brush the top of the pasties with the egg wash and prick with a fork.

Bake on a buttered baking sheet for 30 to 35 minutes. The pasties are finished when the outside crust is golden brown.

Remove the pasties from the oven and serve hot.

Traverse City Cherry Crunch

Traverse City is known as the "Cherry Capital of the World." Every July the town holds the National Cherry Festival to celebrate the harvest.

SERVES 8

FILLING

3 CUPS PITTED BALSTON CHERRIES OR ANY OTHER TART CHERRY

1/2 CUP GRANULATED SUGAR

CRUNCH

1 CUP (PACKED) BROWN SUGAR

1/4 CUP GRANULATED SUGAR

1 CUP QUICK OATS

1/2 CUP ALL-PURPOSE FLOUR

1 TEASPOON GROUND CINNAMON

1/2 TEASPOON GROUND NUTMEG

1/4 POUND (1 STICK) UNSALTED BUTTER

Preheat the oven to 350°F.

FOR THE FILLING: In a medium mixing bowl, fold together the cherries and granulated sugar.

FOR THE CRUNCH: Combine the brown sugar, granulated sugar, oats, flour, cinnamon, and nutmeg. Cut the butter into the dry ingredients with a pastry cutter, fork, or 2 knives.

Firmly press half of the crunch mixture into the bottom of a buttered 8 × 8-inch baking dish. Gently pack the cherry mix on the pressed crunch crust. Pack the rest of the crunch mix on top of the cherry filling.

Bake, uncovered, for 40 to 45 minutes, or until the crunch topping is lightly browned. Remove from the oven and let cool for 10 minutes.

Serve warm with your favorite ice cream.

Autumn Apple Bake

Here's one of my favorite Michigan autumn desserts. It's guaranteed to be a guest pleaser. It combines the great flavors of apples and dried cherries.

SERVES 4

2 LARGE EGGS

1/4 CUP MILK

4 GRANNY SMITH APPLES

1/2 CUP CHOPPED RAISINS

2 CUPS CHOPPED PECANS

1 CUP CHOPPED DRIED CHERRIES

1 TEASPOON GROUND CINNAMON

1/4 POUND (1 STICK) UNSALTED BUTTER, MELTED

5 SHEETS PUFF PASTRY, 6 × 6 INCHES

Preheat the oven to 400°F.

In a medium mixing bowl, whisk together the eggs and milk to make an egg wash.

Peel the apples and completely hollow out the cores with a melon baller.

In a food processor, place the raisins, pecans, dried cherries, cinnamon, and butter. Puree until the mixture has the consistency of a paste.

Fill the apples from both ends with the paste. Wrap each apple with a sheet of puff pastry.

With a paring knife, cut 1 sheet of puff pastry into the shape of leaves. Decorate the top of each apple with 2 leaves. Brush the puff pastry dough with the egg wash.

Bake the apples on a baking sheet until golden brown, approximately 20 minutes.

Serve with ice cream and top with whipped cream.

SEATTLE

SEATTLE IS SLOSH. THERE'S SILVERY GREEN ELLIOT BAY TO THE WEST, LAKE WASHINGTON TO THE EAST, THE CASCADES AN EVER-THAWING BACKDROP IN THE DISTANCE, AND A SATURATED AWNING HOVERING OVER PUGET SOUND THAT SENDS LIQUID TENDRILS INTO EVERY CRANNY AND TURNED-UP COLLAR.

No one likes to pigeonhole or shore up soggy reputations, of course, and according to well-respected locals, Seattle enjoys seccant summers, juiceless Julys, and arid Augusts. They gamely point out that, statistically, Seattle is less cloudy than Eugene, Oregon, that it's far more humid in New Orleans, and that it gets less overall precipitation than Sault Sainte Marie—all of which is like saying you have got the best tan at the Pillsbury Dough Boy convention. For the vast majority of the year (October through June) Seattle is wet. Wetter than wet. Realists don't try to hide it, and the hand-scrawled sign in the window of the Seattle Shirt Company says it all: WE HAVE UMBRELLAS. The motto of the Visitor and Convention Bureau is "Seattle: Soak It Up." Even its ballplayers are Mariners, and Safeco Field was specifically engineered around rain-outs. There's a clinically documented mass hysteria known as Northwest Mania that sweeps the citizenry whenever the sun puts in a cameo. At such times a local colloquialism goes, "Hey, look, the mountains are out today."

None of which is bad, mind you, especially for those of us on culinary odysseys. Relentless chills and soppy clothing produce a driving need for all things warm and toasty. The waxed coffee cup, clutched in the damp mitts of passersby, is indispensable to the Seattle look; even the winos use them. In November, with dull, steady, endless drizzles leaking from a steel-gray canopy and humid cedar-scented winds kicking in from Puget Sound, Seattle is a water world, and there's a collective demand for richly flavored pick-me-ups. Up and down the downtown arteries—Union, Pike, and Pine Streets—the bittersweet and vaguely oily aroma of freshly roasted, freshly ground, freshly brewed java bores through the gloom like a lighthouse beacon, and behind countless steam-spewing storefronts customers chant with straight faces, "Double-tall, no-foam, half-caf, add-a-shot-of-butterscotch in a cup with wings," and are understood.

Trendy lexicon aside, Seattle's caffeine cuddle began early in its history: A front-page ad running in a 1900 *Post-Intelligencer* offers mocha and java beans at forty cents per pound. Precisely when coffee cast aside the aura of a lifestyle and became an all-consuming addiction is less clear. It seems to be a fairly recent phenomenon. In 1989, *New York Times* food writer Marian Burros was so awed by the Svengali hold that the bean had on Seattle that she wrote, "In ordinary American cities the aroma of espresso does not emanate from local department stores, nor can it be purchased on street corners and in libraries. But Seattle is no ordinary American city."

In the years since, New York, along with the rest of the nation, has pretty much contracted espresso fever, and it's a good bet that plenty of cafés don't even serve drip coffee anymore. Seattle's own Starbucks, a now-clichéd success story, had a handful of outlets in 1989, mostly sprinkled throughout the Northwest. Today, they're popping up like chanterelles after an autumn shower. There are more than four thousand to date, with an average of three opening every day. Forget about Burros's libraries and department stores; a Starbucks is currently trafficking Frappuccino inside a church lobby in Munster, Indiana, and the world's busiest Starbucks outlet is in downtown Tokyo, the heart of tea country. Then again, Seattle itself was originally a tea destination, and the first scheduled steamer service between the Orient and the U.S.A. hit these shores in 1896. What goes around . . . ?

Apple Cinnamon Rice Pudding

Growing up in Michigan, I can understand why the people from Washington get excited about autumn. It's apple season, and Washington produces some great varieties of apples, such as Red Delicious and Granny Smith. Washington actually produces over half of all the apples that Americans consume.

SERVES 6

1 CUP LONG-GRAIN WHITE RICE

1 1/2 CUPS WATER

1/4 TEASPOON SALT

3 CUPS WHOLE MILK

1/2 CUP SUGAR

1/2 CUP GOLDEN RAISINS

1 1/2 TEASPOONS GROUND CINNAMON

1 1/2 TEASPOONS VANILLA EXTRACT

2 CUPS PEELED, CORED, AND DICED
   GRANNY SMITH APPLES

In a medium saucepan over medium heat, combine the rice, water, and salt. Cook for 10 to 15 minutes, or until the water is absorbed.

Add the milk, sugar, raisins, cinnamon, vanilla, and apples to the saucepan. Cook, uncovered, for 30 minutes.

The rice pudding is done when the rice and milk have formed a thick porridge.

Serve the pudding either warm or cold.

Brand equity aside, the original idea pioneered by Starbucks visionaries was simple enough: *Brew it right, and they will come.* Come they have, and left vibrating like a tuning fork. So take the quality concept and raise it exponentially, remove the juggernaut licensing strategy, transform *barista* ("espresso maker") from a summer gig into a hallowed calling, and you'll wind up with something like Caffè Vita, where founders Michael Prins and Michael McConnell have been roasting up their own field of dreams since 1995. Compared to Starbucks' industrial supernova, Caffè Vita's expansion has been gloriously unremarkable: To date there are three retail outlets, all fairly nondescript, all in Seattle. The product, however, is a different story. It was precisely the gap left by the mega-growth of "the big guys" (their term) that the duo sought to fill: "We buy and roast our beans in small quantities," explains Prins. "In order to have amazing-tasting coffee, you have to have the highest quality green beans. And freshness is just as important. Our coffee is rotated every two or three days, whereas coffee purchased in grocery stores can be thirty, sometimes sixty days old."

A third and equally vital factor in assuring that coffee reaches its flavor potential is the individual barista who prepares the brew, and making certain that the shot-pulling, milk-steaming front line knows its job is where Mike and Mike earn their most outré notoriety. At Caffè Vita, barista wannabes are compelled to undergo intensive apprenticeships that can last up to a year. Says Prins, "It takes a lot of practice and many months before a barista can consistently perfect all the techniques—especially the latte art." During that time, fledgling baristas learn grinding, extraction, and milk-steaming techniques, and do not fly a joe-jerking solo shift until a mentor confirms that the lessons have sunk in.

A few blocks north of Caffè Vita stands Rachel, the life-sized piggy bank that guards the maw of Seattle's top culinary attraction, Pike Place Market. Rachel has been accepting donations, cooling kids' butts, and generally riding marketplace sentry since 1987, but it's been nearly a century since local farmers, craftsmen, and fishermen first began plying trade throughout this labyrinth of stalls and stores. The massive neon sign and retro clock capping the place are as familiar to Seattle foodies as the Space Needle is to Jetson fans. Nearly a casualty of a newfangled sixties notion (the supermarket), a group of plucky citizens defied city hall's odds and spent years lobbying, protesting, and fund-raising before finally salvaging it from the wrecking crew in 1971. It has repaid the favor many times. Contained by the piers of Elliot Bay and bordered by Virginia Street, Union Street, and 1st Avenue, Pike Place now sprawls across nine funky, frenetic, and food-flooded acres and receives more than 9 million visitors every year.

The best way to tour a local market, of course, is with a

IF YOU EVER GET TO SEATTLE, YOU HAVE TO VISIT PIKE PLACE MARKET, WHERE YOU WILL SEE SOME OF THE FRESHEST SEAFOOD EVER!

local chef, and I track down Chef Michael Weeks of Seattle's incomparable Dragonfish Asian Cafe in the Paramount Hotel as he begins a shopping romp. Each morning he wends among the six-hundred-plus day stalls, high stalls, and storefronts in order to lay essential super-fresh foundations for that day's menu. He's been at it for years and is eager to share advice, explaining some of the market's terminology. Day stalls, for example, are transient farm tables set up by local growers to offer just-picked produce; high stalls are permanent fixtures offering fresh items from around the globe; wet tables are for produce, dry tables are for crafts, and the Sanitary Market was so-named early in the market's history because horses were not permitted inside.

Seattle seafood is the showstopper. Four fishmongers operate daily, offering a succulent selection of indigenous species. Judd Cove oysters, Penn Cove mussels, Manila clams, and Dungeness crabs rest on ice beds; Chef Michael casts his expert eye across the rows of freshly caught fish.

Troll-caught salmon can be found at phenomenal prices (evidently, Seattle trolls work cheap), and the variety is

THE FISH AT PIKE PLACE IS SO FRESH IT'S STILL JUMPING. ACTUALLY, I WAS ABLE TO STEP INTO A LOCAL RITUAL: TOSSING THE SALMON BACK AND FORTH ACROSS THE COUNTER AS A SHOW FOR THE CUSTOMERS.

amazing. Today's Red King catch, with its rosy flesh, is leaner than the Kings—fattier fish that show up with white-colored meat. Chef Michael selects several hefty coho that will be transformed into one of his most popular dishes, grilled and marinated Five-Spice Salmon. Likewise, my own chef's instincts kick in when confronted with such beautiful seafood, and I envision countless dishes, both complex and simple, in which these beautiful clear-eyed fish are sautéed to golden brown alongside fresh chanterelle, shiitake, hedgehog, and porcini mushrooms.

Once our fish selection is pointed out, the mongers go bonkers; that is, they perform the ritual fish toss that began as a practical means to get just-purchased fish back to the processors and has now become something of a Las Vegas floor show. It's shtick, but it's effective shtick, and certainly the most popular happening at the market. The fish "pitcher" seizes the tail and underbelly, and does a softball fling, sending the hapless brute past the counter, over the heads of employees, to his partner, who catches it with a sharp, wet, cold thwack against a sheet of wrapping paper. Seen once, it's impressive; seen again and again, without a miss, it's sort of mind-boggling. It's something I'm obligated to try, if only to prove to my ever-waiting production crew that I'm up to the task of catching one of these 20-pound monsters—and I am. Crowds are omnipresent from the first moment a fish flies, and the humor of the players seems boundless; as a group, they never tire of the accolades, the awe, the admiration—all except one rubber-booted, sopped-apron, scale-speckled teenager on the receiving end, who looks over in a moment of genuine angst after a particularly aggressive toss, saying, "Is this *my* life?"

People watching is as rich a market pastime as food finding. Everywhere, woolen hats gird pates and Annie Hall scarves ring necks, but, oddly, only a few locals are clutching umbrellas. Apparently, nobody who actually lives in this soggy climate wants to be seen as cowed into accessorizing.

Oh, that crazy climate. It's been a human lifestyle factor since time immemorial. At the 1854 treaty negotiation,

PIKE PLACE SQUID WITH ARTICHOKES AND CAPERS

THIS IS A TRADITIONAL ITALIAN DISH INSPIRED BY THE FRESH SQUID I PURCHASED FROM PIKE PLACE MARKET.

SERVES 4

2 TABLESPOONS OLIVE OIL

1½ POUNDS SQUID, CLEANED, BODY CUT INTO RINGS, AND TENTACLES LEFT WHOLE

2 GARLIC CLOVES, MINCED

¼ CUP DICED WHITE ONION

2 TABLESPOONS CAPERS

1 CUP SMALL ARTICHOKE HEARTS, CANNED, DRAINED, AND HALVED

½ CUP PITTED KALAMATA OLIVES

2 PLUM TOMATOES, DICED

½ CUP WHITE WINE

JUICE OF 2 LEMONS

2 TABLESPOONS CHOPPED FRESH FLAT-LEAF PARSLEY

1 TABLESPOON UNSALTED BUTTER

SALT AND BLACK PEPPER TO TASTE

Heat the olive oil in a sauté pan over high heat. Sauté the squid until it begins to brown, approximately 3 minutes. It is very important that the pan be hot. Add the garlic and onion. Sauté for 1 minute. Add the capers, artichokes, olives, and tomatoes, and cook for 1 additional minute. Add the wine and lemon juice, and reduce the liquid by one-half. Stir in the parsley and butter. Season with salt and pepper. Serve hot.

At Tillicum Village, Roland Lucero cooks salmon on cedar planks over an alder wood fire.

during which these lands were first ceded to the settlers, the city's namesake, Chief Seattle, is said to have declared, "Yonder sky has wept tears of compassion upon my people for centuries untold."

In fact, signing that particular treaty cost Chief Seattle and the Suquamish tribe most of their traditional stomping grounds in return for a few small reservations and the promise of government handouts. The subsequent erosion of Suquamish culture is a tragedy that, sadly, offsets some of the magnificent scenery of the Pacific Northwest. In an effort to "Americanize" Suquamish children during the last century, boarding schools adopted them and then forbade them access to tribal traditions. Many of these vital cultural links were lost forever.

Today, however, on a small cedar-studded island in Puget Sound, a group of theatrical whizbangs and Native American dancers, under the direction of acclaimed choreographer Greg Thompson, are working to revive and preserve a modicum of that culture.

The Tillicum experience is a marvelous time machine for exploring the culinary history of north coast Native Americans. As soon as you disembark, you're handed a bowl of juicy littleneck clams, caught seaside and steamed over roaring fires built along the beach. Shells are discarded at your feet and ground into shards by passing shoes, adding to the crunchy white sward that spreads before the longhouse.

Inside, alder fires smolder. This aromatic and hot-burning wood is ideal for roasting and curing fish, and fillets of coho salmon are lashed to cedar posts to form a teepee around the heat source. After an hour the succulent fish is ready and served with lemon butter alongside fresh vegetables and a salad of northwest winter greens. This method of preparing salmon, according to Mark Hewitt, son of Tillicum's founder and current president, is steeped in native prehistory.

The availability of such coastal delights as geoducks, accessible to enterprising clam diggers on inland beaches alongside Pacific oysters (developed locally to replace the native but vanishing Olympias), Dungeness crabs, and chowder-ready cockles, makes Seattle one of the world's shellfish capitals. Add to the mix sparkling blue salmon-heavy waters and the almost limitless bounty of agriculture that surrounds them, and Seattle holds its own against the best food cities to be found. As for the weather, sitting seaside, with waves lapping, gulls squawking, and misty mountains slipping in and out of silver wreaths, who minds a little drizzle?

Henry Wadsworth Longfellow, whose description of Olympic hemlocks remains one of the prettiest passages in his poetry, put it this way: "The best thing to do when it rains is . . . let it rain."

AMID THE BONE-CHILLING WATERS AND HEAVY CURRENT NEAR ORCAS ISLAND, THE CATCH OF THE DAY WAS RED ROCK CRAB.

CRAB AND CORN BISQUE

What a combination! The sweetness of the crab and corn really makes for a delicious bisque. This is a chunky-style bisque as opposed to the creamy-style bisques you normally see.

SERVES 4

GARNISH

2 TABLESPOONS OLIVE OIL

1 EAR OF CORN, KERNELS CUT OFF THE COB

2 TABLESPOONS CHOPPED FRESH FLAT-LEAF PARSLEY

4 TABLESPOONS GRATED PARMESAN CHEESE

BISQUE

1/4 POUND (1 STICK) PLUS 2 TABLESPOONS BUTTER

3/4 CUP ALL-PURPOSE FLOUR

1/2 CUP DICED WHITE ONION

1/2 CUP DICED CELERY

2 CUPS CORN KERNELS

1/2 CUP DICED RED BELL PEPPER

4 CUPS CLAM JUICE

1 CUP WATER

1 CUP HEAVY CREAM

1 1/2 CUPS LUMP CRABMEAT

SALT AND BLACK PEPPER TO TASTE

FOR THE GARNISH: Heat the olive oil in a medium sauté pan over medium heat. Sauté the corn kernels until golden in color. Toss the kernels with the parsley. Keep warm on the back of the stove.

FOR THE BISQUE: In a medium sauté pan over medium heat, melt the 1/4 pound of butter and whisk in the flour until incorporated. Remove from the heat and allow to cool to room temperature. This is a blond roux.

Heat the 2 tablespoons of butter in a 1-gallon stockpot over medium heat. Sauté the onion, celery, corn kernels, and red bell pepper for 5 to 6 minutes, or until tender. Add the clam juice and water, and bring to a simmer. Stir in the roux until fully dissolved. Cook, while stirring, until the bisque begins to thicken.

Stir in the cream and simmer the mixture for 10 minutes to remove the starchy flavor of the roux.

Fold in the crabmeat. Season with salt and pepper. Simmer an additional 5 minutes.

Ladle the bisque into 4 serving bowls. Garnish each serving with a spoonful of the parsley-corn garnish and 1 tablespoon of grated Parmesan cheese.

BREADED RAZOR CLAMS

A RAZOR CLAM IS A SAND-BURROWING CLAM WITH AN ELONGATED TUBULAR SHELL. IT CAN BE COERCED OUT OF ITS BURROW BY BAITING IT WITH SOME COARSE SALT PLACED AT THE ENTRANCE.

SERVES 4

VEGETABLE OIL FOR FRYING
12 LARGE RAZOR CLAMS, SHUCKED
SALT AND BLACK PEPPER TO TASTE
2 CUPS CRACKER MEAL OR BREAD CRUMBS
1 TEASPOON GARLIC POWDER
½ CUP CHOPPED FRESH FLAT-LEAF PARSLEY
1 TEASPOON SALT
1 TEASPOON LEMON PEPPER
3 LARGE EGGS
COCKTAIL SAUCE

Fill a medium stockpot halfway with vegetable oil and heat to 350°F.

Lay out all the razor clams on paper towels to absorb any surface moisture. The outside of the clams must be dry for the breading to stick. Season the clams with salt and black pepper.

In a large mixing bowl, combine the cracker meal, garlic powder, parsley, salt, and lemon pepper.

In a medium bowl, beat the eggs.

Dip the razor clams one by one into the eggs and then into the breading mixture. When all the razor clams are breaded, fry them in the hot oil.

When the clams are golden brown, drain on paper towels.

Serve immediately with cocktail sauce.

Tillicum Salmon and Corn Chowder

Tillicum is a Chinook word meaning "friendly people," which best describes Mark Hewitt and Jim Cacabelos. These individuals helped us experience northwest coast Native American culture and cuisine through their program at Tillicum Village on Blake Island in Puget Sound.

SERVES 6

1/2 CUP DICED CELERY

1/2 CUP DICED WHITE ONION

1 CUP UNCOOKED CORN KERNELS

2 1/2 CUPS DICED RUSSET POTATOES

1 TABLESPOON UNSALTED BUTTER

5 CUPS WHOLE MILK

1 POUND SALMON, CUT INTO LARGE DICE

1 CUP THINLY SLICED SCALLIONS (WHITE PARTS ONLY, CUT ON THE BIAS)

1/2 POUND SPINACH, CHOPPED

1 TABLESPOON CHOPPED FRESH DILL

SALT AND BLACK PEPPER TO TASTE

6 TABLESPOONS GRATED PARMESAN CHEESE

In a 1-gallon stockpot over medium heat, sauté the celery, onion, corn kernels, and potatoes in the butter until the onion is tender. Add the milk and simmer for 25 minutes, or until the potatoes are tender.

Add the salmon and simmer another 8 to 10 minutes. Stir in the scallions, spinach, and dill. Simmer for 2 to 3 minutes. Season with salt and pepper.

Ladle the chowder into 6 serving bowls. Sprinkle 1 tablespoon of cheese over each serving. Serve hot.

Cioppino

Cioppino is the Italian equivalent of bouilla-baisse. In Seattle you can find this dish in many restaurants. One thing is for sure: The seafood will be fresh! Don't forget the crusty French bread.

SERVES 4 TO 6

1/2 CUP OLIVE OIL

1 CUP DICED WHITE ONIONS

2 GARLIC CLOVES, MINCED

1 1/2 CUPS DICED PLUM TOMATOES

1 CUP TOMATO JUICE

1/2 CUP WHITE WINE

4 CUPS CLAM JUICE

12 LARGE SHRIMP, PEELED AND DEVEINED

12 MUSSELS, DEBEARDED

12 MANILA OR LITTLENECK CLAMS

1 CUP LARGE-DICED SALMON

1 CUP LARGE-DICED LINGCOD OR COD

1 CUP BAY SCALLOPS

1/2 CUP DUNGENESS OR LUMP CRABMEAT

1 CUP FRESH SHUCKED OYSTERS

1 TABLESPOON CHOPPED FRESH BASIL

1 TABLESPOON CHOPPED FRESH OREGANO

1 TABLESPOON CHOPPED FRESH FLAT-LEAF PARSLEY

1 WHOLE BAY LEAF

SALT AND BLACK PEPPER TO TASTE

FRENCH BREAD

Heat the olive oil in a 2-gallon stockpot over medium heat. Sweat the onions and garlic until tender, approximately 4 minutes. Add the tomatoes and cook an additional 2 to 3 minutes. Add the tomato juice, wine, clam juice, shrimp, mussels, clams, salmon, and lingcod.

When the shellfish open, add the scallops, crabmeat, oysters, basil, oregano, parsley, and bay leaf. Simmer an additional 8 minutes.

Season with salt and pepper. Remove the bay leaf.

Ladle the cioppino into serving bowls. Serve with a piece of crusty French bread.

Dungeness Crab Salad with Avocado, Cucumber, Tomato, and Basil

While at Rosario Resort and Spa on Orcas Island, Chef Geddes Martin prepared one of his house specialties for me after a long day of scuba diving. You will find that the lemon dressing really pulls the flavors of this dish together.

SERVES 4

BASIL OIL

2 CUPS FRESH BASIL LEAVES

1 CUP CANOLA OIL

SEA SALT TO TASTE

TOMATO OIL

1 RIPE, BRIGHT RED BEEFSTEAK TOMATO

1 GARLIC CLOVE, PEELED

1 CUP WATER

1/2 CUP EXTRA-VIRGIN OLIVE OIL

SEA SALT TO TASTE

LEMON DRESSING

1 TEASPOON CHOPPED SHALLOT

1/2 CUP FRESH LEMON JUICE

ZEST OF 2 LEMONS, FINELY CHOPPED

1/2 CUP EXTRA-VIRGIN OLIVE OIL

1 CUP CANOLA OIL

SEA SALT AND BLACK PEPPER TO TASTE

SUGAR TO TASTE

SALAD

2 RIPE AVOCADOS, PEELED AND CUT INTO MEDIUM DICE

2 RIPE TOMATOES, CUT INTO MEDIUM DICE

1 CUCUMBER, PEELED, SEEDED, AND CUT INTO MEDIUM DICE

1 TABLESPOON CHOPPED FRESH BASIL

1 TEASPOON CHOPPED FRESH TARRAGON

1 TEASPOON CHOPPED FRESH CHIVES

1 TEASPOON CHOPPED FENNEL FRONDS

1/2 POUND FRESH DUNGENESS OR LUMP CRABMEAT

2 CUPS MIXED GREENS

1 CUP CHERRY TOMATOES, CUT IN HALF

SEA SALT AND FRESHLY CRACKED BLACK PEPPER TO TASTE

FOR THE BASIL OIL: Bring about 3 cups of salted water to a rapid boil. Place the basil leaves in the water for 10 seconds, then strain immediately. Plunge the leaves in an ice bath to stop the cooking process and preserve the bright green color. Squeeze all the water from the leaves. In a blender or using an immersion blender, blend the oil and blanched basil until the leaves are finely pureed. Season with salt. You may use this as is, or you can strain the leaves to remove the oil. I prefer to leave the leaves in the oil as long as they remain green. Set aside at room temperature.

FOR THE TOMATO OIL: Core and seed the tomato and cut it into quarters. Place it in a saucepan with the garlic and water. Cook over medium heat until the tomato is very soft and most of the water has been reduced. In a blender, puree this mixture and slowly drizzle in the oil to make an emulsion. Season with salt. This should be slightly thick but pourable and a vivid red color. Set aside.

FOR THE LEMON DRESSING: In a blender, puree the shallot, lemon juice, and lemon zest. Slowly drizzle in the olive and canola oils. Blend thoroughly. Season with salt and pepper. Add sugar to sweeten the dressing slightly.

FOR THE SALAD: Use a tube mold with a diameter of about 2½ inches to build this stacked salad. A piece of PVC pipe will work.

In a small mixing bowl, toss the diced avocados with a little lemon dressing. Season it slightly with salt and spoon one-quarter of it into the bottom of the mold, directly on the serving plate.

Pack a layer of tomatoes into the mold and then pack a layer of cucumbers. Make all the layers relatively even.

In a small mixing bowl, mix together the basil, tarragon, chives, and fennel fronds.

In a medium mixing bowl, toss the crabmeat with some lemon dressing and one-half of the chopped herbs. Place this in the mold and press all the layers down firmly. Lift the ring mold to reveal the layered salad. Repeat these steps for the other 3 salads.

Toss the greens with the remaining lemon dressing and place on top of each stack.

Drizzle the basil oil and tomato oil around the plate. Garnish each plate with cherry tomatoes and the remaining chopped herbs. Sprinkle salt and cracked black pepper over the stacked salad and serve immediately.

Orcas Island Crab Cakes with Eastsound Tomato Sauce

Scuba diving for Dungeness crabs off the coast of Orcas Island inspired me to create this dish.

MAKES 6 CRAB CAKES

TOMATO SAUCE

1 TABLESPOON OLIVE OIL

1/2 CUP DICED RED ONION

1 TABLESPOON MINCED GARLIC

1 CUP DICED PLUM TOMATOES

2 CUPS TOMATO JUICE

1 CUP VEGETABLE STOCK

1 TABLESPOON CHOPPED FRESH FLAT-LEAF PARSLEY

1 TABLESPOON CHOPPED FRESH CILANTRO

PINCH OF GROUND CUMIN

1/2 TEASPOON HUNGARIAN PAPRIKA

1/2 TEASPOON CAYENNE PEPPER

SALT AND BLACK PEPPER TO TASTE

CRAB CAKES

1 POUND DUNGENESS OR LUMP CRABMEAT

1/2 CUP DICED RED ONION

1/2 CUP DICED RED BELL PEPPER

1 CELERY STALK, DICED

2 TABLESPOONS UNSALTED BUTTER

2 TABLESPOONS WORCESTERSHIRE SAUCE

1 1/2 TEASPOONS MUSTARD POWDER

2 LARGE EGGS

1 1/4 CUPS BREAD CRUMBS

1/2 CUP LOW-FAT MAYONNAISE

1 TABLESPOON KOSHER SALT

1 1/2 TEASPOONS GROUND BLACK PEPPER

1/4 CUP OLIVE OIL

FOR THE SAUCE: Heat the oil in a 1-gallon stockpot over medium heat. Sauté the red onion and garlic until tender. Add the tomatoes, tomato juice, and stock. Simmer for 15 minutes. Stir in the herbs and spices, and simmer an additional 3 minutes. Season with salt and pepper.

Place the sauce in a blender and puree until smooth. Return the sauce to the stockpot and bring to a simmer. Once the sauce is simmering, turn off the heat and keep warm on the back of the stove.

FOR THE CRAB CAKES: Preheat the oven to 350°F.

Check the crabmeat to make sure no shells or cartilage are mixed in.

In a sauté pan over medium heat, sweat the red onion, red pepper, and celery in the butter until tender, 5 to 6 minutes. Once the vegetables are tender, remove from the pan and refrigerate until cool.

In a large mixing bowl, combine the cooled vegetables, crabmeat, Worcestershire sauce, mustard powder, eggs, bread crumbs, mayonnaise, salt, and pepper. If the mixture is too dry, add an extra egg. If the mixture is too wet, add ¼ cup more bread crumbs.

Heat some olive oil in a sauté pan over medium heat. Take a small amount of the crab mixture and sauté it. Taste for seasoning and adjust the crab mixture if needed.

Once the mixture is properly seasoned, form into 6 cakes.

Heat the remaining olive oil in the sauté pan over medium heat. Sauté 2 crab cakes at a time. When one side turns golden brown, turn over to brown the other side. When each crab cake is browned, place on a baking sheet.

Bake the crab cakes in the oven for 7 to 8 minutes.

Serve the crab cakes with the tomato sauce.

Cedar-Smoked Salmon with Honey-Mustard Glaze

Cooking the salmon on cedar planks is the method I use to infuse the great flavor of the cedar into the salmon. The wood needs to be soaked in water overnight to prevent it from catching fire. The cedar will smolder to create a smokehouse with your grill. Make sure the wood is not Wolmanized or treated.

SERVES 4

1 CUP HONEY

1/2 CUP BALSAMIC VINEGAR

1 CUP DIJON MUSTARD

4 PIECES CEDAR PLANKS, 5 × 8 INCHES, SOAKED IN WATER
    OVERNIGHT

FOUR 8-OUNCE SALMON FILLETS

SALT AND BLACK PEPPER TO TASTE

Prepare an outdoor grill.

In a medium mixing bowl, whisk together the honey, vinegar, and mustard.

Place the soaked cedar planks on the grill grates.

Place the salmon fillets on the cedar planks. Brush with the honey-mustard glaze. Season with salt and pepper. Close the lid on the grill.

Watch the planks carefully to make sure they do not catch on fire. Be careful when you lift the lid not to breathe in the smoke.

Rotate the planks if necessary.

Glaze the fillets 3 or 4 times before they are completely cooked, which should take 8 to 10 minutes.

Use a spatula to remove the salmon from the cedar planks. If not burned too badly, the cedar may be reused.

Cedar-smoked salmon is best served with grilled vegetables.

HUCKLEBERRY-GLAZED DUCK BREAST WITH SWEET CORN FRITTERS

HUCKLEBERRIES WERE PRIZED BY THE NORTHWEST NATIVE AMERICAN TRIBES. THEY ALSO DEPENDED ON WATERFOWL AND CORN (MAIZE, AS THEY CALLED IT) FOR THEIR DIET. THIS RECIPE BRINGS IT ALL TOGETHER.

SERVES 4

CORN FRITTERS

VEGETABLE OIL

2 LARGE EGGS

1/4 CUP SUGAR

3/4 TEASPOON BAKING POWDER

6 TABLESPOONS WATER

1/2 CUP CHOPPED COOKED CORN KERNELS

1/2 TEASPOON SALT

1/4 TEASPOON GROUND BLACK PEPPER

1 1/2 CUPS ALL-PURPOSE FLOUR

GLAZE

2 PINTS FRESH HUCKLEBERRIES OR BLUEBERRIES

1/4 CUP MOLASSES

1/4 CUP SUGAR

2 TABLESPOONS FRESH LEMON JUICE

DUCK

FOUR 6-OUNCE DUCK BREASTS, WITH SKIN ON

SALT AND BLACK PEPPER TO TASTE

FOR THE CORN FRITTERS: Fill a medium stockpot halfway with vegetable oil. Heat the oil to 350°F.

In a medium mixing bowl, beat the eggs until frothy. Whisk in the sugar, baking powder, water, corn, salt, pepper, and flour.

Drop the batter by 1-tablespoon portions into the hot oil. It is important that you do not make the fritter size any larger because it will burn on the outside before the inside cooks. Turn the fritters frequently so they are golden brown on all sides. Drain on paper towels.

(recipe continues)

FOR THE GLAZE: In a large sauté pan over low heat, combine the huckleberries, molasses, sugar, and lemon juice. Cook for 5 minutes. Place in a blender and puree. Keep the sauce warm.

FOR THE DUCK: Preheat the oven to 350°F. Lightly score the skin of the duck breasts with a knife. Season with salt and pepper.

In a sauté pan over high heat, place the duck breasts skin side down. Render the skin crispy and turn over to sear the other side. Place each seared duck breast on a baking sheet. Brush the huckleberry glaze on each breast. Bake for 10 to 12 minutes, applying the glaze every 3 or 4 minutes. Duck breasts are best served medium-rare to medium.

Remove the duck breasts from the oven and let rest for 3 to 4 minutes before slicing.

Slice the duck and serve with the sweet corn fritters.

ESPRESSO CHOCOLATE MOUSSE

MIKE MCCONNELL OF CAFFÉ VITA IN SEATTLE INSPIRED ME TO MAKE THIS COFFEE-FLAVORED DESSERT. NATURALLY, CHOCOLATE AND ESPRESSO ALWAYS PAIR WELL TOGETHER.

SERVES 4

MOUSSE
1 POUND SEMISWEET CHOCOLATE
1 POUND UNSALTED BUTTER
6 TABLESPOONS ESPRESSO
8 EGGS, SEPARATED
1 CUP GRANULATED SUGAR

CHOCOLATE STRAWS
PARCHMENT PAPER
3/4 CUP SEMISWEET CHOCOLATE, MELTED
4 LARGE PLASTIC DRINKING STRAWS
BAMBOO SKEWER

GARNISH
1 CUP HEAVY CREAM
1 TABLESPOON FRESHLY GROUND COFFEE BEANS
1 TABLESPOON COCOA POWDER
1 TEASPOON CONFECTIONER'S SUGAR
CHOCOLATE-COATED COFFEE BEANS

FOR THE MOUSSE: In a double boiler, melt the chocolate and butter together. Stir in the espresso. Once melted, remove from the double boiler but keep warm.

In a medium mixing bowl, beat the egg yolks and ½ cup of sugar until smooth. Place the bowl over the double boiler and whisk until the egg yolks double in volume. Be careful not to scramble the egg yolks. Set aside at room temperature.

In a separate medium mixing bowl, beat the egg whites until stiff. Sprinkle in the remaining ½ cup of sugar while beating the whites.

Stir the yolk mixture into the melted chocolate. If the chocolate is too hot, it will scramble the eggs. Stir one-quarter of the beaten egg whites into the chocolate mixture. Gently fold in the remaining whites.

Fill 4 coffee cups three-quarters full with the espresso chocolate mousse. Refrigerate for 2 hours.

FOR THE CHOCOLATE STRAWS: Roll a sheet of parchment paper into a cone shape and fill with the melted chocolate. Fill the straws by holding your finger over one end and squeezing the chocolate from the parchment cone into the other end of the straw. Place the chocolate-filled straws in the refrigerator until they harden, approximately 20 minutes.

To remove the chocolate straws, use a bamboo skewer to gently push the chocolate from the straw. Break the straws in half for garnish.

TO ASSEMBLE: In a large mixing bowl, whisk the heavy cream until soft peaks form. Refrigerate.

In a medium mixing bowl, combine the ground coffee, cocoa powder, and confectioner's sugar. Place the mixture in a shaker.

Remove the chocolate mousse–filled coffee cups from the refrigerator. Top each one with a spoonful of whipped cream. Garnish each cup with chocolate-coated coffee beans and 2 halves of a chocolate straw.

Sprinkle the coffee–cocoa powder mix over the whipped cream.

Serve chilled.

Resources

Africa

Mango African Safaris
www.mangosafari.com

Perks Peri-Peri Sauces
www.perksperi-peri.com

Cottar's 1920s Safari Camps
P.O. Box 44191
Nairobi, Kenya
Phone: 254 2 351130 or 577374-81
E-mail: cottars@form-net.com

Cheli & Peacock Ltd.
P.O. Box 39806
00623a Parklands
Nairobi, Kenya
Phone: 254 2 604053
E-mail: safaris@chelipeacock.co.ke

Khaya Nyama Game Restaurant
267 Long Street, City Centre
Cape Town, South Africa
Phone: 27 21 424-2917
www.webdining.co.za/khaya-nyama

The Africa Café
108 Shortmaker Street
Cape Town, South Africa 8001
Phone: 27 21 422-0482
E-mail: africafe@iafrica.com

Australia

Quicksilver Diving Services
www.quicksilverdive.com.au

To purchase Australian spices and
food products, please visit
www.cherikoff.com.au.

Canada

Le Chateau Frontenac
1, rue des Carrières
Quebec City, Quebec
Phone: (418) 691-2166

rain Restaurant
19 Mercer Street
Toronto, ON, Canada
Phone: (416) 599-7246

Susur Restaurant
601 King Street
Toronto, ON, Canada
Phone: (416) 603-9361

Sotto Sotto Restaurant
116 Avenue Rd #A
Toronto, ON, Canada
Phone: (416) 962-0011

Zoom Restaurant
18 King Street East
Toronto, ON, Canada
Phone: (416) 861-9872

Patriot Restaurant
131 Bloor Street West
Toronto, ON, Canada
Phone: (416) 922-0025

Biryani House Restaurant
6 Roy's Square
Toronto, ON, Canada
Phone: (416) 927-9340

Florida

The Tides Hotel
1220 Ocean Drive
Miami Beach, Florida 33139
Phone: (305) 531-8800

Bill Wharton
www.sauceboss.com

B.O.'s Fish Wagon
801 Caroline Street
Key West, Florida 33040
Phone: (305) 294-9272

Blue Heaven Restaurant
729 Thomas Street
Key West, Florida 33040
Phone: (305) 296-8666

Key West Key Lime Shoppe
200 Elizabeth Street
Key West, Florida 33040
Phone: (305) 296-0806

Three Guys from Miami
www.icuban.com

Mangoes
700 Duval Street
Key West, Florida 33040
Phone: (305) 292-4606

To purchase alligator meat, please
visit www.lilsalseafood.com.

South Pacific

Bora Bora Pearl Beach Resort
Phone: (689) 60 52 00
www.pearlresorts.com/bora/
main.htm

Tahiti Beachcomber Intercontinental
Phone: (689) 86 51 10

Jamaica

Beaches Royal Plantation Resort and
Spa—Ocho Rios
Phone: (876) 974-5601

Beaches Negril
Phone: (876) 957-9270

Appleton Estate Jamaican Rum
www.appletonrum.com

Memphis

Bonne Terre Country Inn and Café
www.bonneterre.com

Isaac Hayes Music • Food • Passion
www.isaachayesclub.com

Alcenia's Restaurant
317 North Main Street
Memphis, Tennessee
Phone: (901) 523-0200

Mexico

Chris Haines Motorcycle
    Adventure Co.
www.motorcycleadventure
    company.com

Hotel Finisterra
www.finisterra.com

Momma's Royal Café and Felix's
www.felixcabosanlucas.com

Michigan

Ryba's Fudge Shop
Phone: (800) 447-9227
www.ryba.com

Springbrook Hills Mushroom Hunt
Phone: (616) 535-2944

Macomb SCUBA
Phone: (810) 558-9922

Seattle

Paramount Hotel and
    Dragonfish Asian Café
724 Pine Street
Seattle, Washington 98101
Phone: (206) 292-9500

Caffè Vita
1005 East Pike Street
Seattle, Washington 98101
Phone: (206) 709-4440

Tillicum Village
www.tillicumvillage.com

Rosario Resort and Spa
1400 Rosario Road
Eastsound, Washington 98245
Phone: (360) 376-2289

GLOSSARY

Achiote Seed: See **Annatto Seed.**

Ackee: A bright red tropical fruit that bursts open to reveal three large black seeds and a soft, creamy white flesh. It is poisonous in its underripe stage.

Ahima'a: A Tahitian underground oven. A Tahitian "imu."

Ahuacatle: Translated from the Nahuatl (Aztec) language. It means "avocado."

Ancho Chile: A dried poblano chile. A traditional ingredient in mole.

Andouille Sausage: A Cajun pork sausage that is spicy and smoked.

Annatto Seed: The seed from the annatto tree native to Central America. Used to color cheese, butter, and other food items shades of red. Also known as achiote.

ANZAC Day: Australian memorial day, named for the ANZAC soldiers (Australian and New Zealand Army Corps) who landed on the Gallipoli Peninsula during World War I.

Arbol Chile: A central Mexican chile. Bright red and almost as hot as a cayenne pepper.

Bammy: A Jamaican dough made from yucca and formed into flattened circles and fried.

Bay Bug: An Australian relative of the lobster, yet smaller in size.

Beggar's Purse: A crepe filled with various ingredients to form a ruck-sack, hence the name.

Beurre Manié: Butter and flour in equal parts, kneaded together and used in sauces as a thickener.

Bird's-eye Chile: A dried Thai chile.

Bisque: A thick and rich cream soup, typically made with shellfish and using shells of the fish for stock.

Black Miso: See **Hatcho Miso.**

Blackening Spice: A spice blend used in Cajun cooking consisting of paprika, cayenne pepper, herbs, and spices.

Bobotie: A South African mince-meat casserole made with lamb or beef, fruits, and almonds.

Bolla: A South African pumpkin fritter traditionally served with syrup.

Bouillabaisse: A French seafood stew made with an assortment of fish and shellfish, tomatoes, white wine, garlic, and saffron.

Breadfruit: A large, round, bumpy fruit that has a brown skin and a starchy cream-colored center.

Bucatini Pasta: Long, hollow strands of pasta, slightly thicker than spaghetti.

Caldo Verde: Traditionally, a Portuguese sausage soup with kale.

Callaloo: The patois term for the leaves of the taro plant. Also, a Jamaican soup with taro leaves among the ingredients.

Cardamom: A sweet spice grown on the Malabar coast of India and used in curries.

Carpaccio: A traditional Italian appetizer of beef thinly sliced and usually served with olive oil and capers.

Cascabel Chile: A dried plum-shaped chile that is moderately spicy and has a nutty flavor. Also known as chile bola.

Cassava: See **Yucca.**

Cava Vinegar: A mild vinegar distilled from cava, which is a Spanish champagne-style white wine.

Cavendish Banana: The main variety of banana available in America.

Ceviche: A Spanish salad of seafood marinated in lime or lemon juice. Generally tossed with cilantro and chiles.

Chandi Ka-Vang Silver: East Indian variety of edible silver.

Chanterelle Mushroom: A golden trumpet-shaped mushroom with a nutty flavor and a meaty texture. Grown in the Pacific Northwest and the Great Lakes region.

Chapati: An African dough that is rolled into a circle and fried on both sides. It is commonly rolled with meat like a taco.

Chayote: A green gourdlike fruit that has a large pear shape. It has

white flesh and a neutral flavor. Also known as Christophene or Christophine.

Cherimoya: The fruit of a tree native to Peru. Its flesh has the texture of firm custard. It is now grown throughout the tropics and California. Also known as custard apple.

Chermoula: A Moroccan pesto-like sauce with cilantro as its main ingredient.

Chèvre: A soft goat's milk cheese.

Chiffonade: A cutting technique that produces fine strips of herbs or vegetables.

Chilaca Chile: A moderately spicy Mexican chile that is deep brown and about 6 inches long.

Chile Negro: Another name for pasilla chile.

Chimayo Chile: A select red chile from Chimayo, New Mexico. It can vary in heat from mild to medium.

Chimichurri: An Argentine sauce consisting of herbs, garlic, olive oil, vinegar, and pepper.

Chinois: A fine cone-shaped strainer used to strain sauces.

Chipotle Pepper: A smoked jalapeño pepper available dried as well as canned.

Cho-Cho: Patois for chayote.

Chow Chow: A Chinese-influenced, southern-style relish frequently used as a topping on pulled pork sandwiches.

Christophene: See **Chayote.**

Chutney: A spiced condiment made of fruit cooked with vinegar and sugar.

Clarified Butter: Pure butter fat used for sautéing food. It has been

heated, skimmed, and decanted. To clarify butter, one needs to heat it in a pan until it separates, skim off the scum that forms on top, and remove the "clarified butter" from the water that pools on the bottom.

Compote: A chilled dish of fruit that has been cooked in sugary syrup.

Conch: A mollusk found in the Caribbean that can be eaten raw or sautéed. It is prized for its colorful shell.

Couscous: Granular semolina generally served as a side dish. It is a staple in North African diets.

Cousin Jacks: Michigan's Cornish miners. In the 1850s they would heat pasties on the lamp of their mining hats.

Crepe: A paper-thin pancake that can be filled with sweet or savory fillings.

Cuba Libre: A Cuban-American cocktail made from rum, Coke, and lime juice.

Damper: A simple bread baked in a pot laid in a campfire. Australian bush bread.

Dashi: A Japanese soup stock that is made with kombu, dried bonito tuna flakes, and water.

Demi-glace: A brown stock, usually beef or veal, that has been well reduced and thickened with dark roux.

Drumette: The bone of the chicken wing that is closest to the body.

Dry Rub: A mixture of herbs and spices that are ground and rubbed on meat for flavor.

Egg Wash: A mixture of eggs and milk or water used for breading or coloring dough crusts.

Festivals: A popular Jamaican treat made from flour, cornmeal, butter, and flavorings. They are the size of a hush puppy and fried.

Fish Sauce: A condiment made from fermented fish. Popular in Southeast Asian cuisine.

Five-Spice Powder: A Chinese spice blend generally consisting of star anise, cinnamon, cloves, ginger, and Szechwan pepper.

Foie Gras: The French term for the liver of a fattened goose or duck. Literally, "fat liver."

Fricassee: A dish of meat, usually chicken, that is sautéed in butter and stewed with vegetables and broth.

Fritter: A small, sweet, or savory deep-fried cake that is commonly filled with apple, crab, or corn.

Fufu: Cuban name for a plantain.

Ganja: Jamaican slang word for marijuana.

Gelatin: A colorless and tasteless thickening agent used in desserts.

Glucose: Generally dextrose (corn sugar) in a thick syrup form. Used in candies.

Gnocchi: Italian dumplings commonly made from potatoes and/or flour. They are rolled into small barrel shapes and dropped into boiling water to cook.

Gravlax: A Swedish specialty of salmon cured in salt, sugar, and dill.

Guava: A small, round fruit with a floral flavor. It is native to South America and grows throughout the tropics.

Gumbo: A Cajun stew consisting of seafood or meat and vegetables. Seasoned with gumbo filé and cayenne.

Gumbo Filé: Ground sassafras and thyme blend used to flavor and thicken gumbo.

Habanero: The hottest chile on record. Color ranges from light green to bright orange in its ripe stage. Used in Jamaican cuisine.

Hamachi: Also known as yellowtail, it is a member of the jackfish family. It has soft, fairly fatty flesh that is perfect for sashimi.

Haricot Vert: A French term commonly used to describe a small, tender green bean.

Hatcho Miso: A dark brown miso, made from soybeans. It is very pungent and has a strong flavor. Popular in central Japan. Also known as Black Miso. See **Miso.**

Hoppin' John: A southern dish of black-eyed peas simmered with salt pork and served with rice.

Imu: A Hawaiian underground oven used for pig roasts at luaus.

Jerk Marinade: A Jamaican dry rub made with peppers, garlic, onion, and a variety of spices and herbs.

Julienne: A cutting technique that produces thin "matchstick" vegetables.

Kachumbari: A Kenyan coleslaw made from chopped vegetables, cabbage, and salt.

Kakadu Plum: A small fuchsia-colored plum native to Australia.

Kecap Manis: A sweet, thick, Indonesian soy sauce. It is made from soybeans and has a dark caramel color.

Key Lime: A sweet lime used in pie fillings and other desserts.

King Salmon: A variety of salmon that is fished in northern Pacific waters. It is fattier than Norwegian salmon.

Kohlrabi: A mild-flavored member of the turnip family with edible green leaves.

Kombu: A long, dark brown seaweed that is sun-dried and folded into sheets. Used in Japanese cuisine.

Kowadjik: A South African adaptation of a Malaysian dessert made of rice, almonds, and coconut.

Kung Pao: A Chinese stir-fry with peanut flavor and essence.

Lemon Aspen: A tree found in the Queensland, Australia, rain forest that has edible acidic fruit.

Lemon Myrtle: An herb that has a powerful lemon scent and flavor.

Lemon Sole: A type of flounder. It is low in fat and has a fine texture.

Lemon Verbena: An herb with long, slender leaves that impart a potent lemony aroma and flavor.

Limette: A Mexican tropical fruit similar to key lime.

Maharagwe ya Nasi: Swahili for "beans in coconut sauce."

Mahi Mahi: Also called dolphin-fish, it is a moderately fatty fish with a flavorful firm flesh.

Malanga Root: A mild tuber related to taro and used in Caribbean cooking.

Manchego Cheese: A Spanish sheep's milk cheese. It has a firm, dry texture and a mild, tangy flavor.

Mannish Water: Jamaican goat's head soup. Thought to increase male virility.

Medallions: Small, round cuts of meat, usually pork, beef, or veal, cooked quickly by sautéing or grilling.

Melegueta Pepper: Small, red-brown seeds native to tropical West Africa, mainly Ghana. Pungent and peppery flavor with hints of cardamom and ginger. Pepper mixed with a little ginger can be used as a substitute. Also called Grains of Paradise.

Meyer Lemon: A type of lemon that is sweet and has a slight lemon tartness.

Mille-feuilles: French for "thousand leaves." A classic French pastry with many layers.

Mirin: A sweet Japanese sake made from glutinous rice. Used solely for cooking.

Miso: A fermented soybean paste that has the consistency of peanut butter and comes in a wide range of colors and flavors. Used frequently in Japanese cooking. Pungency increases as the depth of color increases. See **Hatcho Miso, Red Miso,** and **Shiro Miso.**

Mojito: An African rum, lime, and mint drink.

Mojo: A Cuban marinade consisting of sour orange juice, garlic, onion, and olive oil. (Sour orange is a type of orange native to Cuba.)

Molli: Translated from the Nahuatl (Aztec) language, the word means "mixture."

Mop Sauce: A type of basting sauce that can be used as a marinade; it won't burn when cooked because it doesn't contain sugar.

Morita Chile: A type of reddish brown, smoked jalapeño pepper.

Motu: The Tahitian word for "little islet."

Mount: To enhance a sauce with whole butter at the end of cooking.

Mulatto Chile: A dark brown, smoked poblano chile. A traditional ingredient in mole.

Naan: An East Indian flat bread.

Nabe Yaki: A traditional Japanese family-style soup containing shrimp and other seafood. Served in a nabe (pot) in the evening.

Okra: A vegetable native to Africa. It has a gummy texture and is used as much for its thickening qualities as for its flavor.

Pancetta: An Italian bacon that is salted, cured, and rolled. Used to flavor sauces.

Paperbark Tree: An Australian tree with papery bark that is used as a protective wrap for cooking food.

Pasilla Chile: Spanish for "little raisin." A dried chilaca chile. A traditional ingredient in mole.

Passion Fruit: A tropical fruit with a fluid center and a floral and pleasantly tart flavor.

Patois: The slang-heavy Creole language of Jamaica.

Pavlova: A meringue-based dessert popular in Australia. It is named in honor of the famous ballerina Anna Pavlova.

Pawpaw: Both common name used throughout the world for papaya and a North American fruit related to the custard apple, which is not related to papaya.

Pecorino-Romano: An Italian sheep's milk cheese. It is similar to Parmesan but is softer and tangier.

Pectin Powder: Used for thickening jams, jellies, and sauces when fruits don't have enough natural pectin to jell.

Pepitas: Mexican green pumpkin seeds.

Pepperberry: An Australian berry that has a hot peppery bite. It has purple skin and bleeds a light burgundy color.

Pepperpot Soup: A thick Jamaican soup made from tripe, meat, vegetables, and pepper.

Pernod: A French liqueur with an anise flavor.

Piccata: A dish that is quickly sautéed and finished with white wine, lemon juice, and butter.

Pilaf: Technique for cooking rice that can vary from culture to culture.

Pilau: Another name for pilaf.

Pimento: The name for the allspice tree used in Jamaica for cooking fires and spice.

Piquin Chile: A small red hot chile that is dried.

Plantain: A large starchy banana used by Africans and West Indians as a staple carbohydrate.

Poblano Chile: A moderately hot chile that is used for stuffing and sauces. It can be green or red.

Poe: A Tahitian side dish that is made from either taro root or pumpkin that is cooked and mashed to a smooth paste.

Poi: A Hawaiian dish made with taro root. Also the Tahitian term for the method of making *poe* (pounding into pulp).

Poisson Cru: The national dish of Tahiti. It is tuna marinated in lime juice and tossed with coconut milk, peppers, onions, and tomatoes.

Poussin: French term for young, small chicken. A Cornish game hen can be used as a substitute.

Prawn: The name for a freshwater shrimp. Also a common term for a large shrimp.

Quandong: A small peach that is native to Australia. Its skin color ranges from blue to burgundy. It is commonly served stewed.

Quince: A yellow-skinned fruit that looks similar to an apple. It must be cooked to enjoy. It is made into preserves and put into stews.

Ramp: A wild leek that resembles a scallion and has a slight garlic flavor.

Razor Clam: A clam that gets its name because it resembles an old-fashioned folded, straight-edge razor. Popular in Asian cuisine.

Red Miso: A strong-flavored miso. It is made from barley and used in braised items. See **Miso.**

Rima Rima: A dwarfish banana used in Tahitian cuisine. Flavor and texture are similar to the Cavendish banana.

Risotto: A rice dish that is cooked in hot stock with vegetables, meat, or herbs. It is stirred constantly during cooking to ensure a creamy texture.

Roti: A buttery South African flat bread that is fried.

Roux: Equal amounts of fat (generally butter) and flour combined over heat and used to thicken soups and sauces.

Sake: A sweet Japanese wine that is made from fermented rice. It is the national drink of Japan. It is also used in sauces and marinades.

Salomi: A popular South African "fast food" item made of bobotie rolled in a roti.

Saltfish: Cod that is salted and dried. It is a staple in Caribbean and tropical cuisines. It must be soaked before cooking.

Sashimi: Thinly sliced raw fish that is usually served with wasabi, pickled ginger, and soy.

Scotch Bonnet: One of the hottest chiles. It is small and irregular in shape and is yellow, orange, or red.

Serrano Chile: A small, slightly pointed chile that is very hot and savory in flavor.

Shiro Miso: Also known as white miso. See **Miso.**

Simple Syrup: One part sugar to one part water simmered until clear. Used in confections and drinks.

Sour Orange: A type of orange that is native to Cuba. It is now being grown in South Florida as well.

Soy Sauce: A salty condiment made from soybeans and wheat. It is very important to Asian cuisine.

Spiny Lobster: A clawless lobster that is fished in subtropical waters. Also known as rock lobster.

Sucuma Wiki: A Kenyan dish consisting of African spinach, onion, tomato, and cream.

Szechwan Pepper: An aromatic, spicy berry from the Szechwan, China, native, prickly ash. It is not related to black pepper.

Tamarind: The fruit of an evergreen tree, native to India. It is a popular flavoring in Eastern and tropical cuisines.

Tapioca Flour: An extract of the yucca plant. It is used as a thickener in soups, sauces, and desserts.

Taro Root: A large starchy tuber. The main ingredient in poi. It can be fried as chips or baked.

Teriyaki: A Japanese marinade that contains soy, sugar, sake, and ginger.

Thai Chile: A thin red-hot chile used in Thai and Vietnamese cuisine.

Tillicum: A Chinook word meaning "friendly people." It is also the name of a culture and cuisine program in Seattle, Washington: Tillicum Village.

Togarashi: A small red-hot Japanese chile.

Tortas Ahogadas: It means "drowned cakes." It is a pork sandwich with a chile vinegar sauce.

Tuber: The term used to describe the starchy nodules that grow on roots of certain plants.

Udon Noodle: A thick Japanese wheat noodle.

Ugali: A Kenyan side dish made with coarse cornmeal and water. Similar to polenta.

Vegemite: A yeast product that is a popular condiment in Australia.

Venison: Refers to meat from deer.

Vermicelli: Pasta that is similar in thickness to angel hair and is formed into short strands.

Wattleseed: A coffee-flavored seed that is ground and used to flavor both sweet and savory dishes.

White Miso: Mild and sweet miso. Also known as Shiro Miso. See **Miso.**

White Soy: A clear soy sauce that can be found in specialty markets.

White Truffle: A fungus that grows underground and is found by pigs near oak trees. It is beige in color and has an earthy and nutty flavor.

Yucca, or Yuca: A plant with elongated tubers that have white flesh and a waxy texture. It is also called cassava.

ACKNOWLEDGMENTS

This is one of those books that truly could not have been possible without the support and assistance of so many.

Most important are all the passionate cooks—chefs and everyday people who so graciously shared recipes with me, not to mention their lives. But before them there was the great team at Food Network—Judy Girard, Kathleen Finch, and Eileen Opatut. They supported my journeys around the world with great enthusiasm. Jay Mandel, my book agent, as well as Brian Dubin, Jim Ornstein, John Rosen, all from William Morris, play a very intricate part in my adventures.

Roy Finamore, my editor at Clarkson Potter, along with designer Caitlin Daniels Israel, eagerly jumped on board for this book idea and really let me run with my vision.

Mr. Chris Kassel, my buddy, travel compadre, and cowriter. So many stories we shared on so many journeys sadly can't fit in these pages. His style of writing, well, it's just fun to read. Enjoy.

My photographer, Joe Vaughn, is always ready to click away—most important are the ones he gets that you never know he got. Matt Prested is the young man I hired as a cook some years ago and whom I depend on so much. My Visionalist Entertainment Productions team: Jeff Fish, Kevin Hewitt, Vanessa Poma, Bob Berg, Roger Smith, Kerry Brennen, and Jacquelyn A. Engel, all of whom supported this book while it was in the works. Thanks to Barry Feldman and Steve Cole for their solid guidance. My mom, who was taxed with taking care of my father, who has Alzheimer's, every time I left home. My children, Josh and Alicia, who were able to experience some of these journeys with me. And Katrin, my sweetheart, who patiently waited for me to return from all my journeys.

FROM LEFT: STEVE EADS, TOM KASUBOWSKI, TODD GARDNER, ERIN SONNTAG, TODD TROY, ME, MATT PRESTED (MY SOUS CHEF), AND DAVID OGDEN. A SPECIAL THANKS TO THESE INDIVIDUALS, WHO TESTED RECIPES FOR THIS BOOK. ALSO, A SPECIAL THANKS TO SCHOOLCRAFT COLLEGE FOR LETTING US TEST RECIPES IN THEIR KITCHEN.

INDEX

CONVERSION CHART
EQUIVALENT IMPERIAL AND METRIC MEASUREMENTS

American cooks use standard containers, the 8-ounce cup and a tablespoon that takes exactly 16 level fillings to fill that cup level. Measuring by cup makes it very difficult to give weight equivalents, as a cup of densely packed butter will weigh considerably more than a cup of flour. The easiest way therefore to deal with cup measurements in recipes is to take the amount by volume rather than by weight. Thus the equation reads:

1 cup = 240 ml = 8 fl. oz.   ½ cup = 120 ml = 4 fl. oz.

It is possible to buy a set of American cup measures in major stores around the world.

In the States, butter is often measured in sticks. One stick is the equivalent of 8 tablespoons. One tablespoon of butter is therefore the equivalent to ½ ounce/15 grams.

LIQUID MEASURES

FLUID OUNCES	U.S.	IMPERIAL	MILLILITERS
	1 teaspoon	1 teaspoon	5
¼	2 teaspoons	1 dessertspoon	10
½	1 tablespoon	1 tablespoon	14
1	2 tablespoons	2 tablespoons	28
2	¼ cup	4 tablespoons	56
4	½ cup		120
5		¼ pint or 1 gill	140
6	¾ cup		170
8	1 cup		240
9			250, ¼ liter
10	1¼ cups	½ pint	280
12	1½ cups		340
15		¾ pint	420
16	2 cups		450
18	2¼ cups		500, ½ liter
20	2½ cups	1 pint	560
24	3 cups		675
25		1¼ pints	700
27	3½ cups		750
30	3¾ cups	1½ pints	840
32	4 cups or 1 quart		900
35		1¾ pints	980
36	4½ cups		1000, 1 liter
40	5 cups	2 pints or 1 quart	1120

SOLID MEASURES

U.S. AND IMPERIAL MEASURES		METRIC MEASURES	
OUNCES	POUNDS	GRAMS	KILOS
1		28	
2		56	
3½		100	
4	¼	112	
5		140	
6		168	
8	½	225	
9		250	¼
12	¾	340	
16	1	450	
18		500	½
20	1¼	560	
24	1½	675	
27		750	¾
28	1¾	780	
32	2	900	
36	2¼	1000	1
40	2½	1100	
48	3	1350	
54		1500	1½

OVEN TEMPERATURE EQUIVALENTS

FAHRENHEIT	CELSIUS	GAS MARK	DESCRIPTION
225	110	¼	Cool
250	130	½	
275	140	1	Very Slow
300	150	2	
325	170	3	Slow
350	180	4	Moderate
375	190	5	
400	200	6	Moderately Hot
425	220	7	Fairly Hot
450	230	8	Hot
475	240	9	Very Hot
500	250	10	Extremely Hot

Any broiling recipes can be used with the grill of the oven, but beware of high-temperature grills.

EQUIVALENTS FOR INGREDIENTS

all-purpose flour—plain flour
baking sheet—oven tray
buttermilk—ordinary milk
cheesecloth—muslin
coarse salt—kitchen salt
cornstarch—cornflour

eggplant—aubergine
granulated sugar—caster sugar
half and half—12% fat milk
heavy cream—double cream
light cream—single cream
parchment paper—greaseproof paper

plastic wrap—cling film
scallion—spring onion
shortening—white fat
unbleached flour—strong, white flour
zest—rind
zucchini—courgettes or marrow